History by Hollywood

History by Hollywood

THE USE
AND ABUSE
OF THE
AMERICAN
PAST

Robert Brent Toplin

University
of Illinois Press
Urbana
& Chicago

FIRST PAPERBACK EDITION, 1996

© 1996 by the Board of Trustees of the University of Illinois
Manufactured in the United States of America
P 7 6 5 4

This book is printed on acid-free paper.

Library of Congress Cataloging-in-Publication Data
Toplin, Robert Brent, 1940–
    History by Hollywood : the use and abuse of the American past /
Robert Brent Toplin.
        p.   cm.
    Includes bibliographical references and index.
    ISBN 0-252-06536-0 (pbk. : alk. paper)
    1. Historical films—United States—History and criticism.
2. Motion pictures and history. I. Title.
PN1995.9.H5T66   1996
791.43'658—dc20   95-41734
                                                              CIP

CONTENTS

Preface   vii

Acknowledgments   xiii

Introduction   1

PART 1   Exercising Artistic License: Communicating through
a Mix of Fact and Fiction

1 *Mississippi Burning* "A Standard to Which We Couldn't
Live Up"   25

2 *JFK* "Fact, Fiction, and Supposition"   45

PART 2   Drawing Lessons: Making the Past Relevant to
the Present

3 *Sergeant York* "If That Is Propaganda, We Plead Guilty"   81

4 *Missing* "An Assault on the Integrity of the U.S.
Government, the Foreign Service and the Military"   103

PART 3   Reflecting the Present: Revealing Current Controversy
in Portrayals of the Past

5 *Bonnie and Clyde* "Violence of a Most Grisly Sort"   127

6 *Patton* "Deliberately Planned as a Rorschach Test"   155

PART 4   Accenting Heroism: Celebrating the "Great Man" in
the Documentary Style

7 *All the President's Men* "The Story That People Know
and Remember"   179

8 *Norma Rae* "A Female Rocky"   203

Epilogue   225

Notes   229

Selected Bibliography   251

Index   259

Movies dealing with historical themes and personalities have excited public interest through much of the twentieth century. Especially after D. W. Griffith presented what seemed to many to be a transparently prejudiced saga of the Civil War and Reconstruction in *Birth of a Nation* (1915), professional critics, historians, and the viewing public have argued about the way movies reconstruct the American past. They have, for example, criticized *Gone with the Wind*'s moonlight-and-magnolias outlook on the antebellum South; questioned the degree to which movies about demagogues indirectly represented famous figures (as in *Citizen Kane* and *All the King's Men*); complained that filmmakers employed simplistic left-wing perspectives in presenting screen heroes (as in *Reds* and *Born on the Fourth of July*); argued that directors whitewashed history, failing to recognize the contributions of minorities in American life (as in the reactions to *Mississippi Burning*); and maintained that filmmakers distorted the historical record to advance their own agenda (evidenced by responses to *JFK*).

They have debated these and related issues for good reason. Critics of historical movies have recognized that Hollywood's version of the past can make a significant impact on the viewers. Dramatic motion pictures that feature famous stars in the roles of historical characters and present vivid scenes of yesteryear through sophisticated cinematography can make strong impressions. Historical films help to shape the thinking of millions. Often the depictions seen on the screen influence the public's view of historical subjects much more than books do. Americans of the early 1940s knew the story of Sergeant Alvin York not only from York's celebrity status as a war hero but in terms of the role Gary Cooper played in the motion picture about him; many younger Americans in the early 1970s knew little about General George S. Patton until they saw George C. Scott portray the controversial World War II figure in a Hollywood film.

Although it seems obvious that some movies are influential present-

ers of history, it is striking that scholars have given very little attention to their manner of interpreting the past. Research concerning the
media has concentrated instead on analyzing films for insights into the
changing interests of past generations. Students of the movies have
treated dramatic film as a mirror that reflects the conscious and un-
conscious attitudes and concerns of the producers and their audiences.[1] Others have taken inspiration from Siegfried Kracauer, exploring
ways that film may reflect the collective cultural consciousness (or un-
conscious) of a people.[2] Historians also have examined movies to study
the entertainment industry and to understand film's role as an influence on public opinion and as an instrument of propaganda. With
an eye toward the problems of government interference and censorship, for example, scholars such as Garth Jowett, Robert Sklar, Clayton R. Koppes, and Gregory D. Black have investigated the impact of
the Hays production codes, the Office of War Information's role in
overseeing Hollywood's production during World War II, and the House
Un-American Activities Committee's investigations of the movie industry.[3] Others, coming to the subject from the perspective of film studies, bring a host of theoretical constructs to their analysis. They apply
the auteur theories of André Bazin and Andrew Sarris; study semiol-
ogy to understand the cinema as a sign system; seek insights from psychoanalysis, feminist theory, and Marxism; and examine ideological
influences on the movie industry, moviemakers, and audiences.[4]

The phenomenon of film as interpreter of history, however, remains
relatively neglected in the modern age of abundant movie presentations of the past. Only a few scholars, such as John E. O'Connor, Robert A. Rosenstone, and Pierre Sorlin, have examined film's role as a
popular communicator of historical interpretations. This study attempts
to respond to the gap in film scholarship by viewing the way in which
the makers of commercial movies have dealt with American history.

A working title for this book drew on Oliver Stone's reference to
himself as a "cinematic historian." Stone was referring to his role (a
controversial one, to be sure) as a Hollywood filmmaker who has addressed important historical questions and has attempted to make contributions to public thinking by fashioning forceful interpretations of
the past. Stone's reference provides an elegantly succinct way to identify the people who are bringing history to the masses through the
medium of the popular cinema. These filmmakers perform the historian's role. Although their productions are different from the products
of traditional written history, and we may need to entertain new ways

of thinking about their contributions, we cannot deny their impact. In the modern age of electronic media they are delivering abundant information to the public, and they often shape ideas as much or more than those who provide traditional education do. These cinematic historians have become powerful storytellers. They are competing effectively with the schoolteacher, the college professor, and the history book author. Their work deserves attention.

This book focuses on movies about real people and real situations from the American past, because this genre has excited much of the animated discussion about the role of film as a communicator of historical understanding. Such movies spark interest in historical questions, because their attention to the experiences of actual figures suggests a level of authenticity. The films appear to represent reality. Cinema's suggestions of "reality" may be disputed, of course, since the portrayals are strongly manipulated by the filmmakers (indeed, the products of both cinematic historians and book-oriented historians are essentially personal perspectives on the past, not reality itself). Nevertheless, critics and the public raise the most pointed questions about cinematic history in connection with movies that deal with specific personalities and events. Motion pictures that feature largely invented characters and incidents rather than recognizable scenes and figures tend to stir less commentary regarding the treatment of history. For instance, Kevin Costner's fascinating presentation of frontier life and Native American culture in *Dances with Wolves* makes important political and cultural statements, as does Oliver Stone's disturbing treatment of the American soldier's Vietnam experiences in *Platoon*. These motion pictures, however, do not excite interest in the details of the history of the American West or the Vietnam War as readily as movies that portray specific historical figures and situations do.

To say that the films under examination here deal with real episodes from the past is not to indicate that these movies were designed specifically to educate the public about history. Artists created the films to express their thoughts and feelings and to make money. They aimed more to entertain audiences and earn profits than to inform them. But their interest in history should not be underestimated. As an examination of specific production histories makes clear, filmmakers often have approached historical subjects with genuine curiosity about the past. They have committed considerable energy to historical research in the production process and defended their interpretations enthusiastically when critics challenged their portrayals. Although their productions are something less than simple history lessons and something more complex in purpose than works of scholarship, they are, nevertheless, worthy of study. Cinematic history, a curious blend of entertainment and interpretation, needs analysis.

The subject is important, too, because the public takes it seriously. Audiences often argue vociferously about the movies' interpretations of the past and the relevance of their messages for the present. They consider these films to be more instructive than mere entertainment.

This study differs from a number of other examinations of historical films in that it concentrates on a few case studies of filmmaking. An extended analysis of the filmmakers' experiences in production and reception is more satisfactory in addressing questions about cinematic history than is a brief overview of a multitude of films. The pattern of analysis seen in many works in film studies—abundant passing references to a large number of movies to illustrate a variety of points— seems to be of limited value when we consider the broad question: what happens to history when Hollywood filmmakers put their hands on it?

One of the most troubling limitations of the hit-and-run approach is its tendency to offer primarily the finished film as a source of evidence. Discussion typically centers on the movie—its messages, its symbolism, and its techniques of communication. Sometimes the commentators supplement these observations with a few remarks about the movie's possible relationship to other films and the issues of the times. Such analysis is highly speculative, because it does not rest on a larger understanding of the film's production history. The hit-and-run approach does not inform us about the individuals who made the film and why or how they addressed historical questions and adjusted their interpretations as they came under pressure from the marketplace, responded to societal influences, or compromised with other members of their production team. Furthermore, the hit-and-run approach gives us little opportunity to view the film's impact on historical thinking. It cannot tell us much about the way that the public and the critics greeted the movie or how the film's perspective on history sparked debates or affected political attitudes. Brief references also fail to reveal how the filmmakers responded to public discussions of their work. By concentrating on the film rather than on the context in which the film appeared, commentators often miss the fascinating exchanges in which cinematic historians sparred with their critics and defended their treatments of history.

In this book I use case studies to show cinematic history in greater depth and complexity by stepping behind and around the movies. The case studies go *behind* the films in the sense of studying their production histories and the ideas and experiences of the people who contributed significantly to the movies' interpretations of the past. Obviously many individuals can affect a motion picture's presentation. I have concentrated on the roles of three key figures in the production process: the producers, the directors, and the writers. This approach differs somewhat from the one seen in the many film studies that focus primarily on the influence of the director. As I try to indicate in the case studies, writers and producers also play significant roles in shaping the specific genre I call cinematic history (in fact, these individuals often initiate the film projects). I ask the following questions: Which perspectives of history did these individuals bring to their films? What were the mainstream or dissident historical interpretations of the times to which these cinematic historians reacted? How did the filmmakers deal with historical evidence, and to what degree did they adjust their portrayals because of outside pressures? How did these individuals disagree with one another as they tried to fashion interpretations? To what degree did they present history with integrity?

The case studies also go *around* the movies in the sense of placing them in the context of important political and social issues of the day. I consider the way in which historical cinema sometimes excited heated discussions because observers saw lessons for the present in the movies' messages about the past. I ask why these films provoked arguments about interpretation. I consider developments in American society that affected these disputes, and I look at ways in which the critics, the public, and the filmmakers disagreed about interpretation. I also examine the filmmakers' efforts to defend their perspectives of history.

Not all historical movies stimulate wide-ranging disagreements, yet some of the less controversial examples, too, are worthy of investigation. Their production histories may reveal a good deal about the challenges of presenting history on film. For instance, the production records can demonstrate how filmmakers tried to establish realistic visions of the past, seeking to create the look and feeling of specific times, places, and situations. An investigation of these productions can also throw light on some of the pressures the dramatic medium makes on historical interpretation, particularly the pressure to attribute historical change to the actions of a few heroic individuals. Such is the case with two movies considered in this book, *All the President's Men* and *Norma Rae*. These films did not arouse particularly heated debates about their portrayals of the past (although, as I will show, they may have made some impact on historical developments subsequent to their release). A view behind and around their production, however, can illuminate many of the significant challenges involved in portraying history Hollywood-style.

The eight case studies reflect a number of common qualities. All the movies were relatively popular films. Each attracted good to outstanding receipts at the box office. All were critically acclaimed as important films with regard to the artistic accomplishments of their producers and the significance of the subjects they address. All received Academy Award nominations for best picture. Finally, with respect to the challenges of researching behind and around historical movies, a good deal of primary evidence from the production experiences was available for each film. Through work with production documents, interviews with the producers, directors, and writers (as well as interviews with some of the historical figures portrayed in the movies), and examination of a substantial number of published commentaries on the films, it was possible to attempt a broader and more detailed analysis of the popular cinema's approach to history than is found in much of the scholarship.

Despite the availability of primary sources, these case studies can never be as comprehensive as one might wish them to be. There are always questions that cannot be answered fully regarding the filmmakers' motives, the factors that influenced their treatment of history, or any number of other matters. Often important pieces of evidence are lacking; the fragmented data allow conjecture, not certainty. It is not possible, then, to offer these studies as capacious interpretations that completely address all the questions posed by cinematic history. These models can only suggest some ways that we may attempt more informed inquiries into the Hollywood filmmaker's role as historian.

ACKNOWLEDGMENTS

A fellowship from the American Council of Learned Societies allowed me to step away from teaching duties to prepare the manuscript, and two grants from the Faculty Research and Development Fund at the University of North Carolina at Wilmington assisted in meeting travel expenses. Also, several grants from the National Endowment for the Humanities provided an opportunity to produce historical dramas, experiences that awakened my interest in this project.

I am appreciative of support in the formative stages of research from a number of people. John E. O'Connor, a pioneer in the field of history and film and a good friend, did much to excite my interest in the subject, and David Ransel, editor of *The American Historical Review,* gave me a chance to express my initial ideas about the filmmaker as historian in the December 1988 issue of the *AHR*. Several scholars with an interest in film examined a proposal for this research project when I sought a fellowship and gave helpful support. I appreciate the contributions of Natalie Zemon Davis, Louis Harlan, James McPherson, Robert A. Rosenstone, and David Thelen. Also, three perceptive colleagues at the University of North Carolina at Wilmington read the manuscript and raised thoughtful questions: Kathleen Berkeley, Charles Dodson, and Michael Seidman. Also, my wife, Aida, was both an excellent critic and advocate.

History by Hollywood

The Power to Embody Ghosts

Years ago a Hollywood mogul observed that those who wish to send messages should consult Western Union. The view that Hollywood movies are about entertainment and not political argument or instruction has been influential, but the observation ought not to be applied indiscriminately. Many movies carry subtle messages of social and political significance, and some offer rather forceful perspectives on broad public issues. This book is about a particular category of message movies: dramas that tell the story of real people and actual events from American history. Such films constitute a small minority of the thousands of motion pictures released by Hollywood, but they are an important minority. A number of these movies have excited lively discussions about history.

Hollywood's interpretations of American history can make a significant impact on the public's thinking about the past. Historical dramas reach millions of viewers. Often they stimulate wide-ranging debates about their interpretations and lead to the publication of articles and books about the issues they address. Oliver Stone made such an impact with his controversial movie *JFK*. Stone challenged the Warren Commission's conclusion that a lone gunman killed President John F. Kennedy, and for months after his motion picture appeared, newspapers and magazines carried a variety of articles about the film and its view of history. Many criticized Stone severely for taking liberties in his portrayal of the events. Stone welcomed the debates. He aggressively defended his interpretations of the Kennedy murder, saying that he was using film to uncover fundamental truths.

The many people who disputed Stone's use of facts in fashioning a historical interpretation participated in a debate that is almost as old as Hollywood itself. Especially since 1915, the year in which *Birth of a Nation* excited intense arguments because many thought it presented a racist vision of the Reconstruction era, audiences and critics have been engaged in lively disagreements about the way in which cinematic historians deal with their subjects. The debaters have dissected the movies, examining the filmmakers' use of evidence and presentations of images and words to convey interpretations. Some have praised the cinematic historians for their genius in establishing the look and feel of a bygone era and telling dramatic stories that communicate important understandings. Others have lambasted them for exercising too much license and for presenting fiction rather than fact, myth rather than history.

In this book I suggest that both praise and criticism are essential in judging the work of cinematic historians. Filmmakers of necessity face a variety of complex challenges when they interpret history. Even those who are seriously committed to rendering the past with integrity face significant pressures to fictionalize. In view of these pressures, it does not help simply to chastise cinematic historians, expecting them to operate under the most exacting standards of scholarship regarding the presentation of evidence. At the same time, we need to be aware of the dangers of too much tolerance. Artistic creativity can be abused. Filmmakers who see no limits to their imagination may present badly distorted pictures of the past. The matter of how much slack is acceptable in the rope of creative liberty remains an intriguing question.

I have confronted this question personally, and the experience has given me a greater appreciation of the difficulties filmmakers face when they try to interpret history. In my efforts to use drama to throw light on historical issues, I and the production people who worked with me frequently had opportunities to employ creative imagination. These were exciting experiences, but some troubling questions accompanied the sense of stimulation: How far should we go in speculating about the past? To what degree could we invent dialogue and situations to enhance the drama and stimulate the audience's thinking about history? How could we portray historical situations when detailed information about them was lacking? These projects were designed as serious educational efforts, yet we felt some of the same pressures to invent scenes and dialogue that affect Hollywood filmmakers.

The activity involved the development of historical dramas for PBS television (some of the films later appeared on the Disney Channel as well). In creating the projects I planned to relate the stories closely to the historical record. The scripts, I hoped, would be fact-based dramatic portrayals that developed out of careful research into the available

evidence. Throughout the projects I and the other historians and production people who worked with me tried to remain cognizant of this
goal of constructing drama on the basis of scholarship, but we constantly felt the push and pull of the artistic considerations.

Often evidence for the stories was not at hand. For example, we
based a film about a slave conspiracy in Charleston, South Carolina,
largely on the incomplete court records, newspaper reports, and personal correspondence of the 1822 contemporaries, as well as on a broad
reading of the history of slavery in Charleston and in the antebellum
South. Although the documents were wonderfully rich, they could not
possibly provide enough substance to carry the drama fully. Only pieces
of information turned up, and those elements usually constituted reports on the actions of historical figures and revealed little about their
ideas, motivations, or emotions. The archives did not offer much about
the personality of the freed black who planned the insurrection, Denmark Vesey. We did not know precisely how Vesey related to other
people, black and white; what he said to his friends and intimates behind closed doors; or how he felt anticipation, joy, frustration, anger,
or sorrow through his experiences of plotting and capture and his eventual sentencing to execution at the gallows. All these details were essential to the drama, however. To give life to the story of Denmark
Vesey, it was critically important that we cement the pieces of evidence
with mortar of our own construction. To be sure, we tried to construct
that material on the basis of a solid understanding of the published
research on American slavery. The inventive nature of our endeavor
could not be concealed, however; we were fashioning a portrait from
an incomplete puzzle, and other filmmakers might have designed
somewhat different pictures out of the same scattered information.

Interpretation also became a challenge because, even when evidence
was available, it frequently appeared that we could draw a variety of
valid conclusions about it. As storytellers we had to choose among
several possible explanations for behavior. In portraying Denmark
Vesey's conspiracy, for example, we needed to identify the plotters'
goals. What did the African Americans hope to do in Charleston in
1822? Grab control of ships in the harbor and flee to freedom in Hai-
ti? Slaughter the local whites and create their own kingdom in Charleston? Several explanations appeared in the records. Some of the descriptions were complimentary, suggesting that Vesey and his cohort were
motivated by a fundamental desire for liberty; others presented the
conspirators in a different light, suggesting that the blacks hated the

whites and sought vengeance through a bloodbath (we were aware, of course, that virtually all the extant written evidence had been recorded and possibly filtered by South Carolina's whites, and a twentieth-century investigator faces difficulties getting an unmediated view of the African Americans' ideas). No simple answer to the puzzle emerged from the documents. Nonetheless, as cinematic historians we had to provide an interpretation of these vital questions.

If the development of a dramatic program for PBS required considerable exercise of artistic license, it is easy to imagine that Hollywood filmmakers feel much greater pressure to take liberties in their portrayals of history. Not only do the Hollywood figures face the inherent need to fictionalize because available historical evidence is only fragmentary; they also operate in a filmmaking environment that is driven much more by market considerations than is the world of PBS. The Hollywood producers' paramount goal is success at the box office and in video sales. They are pleased if scholars receive their products warmly, but respect from educators is not their primary concern. Above all, Hollywood producers and their underwriters seek movies that will bring handsome profits, and if attention to historical fact gets in the way of relating interesting sagas that will appeal to audiences, many of them will readily compromise the facts.

A recognition of the tremendous commercial pressures operating on Hollywood filmmakers leads many to judge their efforts as significantly flawed. The talented documentary filmmaker Ken Burns communicated this popular viewpoint forcefully when he complained that movie and television dramatists tend to treat the Civil War as a battle between the bosoms (appealing to the audiences' interest in sex rather than to their intellect). Others who have written about history and film have expressed related sentiments. In a chapter entitled "Make-Believe History," for example, Michael Parenti complained that history is usually reduced to personal dramas in movies and television programs. Producers focus on sex and scandal, deviance and depravity, said Parenti, but rarely do they examine truly significant issues such as class power and class struggle.[1] Another historian of film, Daniel Leab, concluded that "truth, accuracy, and a proper respect for history . . . have been routinely subordinated to the need for dramatic effect and even the whim of the filmmaker."[2] The French historian of film Pierre Sorlin also gave a gloomy view of cinema as instruction, observing that the question of "historical truth, which greatly concerns professional scholars, is generally ignored by the producers of historical movies." Popular motion pictures are not truly historical works, Sorlin concluded, and we are wasting time if we pay attention to questions about the accuracy of their depictions.[3]

These critics expressed a feeling that many scholars share when viewing Hollywood's treatment of history, but they are too damning in their dismissal of the dramatic format. Although all historical dramas contain degrees of fictionalization (some of them a considerable degree), they can make significant contributions to the public's appreciation of the past. Their colorful and exciting stories give viewers the look and feel of life in places different both in time and space. Hollywood's dramas also have helped to arouse the public's interest in history. Movies such as *Reds, The Killing Fields,* and *Malcolm X* have stimulated useful discussions about people and issues from the American past.

Indictments of historical dramas also overlook the genre's potential for investigating history in ways that the documentary format may not employ as effectively. Documentary films, which are based on the record of photos, films, newspapers, quotations from historical figures, and other evidence, can be stirring (as Ken Burns demonstrated in his excellent television series *The Civil War*), but the genre does not exhaust the ways in which film can explore historical questions. For a more sustained examination of personalities, emotions, the dynamics of interpersonal relations, and the social and physical conditions of unfamiliar environments, dramatic film may offer more exciting possibilities. Perhaps better than a documentary can, drama permits us to speculate on a historical character's motivation: it lets us imagine the individual's association with friends and adversaries, and it takes us into situations that are not precisely chronicled in the archival records.

The opportunities for imagining the past through drama are enticing, yet many historians are troubled by the conjectural aspect of this enterprise. They prefer to work with what is known; guesswork about the unknown or what is cloudy at best seems to be a very shaky foundation for interpreting history. Some believe the exercise to involve so much fictionalizing that it should not be associated with serious studies of history. Presentations of the past based on speculation appear to be more closely allied to literature than to history.

In many respects this is an appropriate reference, for the work of cinematic historians is related somewhat to the activities of the historical novelists who have done much to excite the public's interest in stories about the past. History-based literature has held a prominent place in Western culture for centuries. From Homer's *Iliad* and *Odyssey*, to Shakespeare's plays about Julius Caesar and English kings, to Victor Hugo's *Les Misérables* and Leo Tolstoy's *War and Peace*, writers have blended fact and imagination to arouse, educate, and entertain. The popularity of these marriages between history and fiction has been evidenced by the public's interest in books such as Marguerite Yourcenar's *Memories of Hadrian*, Henryk Sienkiewicz's *Quo Vadis?* and James Michener's many novels.

Historian Russell B. Nye has suggested that we can learn much from historical novelists (and perhaps his observations apply similarly to the cinematic historians). Both history and literature seek understandings of the reality of the past, said Nye. Novelists assimilate varieties of evidence and speculate about the reasons for thought and behavior. They penetrate the well of "individual consciousness," giving us "an insight into human motivation, a metaphor that adds meaning to experience, a reason for emotion, a perception of a relationship, a cause for an effect."[4] In fact, in some ways literary artists operate with an advantage over the traditional historian. "The artist is permitted to deal with the *internal* currents of men's minds, with the emotions and ideas and motives that run beneath the masks that men assume," said Nye.[5] Often novelists can create a feeling for the past more effectively by resorting to "certain kinds of creative reconstruction denied the historian."[6]

Nye also praised historians who have demonstrated a literary flair, and these observations, too, relate to the cinematic historians' potential for delivering insights. He cited Theodore Roosevelt's writings favorably, noting that the historian-turned-president understood the need to employ a lively imagination when reconstructing the past. Historians, said Roosevelt, need "the power to embody ghosts, to put flesh and blood on dry bones, to make dead men living before your eyes." For Roosevelt, this meant "the power to take the science of history and turn it into literature."[7]

More recently historian Simon Schama has encouraged tolerance for imaginative approaches in an article in the *New York Times Magazine*, using language similar to Nye's. Schama noted that the tension between "popular historians" and the "arbiters of professional decorum" has been long-standing. Unfortunately, too many modern-day commentators praise "a chill, limpid objectivity" in historical presentations and "hit the panic button at the least sign of literary playfulness." Schama said that these critics fail to recognize that much of the new history cannot give us the same "dramatic immediacy" as the older, more emotionally powerful narrative works by the nineteenth-century writers such as Thomas Carlyle, Thomas B. Macaulay, Francis Parkman, George Bancroft, and William H. Prescott. Schama praised not only the historians who wrote colorfully and with texture but also novelists such as Leo Tolstoy and Victor Hugo, who brought the past to life in poetic fashion. We must do more to explore the subjective and interpretive, Schama insisted, noting favorably that Alexandre Dumas "congratulated Lamartine (only half in jest) for having raised history to the status of a novel."[8]

In a fascinating experiment in historical writing called *Dead Certainties: Unwarranted Speculations,* Schama tried his own hand at a blend of fact and fiction. Noting that the Greek word *historía* originally meant "an inquiry," Schama invited readers to experience the uncertainties of historical investigation. He drew attention to the gap between historical events and their subsequent interpretation and narration. In looking at two deaths in North America, one from the eighteenth century and another from the nineteenth, Schama revealed the interpreter's difficulties in working with inadequate or conflicting factual evidence and testimony. His inquiry showed that historical viewpoints can be imagined in a variety of ways and that much of what is presented as history is really a form of speculation. "Historians are painfully aware of their inability ever to reconstruct a dead world in its completeness, however thorough or revealing their documentation," said Schama.[9] Aware of this shortcoming, Schama nevertheless explored possibilities of interpretation that mix informed understanding with poetic imagination.

Schama did not apply his ideas to cinematic history (his references to film in the *New York Times Magazine* article, for example, were limited to a few words of praise for Ken Burns's work), but the essentials of his argument are relevant to a consideration of historical dramas. Cinematic historians engage forms of poetic speculation much as historical novelists employ artistic devices. When filmmakers practice this art with a well-informed and sensitive appreciation of history, they can make useful contributions to the public's thinking.

Some historians have discussed this potential, expressing interest in the imaginative ways in which dramatic film can explore the past. Although intolerant of some movies' gross distortions of history, these scholars urge greater openness to the work of the more sophisticated filmmakers. Cinematic history can deliver important insights, they say, and to recognize the medium's possibilities we need to think openly and differently. Conventional suspicions about the treatment of history in film and television frequently blind us to the rich possibilities.

One of the important figures in these discussions is Daniel Walkowitz, a specialist in U.S. labor and social history who eventually became a filmmaker. Walkowitz developed his interest in film particularly when he found an opportunity to turn his historical monograph into a "docudrama" for television. With funding from the National Endowment for the Humanities, Walkowitz helped to produce *Molders of Troy*, a drama about industrial workers in New York State. Working with a team of filmmakers, Walkowitz crafted a fictional story based on the facts he discovered in the research for his book *Worker City, Company Town*. Walkowitz invented characters for the drama but based the portrayals on evidence from the lives of people who lived in Troy, New York. He defended this strategy as a valid approach to interpreting history through drama. The program delivers important truths, said Walkowitz, even if its principal characters are fictional. "A sense of verisimilitude must be established," he observed; "after that, any given fact may be negotiated so long as the overriding conceptual framework remains inviolate."[10] Walkowitz suggested that the critics of docudramas who focus on minutiae miss the big picture: "I am less concerned with the authenticity of the details in a scene—for example, whether the shoes are authentic—than with the pattern of a set of social relationships that exists in a period of time."[11] Walkowitz hoped to capture the essence of the past through fiction based on fact.

Another historian, Robert A. Rosenstone, has also been influential in encouraging open-minded consideration of film's usefulness in presenting history. In the lead article of a forum on film and history published in the December 1988 issue of *American Historical Review*, Rosenstone commented enthusiastically about the growing "opportunity to represent the world in images and words rather than in words alone."[12] He claimed that film "suggests new possibilities for representing the past, possibilities that could allow narrative history to recapture the power it once had when it was more deeply rooted in the literary imagination."[13] Like Walkowitz, he expressed tolerance for artistic creativeness that contributes to the audiences' understanding of broad historical issues. Rosenstone drew attention to Richard Attenborough's *Gandhi* to point out how a director's inventiveness can enhance a movie's presentation of history. He noted that near the beginning of the movie Attenborough showed a South African railroad conductor pushing Gandhi out of a train compartment for whites. Details of this event were not described in Gandhi's autobiography, said Rosenstone, but the movie's dramatic episode gives audiences a strong sense of the pain of discrimination. Such an artistic embellishment does not do violence to history, "at least not so long as the 'meaning' that the 'impersonators' create somehow carries forth the larger 'meaning' of the historical character whom they represent."[14] In a later commentary Rosenstone applied his tolerance for artistic creativity to a more controversial example of story manipulation. Speaking about Oliver Stone's *JFK*, Rosenstone praised the director for provoking thought and arousing audiences to question official truths. He saw a larger lesson in the case of Stone's contribution. "The Hollywood historical film," said Rosenstone, "will always include images that are at once invented and yet may still be considered true; true in that they symbolize, condense, or summarize larger amounts of data; true in that they carry out the overall meaning of the past that can be verified, documented, or reasonably argued."[15]

Rosenstone also questioned popular impressions about the superiority of written history over filmed history. He noted that many scholars are more comfortable with the printed medium, because they believe that it comes closer to the truth in portraying the past. They think that a book is more effective than a film in showing the complexities of motivation and causation. To them, historians of the printed word are committed to working with facts and reconstructing reality, whereas filmmakers seem to show reckless disregard for the facts as they construct their own versions of reality. Rosenstone pointed out, however, that those who accept this viewpoint overlook the creative nature of all historical interpretation, whether in writing or in film. Addressing issues similar to the ones Schama raised, Rosenstone observed that people and nations do not really live historical "stories" or narratives that are coherent tales with beginnings, middles, and endings. Historians construct these narratives "as part of their attempts to make sense of the past." Written history "is a representation of the past, not the past itself."[16] In short, scholars do much imagining about the past when they attempt to understand history, and a recognition of this process suggests a need for appreciating the filmmaker's efforts to imagine history.

Walkowitz, Rosenstone, and other historians have awakened us to the need to greet cinematic history with more tolerant and curious eyes, but there is a danger in pursuing their logic to an extreme. A consistently open-minded view of the filmmaker's efforts to fictionalize would leave us unprepared to discriminate between an admirably filmed presentation of history and a poor one. It would lead us toward treating almost any fabrication or distortion as a legitimate artistic exercise as long as it contributes in some way to the audience's thinking about the past. Any manipulation of evidence would seem fair game if it educates moviegoers in a broad sense. Marcus Raskin articulated this excessively generous view in an evaluation of the movie *JFK,* saying, "it does no good to pick apart the rendering of an event by an artist. His or her purpose is not the particular but the general."[17] Such a sweeping statement seems to leave little room for consideration of integrity in dealing with historical evidence. It makes the scholars' efforts to evaluate cinematic history seem to be irrelevant. Raskin's words suggest that historians who are sensitive to the rules of traditional scholarship cannot fruitfully comment on a movie's handling of particulars, because the makers of docudramas cannot be held accountable to facts in the same way as the producers of written history are.

Excusing *any* manipulation in the name of artistic license is indefensible, and certainly this is not the purpose of most analysts who have praised sophisticated exercises in cinematic history. They do not sanction filmmaking activities that treat the subject irresponsibly; rather, they ask us to recognize that the visual media may provide exciting and different ways to explore historical truths.

What, then, is a "responsible" manner in which to work with dramatic film? To what degree should we tolerate manipulation of evidence so that the filmmaker can touch the viewers' feelings and stimulate their thinking? These questions cannot be answered by making broad indictments that demonstrate no sensitivity to the realities of filmmaking. If we hold cinematic historians strictly to the standards of most written history, we are almost certain to be disappointed, for filmmakers must attend to the demands of drama and the challenges of working with incomplete evidence. In creating historical dramas they almost always need to collapse several historical figures into a few central characters to make a story understandable. Often they are pressed to simplify complex causes so that audiences will comprehend their movies' principal messages and not lose interest, and the dramatic medium often leads them to attribute changes in history to the actions of dynamic individuals rather than to impersonal forces. Cinematic historians often lack detailed evidence about situations in the past, so they invent dialogue and suggest impressions about the emotions and motivations of historic figures. Also, they suggest closure on a story, revealing few doubts, questions, or considerations of alternative possibilities.

Critics of docudramas may not be comfortable with these practices, but it is important that they understand that they, too, would experience pressures to manipulate stories if they were to try their hands at docudrama. The challenge in assessing cinematic history involves much more than leveling sweeping criticism at liberties taken. It calls for sensitivity to important questions about historical interpretation and an understanding of the world in which cinematic historians operate. Out of this balanced appreciation of goals and realities—of the potential and the difficulties of doing cinematic history—a more sophisticated discussion of the genre may emerge.

The work of historian James M. McPherson offers an example of the kind of balanced assessment that can advance our understanding of the subject. His informed and elastic evaluation of the movie *Glory* illustrates the value of combining critical judgments with an awareness of the unique nature of docudrama's approach to history. In a lengthy review of the 1989 movie dealing with the African Americans fighting for the Union in the Civil War, McPherson assessed the way in which director Edward Zwick and other members of the production team interpreted the past. McPherson, author of the Pulitzer Prize–winning history of the Civil War *Battle Cry of Freedom,* identified both the achievements and the shortcomings of the motion picture. He criticized the filmmakers for specific errors and misrepresentations, but he also tolerated some rearrangements of facts when they serve what seem to be legitimate purposes. For instance, *Glory* leaves the impression that the men of the Massachusetts 54th were largely escaped slaves. They were, in fact, mostly free blacks. *Glory* misrepresents the facts in this case, but McPherson claims that the moviemakers made a defensible artistic decision. After all, *Glory* really is about the general subject of "blacks in the Civil War" and "not simply about the 54th Massachusetts." Most of the African-American soldiers in the war "were slaves until a few months, even a few days, before they joined up." Thus, the film makes an important contribution to understanding by making many of the principal characters in the story represent the more than 100,000 African Americans who changed quickly "from an oppressed to a proud people" who fought for freedom. Ultimately the movie presents a powerful, inspiring perspective on history.[18]

McPherson's approach to *Glory* provides some useful thoughts for examining other movies that deal with historical subjects. As his analysis demonstrates, it is worthwhile to observe errors of fact and to point out misleading representations that serve no important dramatic pur-

e thugs / to communicate / broad truths.

pose. In instances where the movie's evidence is incorrect or unrepresentative but is placed in the story to convey a particular message, however, the task of assessment is more challenging. It is worth considering whether the manipulation of evidence developed out of genuine and laudable efforts to communicate broad truths.

Questions about a film's potential for delivering transcendent truths relate also to the tendency of Hollywood movies to deal with powerful myths about the American past, and here, too, the observations of some historians suggest the grounds for a complex rather than a simplistic reaction to cinematic history.

Hollywood's filmmakers have long demonstrated an enthusiasm for building their stories around myths. Their dramas draw on a great reservoir of popular images about the nation's heritage. Motion pictures invoke tales about the frontier, the South, and the West. They give life to popular images of the Native American and the cowboy. Myths about struggles for freedom, rights, justice, and progress are often at the foundation of movie treatments. In short, cinematic historians do not simply create plots out of the documentary record of specific incidents or incorporate their own personal impressions; they also establish and dramatize their portrayals through images drawn from the rich mythology of American culture. Some of the myths they employ developed in popular oral traditions, works of literature, or fashions of the theater; others emerged especially from the movie culture itself. These visions wield tremendous emotional force in the present day. Consequently, the filmmakers produce part history, part myth.

Recognition of this mythic quality may appear to suggest cause for casting suspicion on cinematic history, but scholars such as the late Warren Susman have urged a more appreciative response. Susman noted that myth and history relate significantly to each other. "History becomes myth and myth becomes history," said Susman.[19] Myths express the vision, hopes, and dreams of a people (often utopian visions); they define the fundamental goals of the society, whereas historical interpretations illuminate the processes for achieving those goals. "Myth provides the drama, and history puts the show on the road," he wrote. The two serve related purposes and are not necessarily in conflict with each other.[20] Richard Slotkin, author of a trilogy about myths and American culture, also sees a connection. Slotkin acknowledges that myth can feed our nostalgia for an idealized past, but he also sees a positive aspect, observing that we can make mythic discourse a way of imaging the truth." Slotkin does not see myths as static conceptions. Mythical ideas are constantly reworked as the storytellers try to bring them into line with changing realities in American society. In this sense myths become a vehicle for reimagining America and revising and transforming our culture.[21] The modern mass media offer the broadest base and most pervasive means for communicating these evolving mythic visions, said Slotkin, and he probed examples of Hollywood productions for evidence of the way in which myth and history interact and influence each other.

Clearly the filmmakers examined in the eight case studies featured in this book drew on many of the familiar myths from American history. Their stories relate tales of Davids fighting Goliaths, of the dignity of the poor in confronting the rich, and of the moral superiority of individuals who fight for justice. Their films also convey broad critical judgments. They invoke traditional suspicions about people in power, whether these well-positioned figures are situated in business or in government. They raise questions about the behavior of individuals in seats of authority, such as manufacturers, bankers, presidents, generals, or government bureaucrats—even southern rednecks, if the scene of presentation is the racist South. Most fundamentally, their histories communicate lessons about the struggle of the little person versus the big one, the weak versus the powerful.

The movies' relationship to myth does not destroy their value as communicators of historical interpretations. References to myths strengthen the dramatic force of Hollywood's storytelling and help audiences to sense the relationship of specific problems to broader issues. Invocations of myths facilitate the filmmakers' efforts to draw attention to larger truths. Dramatic cinema is a particularly attractive instrument for realizing myths' value in communicating, and not surprisingly, myth has found a prominent place in movies about the past. In studying the record of cinematic history, the challenge is not simply to denounce myth's presence but to distinguish between falsely distorted myths and the impressively imaginative efforts to speak the truth through mythic images.

The Practice of Cinematic History

This book explores ways in which filmmakers treat history. The following chapters examine four principal methods of cinematic history: mixing fact with fiction, shaping evidence to deliver specific conclusions, suggesting messages for the present in stories about the past, and employing a documentary style to develop the "Great Man" perspective on the past.

Each of these approaches helps the filmmaker to render history in engaging and intelligible ways. Sometimes, however, the techniques elicit objections. Moviegoers as well as film reviewers and historians are often troubled by these modes of interpretation. Aware that the dramatic format offers creative artists abundant opportunities to design stories that satisfy their own wishes, these critics are suspicious of Hollywood's handling of history. They complain that filmmakers seem too eager to paint their own version of events and that they lack strong commitments to rendering truthful pictures of the past.

In discussing the four approaches to cinematic history, it seems wise not to prejudge the techniques as inherently effective or flawed. Each way of telling stories has value as a means of communication. Each enables artists to make history exciting and comprehensible to audiences. Nevertheless, the techniques can be abused. Filmmakers may go to extremes in manipulating evidence and suggesting messages. They can recklessly interpret events. In assessing these approaches, then, it is useful to keep an open mind. More can be gained by judging individual production activities than by condemning the techniques indiscriminately. Attention to specific experiences in filmmaking throws light on both the strengths and weaknesses of cinematic history.

A glance at Robert Redford's *Quiz Show* (1994) demonstrates some of the benefits and liabilities. *Quiz Show* portrays the scandals involving Charles Van Doren and others who pretended to be uncoached contestants in a popular 1950s televised game program called *Twenty One*. Van Doren secretly received information about the questions he faced in the programs, and he suffered great humiliation when his involvement in the deception came to light.

First, Redford (working with his screenwriter, Paul Attonasio) exercised considerable artistic license in designing the story for the cinema. He compressed time, collapsed several historical figures into one, and took other liberties to simplify the portrayal and make it dramatically engaging. His efforts enhanced the performance, but the technique also drew fire from some critics. They complained that Redford speculated excessively when he suggested that Van Doren participated in the deception especially to compete with his Olympian father. Critics also objected to the way in which the movie suggests that a specific executive representing Geritol (which sponsored the quiz show) and an executive at NBC were major participants in the scandal (these figures served the drama nicely as villains, said the critics, but they were not principal culprits in the real case).[22]

Second, Robert Redford drew lessons from history by making his story of the quiz show scandals a metaphor that represents many deceptions in American life. Redford hoped that the drama would bring to mind other examples of wrongdoing in recent U.S. history, such as Watergate, the Iran-Contra scandal, the Bank of Commerce and Credit International (BCCI) scandal, and the savings and loan scandal. He hoped that *Quiz Show* would raise questions about immorality and suggest that Americans need to be more alert and angry about large-scale violations of the public trust. Some praised Redford for this display of conscience; others took issue with his interpretations, claiming that he practiced his own form of deception by playing loosely with the facts.

Third, *Quiz Show* contains some ambiguous elements that allow viewers to read a variety of contemporary meanings into the story. For example, the movie features images that suggest a causal connection between the American capitalistic ethos and the fall from grace that wrecked the lives of Charles Van Doren and various other contestants and business executives involved in the scandal. In this manner *Quiz Show's* vague references to the dollar nexus provides a lively sounding board for debates about the role of materialism in modern American life.

Finally, Redford dramatized the story about the discovery of corruption in television game shows by focusing on the exploits of one investigator. As Redford portrayed the events, the hero of the story was Richard Goodwin, a bright, young lawyer out of Harvard who worked for the Federal Communications Commission in the 1950s. Redford based much of his account on Goodwin's book, *Remembering America: A Voice from the Sixties.* Chronicling Goodwin's activities in a realistic, documentary style, Redford stressed the investigator's tenacity in pursuing truth against difficult obstacles. In the manner of many other makers of Hollywood dramas, Redford accented the achievements of this single person to strengthen audience interest in the story and to simplify the details of a complex situation. Goodwin's actions in the movie symbolize the contribution of a number of different individuals, Redford explained.

Some observers of the film could not accept this reconstruction of events. They complained that the movie grossly exaggerates the importance of Goodwin's role and fails to give credit to other key figures, particularly Joseph Stone, the head of the Manhattan district attorney's complaint bureau, who did more to unravel the mystery than Goodwin. In fact, said the critics, most of the key evidence about the corrupt game shows had already come into the open when Goodwin pursued his investigation. Thus, *Quiz Show*'s focus on a single, dynamic personality enhances its dramatic quality but stirred questions about representativeness and authenticity.

Just as all four approaches to viewing history through the cinema are evident in *Quiz Show*, they are visible, to a degree, in all the motion pictures under consideration in this book. Each film contains examples of artistic license, evidence of the filmmakers' attempts to make the past relevant for the present, reflections of modern-day controversies, and indications of the "Great Man" style of historical interpretation. Of course, some motion pictures serve better than others to illustrate each approach. To explore further the strengths and weaknesses of these applications of cinematic history, I examine two films for each category.

Exercising Artistic License: Communicating through Fact and Fiction

Filmmakers often simplify and fictionalize their stories. They envision scenes from the past for which they lack detailed information. They put words in the mouths of historical figures and imagine moments of argument and conflict that may never have existed in the way shown on the screen. As in *Quiz Show*, cinematic historians often collapse several different figures into one or two representative ones, and they stress the importance of only one or two factors in explaining the causes of historical problems rather than many possible complex causes. Filmmakers also compact time, giving events that took place over months or years the appearance of occurring in a relatively brief period.

These devices aid communication. Inventing scenes and dialogue, cinematic historians speculate on intriguing questions about causation and motivation. Manipulating facts, they try to render detailed information comprehensible to audiences and make the past come to life in compelling drama. The productions that result from such artistic license may prove to be interesting to the audiences, but are they really history? Does the use of literary imagination destroy authenticity? How much creative liberty should be tolerated when judging movies for their contributions to the public's thinking about the past?

These questions are applied to two specific cases of filmmaking. *Mississippi Burning* and *JFK* came under fire for the panache their filmmakers demonstrated in telling colorful tales. Some critics insisted that these movies do not present serious examinations of the past and that to treat them as versions of history is an insult to anyone truly committed to ideals of scholarship. The filmmakers were sloppy in their use of evidence, said the critics, and when they invented material for their dramas, they demonstrated very little interest in telling truthful stories. *Mississippi Burning* and *JFK* are essentially fictional forms of entertainment. Others praised these filmmakers for communicating higher truths in the course of designing stimulating portrayals that mix fact with fiction. The makers of these movies succeeded in getting the public to ponder important questions, they argued; the artistic flourishes make audiences think about history. Indeed, said the defenders, these individuals demonstrated some of the exciting ways that film can stir us to feel and conceptualize the past.

Although questions about artistic license are relevant to all the movies under review in this book, they are most pertinent in the cases of *Mississippi Burning* and *JFK*. These films tested the dimensions of creative imagination most strikingly. Controversies that swirled around these films particularly concerned the filmmakers' mixing of fact and fiction.

Mississippi Burning powerfully portrays the frightening environment of racist terror that troubled African Americans and their white supporters during the years of the struggle for civil rights in the South. The first half of the movie sensitively chronicles the brutal murder of three campaigners in Mississippi and the frustratingly difficult search for the culprits, but the second half veers away from the historical record and becomes a Hollywood-style action/adventure film about two fictional FBI agents. This diversion provoked strong attacks, as did the concentration on the actions of whites in Mississippi instead of the important activities of blacks in the fight for civil rights. Is *Mississippi Burning* a historical film? Does it provide insights on the past as well as entertainment?

Oliver Stone's *JFK* appears to have excited the most praise and criticism regarding artistic license. With dazzling technical skill, Stone examined a great variety of details concerning the assassination of President John F. Kennedy. This fast-paced drama throws an abundance of information at the viewers over a period of more than three hours. But is the information true? Stone liberally mixed actual news footage with simulated footage. He designed scenes for the movie based on rumors and speculation. Not surprisingly, many asked whether *JFK* offers a legitimate perspective on history. Indeed, they questioned whether the movie represents history at all.

Drawing Lessons: Making the Past Relevant to the Present

When the director D. W. Griffith promoted *Birth of a Nation* in 1915, he confidently identified his movie as an objective and authentic picture of the past. Griffith boasted that his film presents the experience of civil war and Reconstruction with stunning realism. "You will actually see what happened," said Griffith. "There will be no opinion expressed. You will merely be present at the making of history." Griffith's claims about the movie were ridiculous, as modern students of film and history are well aware. *Birth of a Nation* is not a value-neutral examination of the past. The movie casts the Radical Republicans and their African-American friends in the role of villains, portrays the gentry of the Old South and members of the Ku Klux Klan as heroes, and depicts the Reconstruction as a tragic experience in which aggressive Yankees wrongfully interfered in the white southerners' way of life. Historians have recognized that Griffith's movie carried biased messages for Americans in 1915 that suggested a critical view of campaigns for racial integration. They also have understood that Griffith's cinematic history suggested a need for northerners of 1915 to move past the sectional enmity that grew out of the Civil War and to feel sympathy for the white southerners who suffered greatly in their lost cause. In short, a study of *Birth of a Nation* strikingly illustrates the way that filmmakers often use history to make a point about the present. Like Griffith, many cinematic historians have examined stories from the past to suggest lessons concerning modern-day controversies.

Two films addressed in this book, *Sergeant York* and *Missing*, particularly represent partisan attempts to seek lessons for the present from the past. *Sergeant York* (1941) offers a moving story about a World War I hero in a manner designed to deliver a powerful message for Americans trying to decide what their country's role should be in World War II. The popular motion picture drew strongly positive conclusions about the United States' fighting role in Europe in 1918, and this interpretation provoked heated criticisms from Americans who demanded a more isolationist position for their country in 1941. *Missing* (1982) suggests lessons about the history of U.S. intervention in Third World countries by examining a specific tragedy in a South American nation. In pointing to the case of an American who was killed during a military coup in Chile, the movie raises broad questions about the United States' role in subverting democracy in the name of anticommunism during the Cold War years. As in the case of *Sergeant York,* this example of partisan interpretation of history also drew fire, illustrating the ways that cinematic history can make poignant and debatable political statements.

Reflecting the Present: Revealing Current Controversy in Portrayals of the Past

Whereas the makers of historical cinema such as *Sergeant York* and *Missing* designed their films with specific lessons for the present in mind, some filmmakers are much more vague about suggesting lessons. Their movies examine the past with considerable complexity and subtlety, featuring evidence that can seem appealing to viewers who entertain quite different thoughts about history's meaning for modern times. These films serve as reflections that allow audiences to draw their own conclusions from the stories. They suggest that there may be more than one good answer to questions about the past and present, and they hint at some of the possible conflicting perspectives. They achieve, in a sense, what the noted Japanese director Akira Kurosawa attempted to do in his classic film *Rashomon* (1950). Kurosawa showed four different accounts of a rape and murder in the movie. Instead of choosing a specific explanation for the event, Kurosawa left audiences to reach their own conclusions. Of course, most American filmmakers are not as overt in their presentation of multiple perspectives. Rather, they stay close to a chronological story, preferring to juxtapose positive and negative images within the context of a more traditional dramatic format.

The first film under consideration in this category, *Bonnie and Clyde,* had its genesis in the 1960s. The motion picture's developers planned to appeal to the 1960s generation's fascinations with unconventionality and independence, its concern for the poor, and its suspicion of the "Establishment." The filmmakers touched a sensitive nerve, though. To their surprise *Bonnie and Clyde* grew into more than just an innovative adventure story. It became an important point of reference in a lively debate about the impact of the visual media in a crime-ridden society.

The makers of the second movie in this category, *Patton,* showed more awareness of their film's potential for controversy. These filmmakers were, after all, designing a biographical drama about a headstrong general who had attracted a long list of admirers and detractors. Had they been able to bring off their movie as planned, they might have succeeded in eluding the political fires. During the latter part of the production period, however, the United States became deeply involved in Vietnam. By the time of *Patton*'s release (1970), the American people were sharply divided about the role of their country's armed forces in Southeast Asia. In this context critics and audiences were not prepared to view *Patton* as just another war movie. *Patton*'s story excited positive and negative emotions about the contributions of the U.S. military establishment, and the movie's producers had to steer their way through stormy debates. Like *Bonnie and Clyde, Patton* served as a sort of Rorschach test that invited Americans to express their tensions and frustrations.

Accenting Heroism: Celebrating the "Great Man" in the Documentary Style

In presenting stories about the past, filmmakers usually focus on the exploits of one or two individuals. This approach brings history to a personal level, portraying it through the experiences of fascinating and often heroic people for whom audiences are encouraged to show sympathy. The practice of reporting on good people's struggles against adversity produces attractive drama, but it also raises some problems. Personality-oriented movies give short shrift, for example, to the effect of collective action from the masses or to the impact of long-term economic changes. Instead of recognizing subtle, complex factors that foster change, they see developments resulting almost exclusively from the actions of dynamic individuals. In this respect they borrow ideas from the "Great Man" theory of history and stretch them to an extreme.

Both movies identified here with this approach relate how determined, aggressive individuals worked hard and eventually succeeded in promoting important reforms. *Norma Rae* suggests that unions won a significant victory in the North Carolina textile mills especially because a determined female mill worker and her union agent showed the perseverance to pull off a victory. The movie fails to reveal that many other people contributed to the gains in Roanoke Rapids, North Carolina, or even that the victory constituted just a small part of a larger wave of organizing activity that was beginning to bring the protection of collective bargaining to southern mill workers in the late twentieth century. Similarly, *All the President's Men* leaves the impression that two *Washington Post* reporters, Bob Woodward and Carl Bernstein, almost single-handedly brought down the Nixon administration. The movie gives little notice to the way in which other journalists, as well as special prosecutors, judges, members of Congress, and even one of the jailed burglars, helped American society to discover the dimensions of the scandal.

Both movies under study in this section present history in realistic, documentary-style formats. The makers of *All the President's Men* and *Norma Rae* gave careful attention to detail, appearing to reproduce the past as it really was. This emphasis on what may be called "cinematic realism" is evident in many films that chronicle individuals' struggles against difficult odds. Such movies have the appearance of muckraking dramas. They portray the past in fine detail to establish the audience's belief in the legitimacy of their reports. They make their case by stressing authenticity. Such films appear to express their own authenticity, as if saying, "This is not just an interesting personal story; it is a very realistic picture of actual problems that badly needed attention." By drawing viewers into a richly documented look at society's troubles, the motion picture hints that related difficulties are still present in America and need correcting. Verisimilitude received attention in all the productions addressed in this book, but for *All the President's Men* and *Norma Rae* realism became a defining characteristic.

Of course, attention to verisimilitude does not in itself guarantee that a movie will present a sophisticated picture of history. The expensive efforts to design historical scenes in careful detail are of little value if the filmmakers fail to address significant issues in their movies or if they radically distort the historical record. A more important test of their production's quality relates to the intelligence and seriousness of the interpretations of history. Fortunately, the makers of *All the President's Men* and *Norma Rae* performed well in this regard, rendering sensitive and informed perspectives on events.

It is difficult to assess the filmmakers' practice of historical interpretation when limiting the analysis to the words and images that appear on the screen. Such an approach can yield only limited insights into the filmmakers' uses of artistic license, their efforts to draw lessons for the present, their attempts to relate historical subjects to modern-day controversies, and their attempts to make judgments by celebrating the heroic actions of individuals. A filmmaker's approach to each of these four practices becomes somewhat clearer when we step outside the film and view a movie's production history and reception. Our judgments about the film's treatment of history are better grounded when we know something about the producers, directors, and writers—their backgrounds, their ideas, and their motivations. Our observations also profit from an awareness of the planning experience—the conditions under which moviemakers designed their stories and the manner in which economic, social, and political factors influenced construction of their dramas. Finally, it is helpful to know how cinematic historians responded to controversies and defended their interpretations in the face of criticism. The following eight case studies provide this broader view of the practice of cinematic history.

PART 1

EXERCISING ARTISTIC LICENSE

Communicating through a Mix of Fact and Fiction

1

Mississippi Burning
"A STANDARD TO WHICH WE COULDN'T LIVE UP"

Rupert Anderson (Gene Hackman) and
Alan Ward (Willem Dafoe) investigate the
murders of civil rights workers in *Mississippi
Burning*. Courtesy of the Museum of
Modern Art/Film Stills Archive.

W hen the time came for announcing the Academy Award for best picture of 1988, Hollywood suspected that one of the nominees was unlikely to get the Oscar because of its controversial treatment of history. The manipulation of facts and fictionalizing in *Mississippi Burning* had angered many citizens, journalists, and professional historians, sparking lively debates about the degree to which filmmakers ought to feel obligated to produce reasonably authentic and representative pictures of the past. *Mississippi Burning* does not tell the true story of the Freedom Summer of 1964, said the critics; it tells Hollywood's distorted version. Some of the harshest criticism came from African Americans who complained that the movie largely overlooks the important role of blacks in the civil rights struggle. *Mississippi Burning* makes the civil rights victories in the South seem to have been almost totally the result of work by whites, they said. In this context director Alan Parker's moving examination of the murders of three civil rights workers in the Deep South fell into trouble. Popular objections appeared to taint the film. As expected, when the Academy of Motion Pictures Arts and Sciences got around to delivering Oscars, *Mississippi Burning* did not receive the prize for best picture.[1]

This run-in with history was unfortunate, for when the movie portrays events from the historical record, it offers riveting drama. *Mississippi Burning* communicates the ugliness and viciousness of racial prejudice in the South about as well as any Hollywood film of the post–World War II period. It focuses on a murder case that was naturally appealing as the source for a motion picture screenplay. The killing of a black civil rights campaigner and his two white companions had outraged the nation in 1964 and provoked a massive response from the federal government. President Lyndon B. Johnson threw numerous federal agents into the effort to capture the murderers. Congress reacted to the tragedy by voting a wide-ranging civil rights bill into law. After a tremendous effort the FBI found the bodies and identified the culprits. Conviction was difficult, because all-white juries in Mississippi tended to look the other way regarding such crimes, but eventually a number of the conspirators went to prison for civil rights violations. This was the stuff of good Hollywood storytelling, a historical case that offered fascinating possibilities for dramatic portrayal.

To appreciate how *Mississippi Burning*'s handling of this story provoked heated controversy, it is useful to consider a brief chronicle of the principal events in Mississippi during the historic summer of 1964. This is the record on which the filmmakers drew to create their movie; this is the evidence that they incorporated with considerable detail and yet sometimes contradicted and distorted.

The tragedy that *Mississippi Burning* dramatizes occurred during the summer of 1964, after civil rights workers launched a broad campaign to register black voters in the state. The campaigners hoped that their efforts would draw national attention to the racial problems in the Deep South. To win sympathy from the American public, they practiced a strategy of nonviolent resistance, even when confronting physical abuse from segregationists. A number of white Mississippians did not look kindly on the intervention from Yankee do-gooders or the evidence that local African Americans were organizing politically. Some of these whites took action, practicing intimidation and terror as members of the Ku Klux Klan. These racists harassed civil rights activists and attacked homes and churches where the organizers congregated. In 1964 they burned thirty-one African-American churches in Mississippi.

The tragedy occurred near Philadelphia, Mississippi, after three young men left Meridian to drive into the countryside and investigate the burning of a black church. One of the travelers was Michael Schwerner, a white social worker from New York City who had moved to Mississippi with his wife to coordinate community programs for the Congress of Racial Equality. The second was Andrew Goodman, a student at New York's Queens College who arrived in Mississippi just a day before the fatal trip. The third was James Chaney, a black youth associated with the Congress of Racial Equality who worked with Schwerner in the drive to register black voters. Local members of the Ku Klux Klan were determined to attack these campaigners and send a message of fear to other such activists. The Klansmen believed that they could act almost with impunity, for whites in Mississippi were rarely brought to trial for injury to African Americans or harassment of whites who operated as allies of black "troublemakers."

While the civil rights workers were driving along a Mississippi high-way, the Neshoba County deputy sheriff took the three to the local jailhouse and then released them. With the deputy sheriff's assistance, members of the Klan later assumed control. They forced Schwerner, Goodman, and Chaney into the woods and shot them. The murderers hid the car near a river and buried the three bodies. When FBI investigators began to look for the missing persons, the local sheriff of Neshoba County, who knew about the murders, said that the civil rights campaigners probably were hiding out somewhere to get publicity. This idea became popular across the state of Mississippi; many segregationists laughed and claimed the disappearances to be a publicity stunt.[2]

The Mississippi case did not seem a laughing matter in Washington, D.C. President Johnson saw this tragedy in the Deep South as a stain on the nation's record, and he wanted the spot removed quickly. Johnson pressured the FBI to beef up its activities in Mississippi. The bureau's director, J. Edgar Hoover, was unsympathetic toward the rights movement and reluctant to intervene much in the affairs of the Deep South. He responded to Johnson's appeals, however, and suddenly threw the bureau's weight into Mississippi. As the search for the bodies expanded, three busloads of sailors from the U.S. military arrived to aid the effort. The sailors searched over a large and marshy area of the Pearl River in a busy weekend of body hunting. Nothing turned up. The search continued, as FBI agents gathered over 150,000 pages of information in the search for clues.

Collecting documents and scouring the Mississippi terrain in the heat of summer did not prove to be as useful as the FBI's efforts to bribe informers. The news that helped to break the case came from Klan members who responded to rewards for information (informants received $30,000 for cooperating; plea bargaining for reduced sentences also helped to bring out evidence). Eventually agents found the three bodies at the base of a dam. Investigators were able to pry more information loose by telling various Klansmen what they knew about their activities. When it became evident that the investigators were beginning to learn the identities of the culprits, several of the Klan members became suspicious of their fellow conspirators. Fearing arrest, they related valuable information about their associates in the crime. Several arrests followed, including that of the sheriff and deputy sheriff of Neshoba County. Eventually a jury of Mississippi whites found the two law enforcement officers and six others guilty of depriving Schwerner, Goodman, and Chaney of their civil rights (a more serious conviction on murder charges could not be obtained in the state, because local jurors of whites would not convict).[3]

This is the history that served as the basis for *Mississippi Burning*'s story. The case of violence in Philadelphia, Mississippi, contained abundant elements suitable for portrayal in a motion picture. The film's developers did not need to stray far from the facts to create a compelling drama. Indeed, the individual who first developed the movie project intended to design a script that stayed relatively close to the evidence. Over the course of production planning, however, his project began to spin away from history and move considerably into the realm of fiction. By the time *Mississippi Burning* reached the screen, it had become a melding of sophisticated re-creation and regrettable distortion, exposing its makers to claims that they had abused their artistic license.

The individual who thought that this historical case could serve as the foundation for attractive Hollywood entertainment was Chris Gerolmo. He initiated the planning and followed the project through to completion. Gerolmo had studied at Harvard and taught documentary film production there for a few years. He had been enthusiastic about the direct cinema of Frederick Wiseman and encouraged students to make documentaries about social issues such as the problems of the handicapped. Eventually Gerolmo moved into theater production (his father was already a noted producer). He wanted to develop a career as a director in Hollywood but sensed that he would have to enter the movie business on the basis of his writing talents. Gerolmo began looking for a story that offered potential as a screenplay and discovered an intriguing possibility in an article in the *New York Post*. The selection was a chapter excerpted from a book by Neil J. Welch and David W. Marston entitled *Inside Hoover's FBI*. It describes how J. Edgar Hoover encouraged FBI agents to "take the gloves off" and infiltrate the Ku Klux Klan to find the murderers of civil rights campaigners in Mississippi. Gerolmo then decided to approach a friend, theatrical producer Fred Zollo, for help with the project. He made Zollo the producer. Together Gerolmo and Zollo went off to Hollywood to sell the concept for the movie.[4]

Marketing the concept proved difficult. Some young studio executives had never heard of the murder cases in Mississippi and wondered whether audiences would show much interest in what seemed like an obscure story about racism in the South. Others simply were not convinced that the film could make money. Unable to get a financial com-

mitment, Gerolmo returned to New York and decided to write the script
"on spec." He investigated the historical evidence related to the cases,
prepared a screenplay, and tried to get the necessary financing by sub-
mitting a more complete proposal. His perseverance paid off, but he
needed four and a half years to bring the project to completion.[5]

As production planning moved forward, Orion Pictures secured the
services of Alan Parker, a talented British director who brought strong
personal views about ways to depict racist terrorism in the South. Parker did not have much personal knowledge of the civil rights confrontations in Mississippi in the 1960s (he had been living in England at
the time), but he had firsthand experience with class tensions and
economic inequality from his youth in a working-class area of North
London. Building on these memories, he stressed the notion that class
antagonism was at the core of much of white racist thinking in Mississippi. Parker also brought a reputation for making films that dramatically contrast "good" and "bad" characters, and he pursued this approach in portraying the Mississippi figures. In adjusting the script and
selecting actors, Parker took care to characterize many of the Mississippi whites as ignorant and prejudiced. Members of the Ku Klux Klan
got particularly emphatic treatment, appearing as vicious, contemptible bigots.[6]

Parker's contributions toward script design added tension and excitement to the story, but they also pulled the portrayal from its historical base and pushed it in the direction of fiction. Some of these
adjustments disturbed Gerolmo, who felt that the changes could lead
to a kind of story different from the one originally intended. Gerolmo
was troubled, for example, about Parker's decision to alter a scene
depicting FBI-sponsored intimidation of a Mississippi white man. Gerolmo's script has a Mafia member who owes the FBI a favor threatening a white racist conspirator by holding a gun to his mouth. Gerolmo
based this depiction on rumors he heard about the FBI's tactics. Parker redesigned the incident so that the movie shows a black FBI agent
using a razor to threaten the town's mayor with castration if he does
not reveal what he knows. This powerful image seemed to offer great
potential for exciting movie audiences, because it suggests a nightmare
for a white Mississippi racist. The scene reverses the predator/victim
relationship evident in much of southern history. Americans were familiar with stories about white racists castrating southern blacks; now
Parker intended to symbolize a form of revenge by depicting a black
intimidator with a knife to the groin of a white man. Gerolmo was

uncomfortable with the change. He knew that there had been no black agents in the FBI in 1964, and nothing existed in the records or the rumor mills that even remotely resembled the proposed scene. Inclusion of Parker's idea might draw unwanted criticism.[7]

Gerolmo had tried to base much of his screenplay on actual events. He supplemented material from *Inside Hoover's FBI* with material from William Bradford Huie's book on the Philadelphia murder case, *Three Lives for Mississippi,* and another book that deals, in part, with the history of the period, *Attack on Terror.* Additionally, Gerolmo examined newspaper reports from 1963 and testimony from the lengthy court case against the Klansmen.

Gerolmo had decided to focus the screenplay on the FBI's fight against the Klan. His story was not to be about the civil rights movement; rather, it would deal with the struggle of law enforcement agents to catch the racists responsible for the deaths of Schwerner, Goodman, and Chaney. The general shape of his drama would "be a lot like what really happened," he explained later, but he intended to condense the action in time and collapse several FBI characters he read about into two principal figures (and then add fictional material about their exploits). In the movie Gene Hackman and Willem Dafoe play the two FBI protagonists (under the fictitious names of "Anderson" and "Ward"). Gerolmo's original draft uses many real names from the Mississippi case, but later versions substitute fictitious names throughout ("to protect the guilty," as producer Fred Zollo put it).[8]

The movie's focus on the exploits of two fictitious FBI agents made interesting drama, but this approach created grounds for controversy once the movie reached the theaters. Critics observed that the two principal characters in the story are fictional and that their prominent roles tend to exaggerate the FBI's importance in the civil rights case.

The relationship between Anderson and Ward portrayed in the movie came not from historical evidence but from the theme of a popular Western, *The Man Who Shot Liberty Valance.* Gerolmo liked the plot to the movie, which features Jimmy Stewart as a young peace-minded lawyer toting books and John Wayne as the tough cowboy who befriends him. When one of the meanest bad men in the West (played by Lee Marvin) intimidates the lawyer, destroys the town newspaper's press, and beats up the editor, the lawyer finally recognizes the need for a violent response.[9] He goes for his six-gun. With assistance from the cowboy, the lawyer ends the threat from the bad man. Building on this idea of two men with different outlooks learning to cooperate and catch a criminal, Gerolmo accentuated the contrast between Anderson and Ward. He made Anderson a native-born Mississippian with little tolerance for by-the-books crime solving. Gerolmo portrayed Anderson as a practical man who sees that legal procedures against the Klan are useless. In the story Anderson believes in fighting fire with fire. He urges Ward to allow him to hit the Klan with the FBI's own forms of threat and intimidation. Ward, on the other hand, is a neatly dressed agent with a Harvard education and a Kennedyesque point of view. He is a liberal, one of the "Best and the Brightest," and his approach to solving the case is to throw more law enforcement personnel and more money at the problem. Eventually he sees the wisdom of Anderson's extralegal approach and reluctantly sanctions the FBI's own brand of vigilantism. The rough tactics quickly succeeded in breaking the Klan's resistance.

Although much of the screenplay for *Mississippi Burning* contains fictional material about a battle between the FBI and the Klan, a substantial portion of the movie features authentic evidence from the actual murder cases. Throughout the film there are numerous references to real people and real situations associated with the tragedy near Philadelphia, Mississippi. This hint of authenticity appears in the opening seconds of the film, when the caption "Mississippi, 1964," clearly identifies the time and place of the story. Audiences then watch the Ku Klux Klan's cat-and-mouse chase of the three civil rights workers on a dark Mississippi highway, and they see the first of the brutal murders at gunpoint. As in the actual case, federal law enforcement authorities learn about the missing car from a Choctaw Indian, naval personnel hunt for the bodies in a marshy region, and investigators keep a paper bag over the head of a witness so that he will not be recognized as he is driven through the streets of Philadelphia. Some of the dialogue is a verbatim reproduction of language recorded in the court records. Also, the characters often resemble the real figures. Michael Schwerner wore a goatee, as does the actor in the movie who portrays him, and the actor representing Deputy Sheriff Cecil Price resembles him in appearance and mannerisms. Even the title of the movie reflects historical authenticity. The FBI gave its investigation the code name MIBURN (for "Mississippi Burning"). In these and other ways the filmmakers gave the audience abundant signals that *Mississippi Burning* is Hollywood's representation of a true story.

Director Alan Parker worked carefully to incorporate a number of authentic details. He traveled to Mississippi with coproducer Bob Colesberry, for example, and tried to retrace the steps of Chaney, Schwerner, and Goodman. The two filmmakers located a spot where they believed the murders to have been committed and spent some moments of silence. Parker then traveled extensively across the state of Mississippi, talking with people from a variety of backgrounds. His location department labored for weeks trying to identify numerous towns across Mississippi, Alabama, and Georgia that might serve as the principal location for the filming. Parker and Colesberry eventually chose Lafayette, Alabama, as the site to represent Philadelphia, Mississippi. In the production notes for *Mississippi Burning* (a portion of the press kit) Parker identified the choice of Lafayette with an apparent note of apology, pointing out that the bulk of shooting for the movie was in Mississippi. Moreover, Parker could boast that for some scenes he used authentic settings (for example, the morgue at the University Medical Center, where the bodies of Chaney, Schwerner, and Goodman were taken). Thus, the director articulated a sense of pride concerning the attention to historical detail.[10]

Parker's finished product effectively conveys a strong feeling for the social tensions that troubled Mississippians in 1964. *Mississippi Burning* communicates a sense of the terror that blacks and whites felt when they worked together in the state for civil rights. Scenes showing the highway chase, the murder, the nighttime attacks on African Americans and their homes, and the burning of churches contributed an understanding of the troubles civil rights advocates experienced when confronting racist vigilantism. Much of the drama has the appearance of a horror picture, except that it deals with actual dangers created by real people rather than threats carried out by imaginary monsters. Indeed, during the tense summer of 1964 there were four shootings, fifty-two serious beatings, 250 arrests, and ten cars damaged or destroyed in connection with the civil rights campaign.[11]

The movie also correctly portrays ways in which representatives of the media were intimidated in Mississippi. Newsmen did worry about physical harm as they covered events during the summer of 1964. David Halberstam, who had worked for a small-town newspaper in Mississippi in the 1960s, later recalled the tensions. Writing about the movie in 1989, Halberstam remembered, "There always seemed to be a pickup truck . . . following me as I left a small town, threatening to bump me off the road."[12] Bill Delgado, an NBC camera operator, suffered more direct intimidation. He covered the Philadelphia murders for the television network and discovered that some Mississippi whites were determined to frighten the press away from their community. A segregationist drove a car into Delgado's automobile and then chased him with a hunting knife. When a police officer arrived on the scene, he issued Delgado a citation for reckless driving. Later Delgado tried to get television footage of the countryside from a helicopter, and a farmer aimed a gun at him. After that experience Delgado asked NBC to transfer him to a new assignment.[13]

Although *Mississippi Burning* effectively demonstrates some of the ugly incidents of intimidation and violence in the Philadelphia area, it also provides some insights into the kind of thinking that supported racial bigotry. The movie's attention to this subject is brief, but the dialogue does manage to convey a thesis. The message comes across particularly in a scene in a motel when Ward asks Anderson where all the terrible hate comes from. Anderson recalls his father's prejudices and suggests an explanation based on economics. The old man used to ask, "if you ain't better than a nigger, who are you better than?" Anderson explains that his father took comfort in knowing that blacks were worse off than he was. Racial prejudice blinded him to the larger realities. The old man was so full of hate, says Anderson, that "he didn't know that being poor was what was killing him."[14]

The movie does an impressive job of communicating a feeling for the conditions in Mississippi in 1964 and the attitudes of the segregationists, but its presentation of the events raised serious questions from critics in three important respects. Detractors said that the movie portrays blacks essentially as sheeplike victims who took almost no steps to influence the course of events in Mississippi; they argued that *Mississippi Burning* creates a distorted view of the FBI's tactics in the murder case; and they claimed that it misinterprets the role of violence in bringing social change to the South. These criticisms sparked a lively debate about Hollywood's responsibility to represent history authentically.

A number of observers, particularly African Americans, charged that almost all the black characters in the movie look like passive victims. They said that the blacks seem frightened, withdrawn, and unaware of how to change their fortunes. With the exception of the fictional African-American FBI agent, black characters in the movie stand on the periphery of events, patiently watching and hoping for a better day while white FBI agents and Klan members battle each other. Critics especially pointed to the example of the chase scene in the opening moments of the movie. *Mississippi Burning* shows Michael Schwerner driving the car containing the civil rights workers, while James Chaney, the black, sits in the back seat. Actually Chaney drove the car, said the critics. Furthermore, Chaney was not just a passive black youngster who looked to the whites to give direction to the fight for justice, as he appears in the film. Chaney was a dedicated civil rights campaigner and full-time organizer for the Congress of Racial Equality (CORE).[15]

Critics argued that the movie's portrayal overlooks the major role African Americans played in shaping their own destiny in Mississippi during the important civil rights campaign of 1964. Hundreds of African Americans who were trained in the tactics of nonviolent resistance worked bravely for their rights in Mississippi through the summer project, they noted. The Klan-led assaults on black churches revealed how successful blacks were becoming: segregationists observed their progress and then tried to frighten them into retreating from their campaign. The civil rights crusaders did not give up, despite the intimidation and physical injuries they suffered, and they made a significant impact on the nation's thinking about conditions in the Deep South. *Mississippi Burning* fails to show these contributions, said the critics. Vernon Jarrett, an African American and member of the *Chicago Sun-Times'* editorial board, summed up the reaction when he said, "The film treats some of the most heroic people in black history as mere props in a morality play."[16] Similarly, Coretta Scott King, wife of Martin Luther King Jr., asked, "How long will we have to wait before Hollywood finds the courage and the integrity to tell the stories of some of the many thousands of black men, women, and children who put their lives on the line for equality?"[17]

Julian Bond, a prominent African American in the Democratic party who had served as a Georgia state senator, found an opportunity to articulate these objections on ABC Television's *Nightline*. A few years later he reviewed his objections to the movie, recalling that he found it to be "condescending" in its treatment of blacks. *Mississippi Burning* leaves the impression that African Americans in the South did not exercise any leadership, he observed. The blacks that appear in the movie seem to be set up to be victims. Bond said that when he saw an African-American character portrayed on the screen as a passive figure, he thought, "That person's gonna die." In making the FBI agents the heroes of the story *Mississippi Burning* badly distorts history. Clever police work had nothing to do with the victory against the Klan, argued Bond; the FBI simply paid informants, "as police often do," and obtained leads that led to prosecution. By misleading audiences regarding what really happened in Mississippi, the movie turns history "upside down." The main characters in the Mississippi story were not the whites but the African Americans from the South, as well as the young workers for the Student Non-Violent Coordinating Committee (SNCC) and CORE who had been putting their lives in danger for civil rights long before the tragedy occurred in Philadelphia, Mississippi. In short, the movie fails to give the blacks credit for winning their own freedom.[18]

Chris Gerolmo and Fred Zollo, the writer and producer, believed that charges about the movie's insensitivity to the role of blacks were unfair. They said that they were well aware of the heroism of many black Mississippians in challenging white supremacy under very dangerous circumstances. They noted that the African Americans' contribution to the fight for equality is well documented in the history books. Gerolmo and Zollo emphasized, however, that they were not making a movie about the civil rights movement. *Mississippi Burning* is about the fight between the Klan and the FBI, which was essentially a drama about the activities of white men. Zollo took particular issue with the claims that *Mississippi Burning* should have shown the black figure, James Chaney, driving the car. The criticism came to him in an emotional way one day when he was lecturing about the movie at Queens College. Chaney's sister was in the audience, and she protested the fact that the movie shows her brother as a passenger in the car, not as the driver. Zollo maintained that Schwerner did drive the car during *some* of the civil rights workers' travels.[19] He argued, however, that evidence about which person was driving at specific times was contradictory and subject to debate (to support his position, Zollo referred to pages in the book *Three Lives for Mississippi*, as well as to testimony by the white conspirators).[20]

Mississippi Burning focused on whites for purposes of box office popularity, and Alan Parker acknowledged the reasons for the decision openly. "Our heroes are still white," the director explained. "And in truth the film would probably never be made if they weren't." He, as well as Gerolmo and Zollo, understood that the movie's primary audience was going to be whites (both in the United States and abroad). The filmmakers believed that a movie about white FBI agents trying to solve the murders would constitute a much stronger attraction than a movie that focused on the African-American struggle.[21] Furthermore, "one of the perverse ironies of the case was that two white kids got killed and the whole of America was interested suddenly, because it wasn't just a black problem." This reality undoubtedly disturbed many black activists, Parker noted, "because it underlined a national hypocrisy."[22]

A related complaint concerned how *Mississippi Burning* attributes the ultimate victories over Mississippi racists to vigorous actions by the FBI. Critics said the movie implies that FBI investigators were the real heroes of the summer campaign, not the black civil rights organizers and their white colleagues. *Mississippi Burning* suggests that the campaign succeeded because men like Anderson and Ward demonstrated the skills necessary to trick racist criminals. Historian Harvard Sitkoff summarized the plot sarcastically by saying that it shows blacks in the South winning their civil rights because "two white guys learned to work together and like each other."[23] The film gives particular credit to Anderson (Gene Hackman) for finding a way to catch the guilty men. "These people crawled out of the sewers," he tells Ward in the movie. "Maybe the gutter is the place we have to be." When Ward fails to find the criminals (and makes conditions worse for the blacks through his naive intervention), he reluctantly accepts Anderson's plan for a no-nonsense assault on the Klan; Anderson and other FBI agents then assault suspects, threaten castration, participate in kidnapping, and fake a lynching to get the information they want. Anderson emerges a hero for these efforts. The FBI's extralegal measures force confessions and send the criminals to prison.

Critics of the movie were quick to point out that these scenarios were fabrications and had little to do with the actual FBI operations in Mississippi. They emphasized that the FBI initially played an insignificant role in investigating violence in the South, because bureau director Hoover loathed blacks. Hoover was deeply suspicious of the civil rights movement, they noted, and he worried about the possible involvement of communists in its organizations. Hoover also disliked Martin Luther King Jr. and authorized wiretaps of his phone conversations. Under Hoover's leadership the FBI seemed to be on friendlier terms with segregationist law officers than with the civil rights campaigners, they observed. President Johnson then intervened and forced the bureau to take an active role in solving the case. As for the violence and intimidation Anderson practices in the movie, nothing of the kind occurred in Mississippi, the critics pointed out. The FBI did not break the case in the manner of action-adventure movie heroes. Instead it used a form of bribery—the payoffs of $30,000 that helped to squeeze information from informants and bring indictments.[24]

Gerolmo acknowledged that the FBI had been dragging its feet in civil rights cases and that Hoover was bigoted and promoted reprehensible acts of intimidation against Martin Luther King Jr. Nevertheless, argued Gerolmo, Hoover responded quickly to LBJ's insistence that the bureau help to apprehend those guilty of the Philadelphia murders. The director put numerous agents on the case, and in this instance, his organization performed admirably in its detective work. *Mississippi Burning* was not intended to be a representative picture of FBI activities in the civil rights era, Gerolmo insisted; it is about the bureau's success in breaking the Klan's silence and intimidation in one specific case.[25]

In this respect Gerolmo regretted that director Alan Parker cut a particular scene from the early drafts of the script. The scene takes place at a church where a small group of blacks and white civil rights organizers meet Anderson and Ward. When one of the youngsters says that he does not trust the FBI, Anderson becomes hostile and Ward has to ask him to step outside. "That would have helped us a lot," Gerolmo believed; it would have given some voice to reservations about the FBI's role in civil rights matters. Without that scene the movie seems to paint the FBI agents as fully welcomed heroes in the minds of civil rights workers.[26]

Alan Parker took a very different view of the moviemakers' relationship with history. He maintained that Gerolmo's original draft was a very simplistic, superficial, and fictionalized story. When taking the director's assignment, said Parker, he immersed himself in the factual materials, attempted to get back to the truth of the story, and politicized the drama with his own "voice." The result was "a better and more meaningful film" than the one Gerolmo originally designed. Parker said that he took what looked like just another buddy cop film and turned it into a new form, imbuing "it with detail based on actuality." At the beginning, explained Parker, "I was presented with fiction and marginal historical background, and I reversed this balance when I re-wrote the script."[27]

Whether Gerolmo or Parker showed more consideration of historical truths is not clear, but certainly the story presented in *Mississippi Burning* could not have placated all the critics. The movie features far too many fictional situations to escape objections from the champions of authenticity. Most of the FBI activity that dominates the second half of the movie is simply invented. Indeed, Welch's and Marston's book, *Inside Hoover's FBI*, which according to Gerolmo inspired the movie project, only vaguely suggests the use of extralegal tactics by the bureau's agents and says nothing about the specific FBI actions seen in the movie.[28] Furthermore, *Mississippi Burning* gives too much credit to the FBI for defeating the Klan and too little credit to the black and white civil rights workers whose actions provoked the Klan to commit atrocities in the first place. The movie confuses the lessons about history, for it fails to show the impact of public opinion in forcing integration on the South. Essentially, the film delivers an incorrect message about the role of violence in effecting change. *Mississippi Burning* leaves the impression that the forces of progress defeated the forces of tradition in the Deep South by adopting the very tactics of violent vigilantism that civil rights campaigners had been denouncing. It appears to argue that segregationist terrorism could not be stopped in legal ways; therefore, the FBI *needed* to resort to extralegal coercion.

In taking this approach the filmmakers overlooked the political context of events and lost sight of one of the most important lessons historians can draw about the murders' effects on the nation. Racist violence backfired in Mississippi. Its effect was opposite to what the assailants expected. The murderers hoped to frighten away the civil rights campaigners, but instead, they prompted the federal government to intervene in Mississippi's affairs. News about the tragedy near Philadelphia, Mississippi, as well as reports of other violent acts, aroused the nation. The public became upset with the evidence of physical intimidation and murder. Televised news footage and photographs in newspapers featured graphic evidence of the segregationists' abuses. In the years before the triple murder in Mississippi, the media had shown police dogs biting civil rights demonstrators and firehoses blowing them across streets; the media also revealed pictures of burned-out buses and homes and churches in ashes. As the reports of new outrages mounted, the political environment in Washington turned toward reform. Members of Congress began to sense a need for stronger federal action to protect citizens and to save the country from additional embarrassments. The reports from Mississippi and other states in the Deep South were disturbing for a society that advertised itself to Third World nations as an attractive example of freedom. It certainly represented bad press in the global competition with the Soviets for respect and influence. Reports of racist killings also made political moderates and business leaders in the South cringe. People who were working hard to promote the image of a modern South believed that the ugly reports about white violence badly undermined their efforts.

Thus, it was not violence by law enforcement agents that brought progress to the civil rights movement (as *Mississippi Burning* implies) but the terrorist violence of southern white racists. That aggression excited revulsion. The 1964 cases came relatively late in this sequence of disturbing news; reports of atrocities in the Deep South had been building for years. When news broke about the Mississippi murders, President Johnson came under tremendous pressure from the victims' relatives and the public to crack the case. Public outrage then helped to put teeth in the Civil Rights Act, which had passed the Senate shortly before the murders and became law a few weeks after the tragedy. Violent events of the next year, such as the killing of Mrs. Viola Liuzzo, helped to build political support for the Voting Rights Act of 1965. In sum, segregationist violence contributed to the extraordinary passage of major civil rights reform that had been delayed for years. Ironically, the enemies of civil rights helped to bring about the very changes they were trying to prevent.

Mississippi Burning not only misses this conclusion but also suggests that journalism and public opinion had little influence on events in the era of the civil rights campaign. The film conveys this assessment in an especially important scene. Toward the end of the story Anderson concludes that the effort to find the killers was frustrated because it "turned into a show for the newsmen." The historical record of that turbulent period, however, demonstrates that the violence of white racists and extensive newspaper and television coverage of their atrocities contributed significantly to the gains realized by the fighters for racial justice. The "show for the newsmen" was critically important.

When details began to appear in the press about *Mississippi Burning*'s liberties with history, harsh criticism quickly emerged. The *New York Times* argued in an editorial that the filmmakers tampered with the facts, for the FBI never used the tactics displayed in the movie. "It's disturbing to think that people will leave the theatre believing that lawlessness is just if it serves a good cause," said the editorial. "Legitimizing that idea traduces the principles for which so many sacrificed so much to advance civil rights."[29] A letter writer to the *Los Angeles Times,* who was himself the author of screenplays for the entertainment industry, called *Mississippi Burning* an insult to the memory of "the real people who were not afraid to risk their lives while acting with moral integrity." The writer said that it was all right to alter some facts from history to enhance or clarify the story, but *Mississippi Burning*'s designers did not understand the crucial difference between "art" and "a lie."[30] Historian Harvard Sitkoff also gave a damning assessment in a review published later, concluding "this film does such injustice to the events with which it deals that its ultimate lynching is of history itself."[31]

Conservative columnist Patrick Buchanan criticized the film for entirely different reasons. Buchanan said that *Mississippi Burning*'s portrayal of southerners reveals how intensely "Hollywood hates the South." He claimed that Mississippi was not one-tenth as dangerous in 1964 as Washington, D.C., was in the 1980s. Buchanan said that Parker's film "slanders an entire state" and "indicts an entire region for a single atrocity committed there."[32]

Mississippi Burning's treatment of the historical issues sparked a lively debate about the artist's responsibility in interpreting the past through film. A reviewer for *The Economist* recognized that questions about fictionalizing history had been asked since Shakespeare's time. "But now television and films are fast replacing books as the chief source of information," said the reviewer, making the questions more vexing.[33] Some commentators excused the filmmakers for their excesses, arguing that a Hollywood movie does not intend primarily to be a documentary. "The truth of its testimony is not so much literal as gospel," explained Richard Schickel in *Time*.[34] David Halberstam was less comfortable with the idea of defending the filmmakers. Halberstam acknowledged that Hollywood is a city more of fantasy than of reality, and artists must enjoy considerable flexibility if not poetic license. "But in the making of this film there is a carelessness, a lack of accountability, that is simply unacceptable," wrote Halberstam. The moviemakers had a right to create a fictional vision of Mississippi, Halberstam thought, but they chose to use the specific case of the three slain civil rights workers for their centerpiece, and that significantly changed their responsibility to history.[35]

Alan Parker took the most active role in promoting the movie with the media, and he found himself facing numerous questions about historical representation. Reporters constantly asked him about an artist's responsibility to present the past with a degree of authenticity. Parker responded in the manner that many directors before him had handled such queries: he danced around the questions. Sometimes Parker implied that *Mississippi Burning* is based in fact, and at other times he suggested that it is a work of artistic imagination. Parker boasted, for example, that he had made the movie "in a realistic way" and claimed *Mississippi Burning* has "a truthful ring to it" because it is fiction based on fact.[36] More typically Parker tried to remove himself from questions about authenticity, appearing to regret that the movie's story was being compared with the historical record. *Mississippi Burning* is not the definitive story of the civil rights movement or the FBI's involvement in it, he said. "It's one story, our story and very obviously fiction."[37] Like Gerolmo, he pointed out that the movie is not really about the civil rights movement, and therefore, it is unfair to expect it to re-create the campaign's history exactly as it occurred in Mississippi. The movie is really about why there was a *need* for a civil rights movement, Parker explained. He said that he had a good purpose in mind when making the film: to get the public to pay attention to an important subject that had been ignored by moviemakers. "I'm trying to reach an entire generation who knows nothing of that historical event," said Parker, noting that young people needed to react viscerally to the movie's message because of the racism that was around them.[38] Arguing essentially that the ends justify the means, Parker said that it was better to alter the facts to make audiences think about racial injustice than to be fastidious about details and risk never getting the message across at all. "There have been a lot of documentaries on the subject" on PBS, Parker observed, but "nobody watches them." *Mississippi Burning*, on the other hand, was going to reach millions in fifty countries and arouse their emotions about racial injustice. "And that's enough of a reason, a justification, for the fictionalizing," he concluded.[39]

Chris Gerolmo, the originator of the film project, found the assaults on *Mississippi Burning*'s treatment of history disheartening. He had wanted to create "a great detective story with a lot of heart." He had hoped that the exciting drama would stir the audience's interest in history, encouraging viewers to think seriously about the relevant moral issues. Gerolmo planned to make the story "relatively consistent with what had happened." It would be close to history "in spirit," communicating history's important messages with fictional flourishes. He believed that the initial advertisements for *Mississippi Burning* undermined this goal. The ads announced boldly that director Alan Parker had examined the rights struggle in a dramatic film, implying that the movie would be Hollywood's first major statement on the history of the civil rights movement. In this manner the promoters "set a standard to which we couldn't live up," Gerolmo lamented. Had the advertising been less ambitious about the film's connections with history, audiences would not have expected *Mississippi Burning* to be a precise historical re-creation.[40] Zollo agreed that audiences and critics were judging the movie with criteria that were difficult to meet. Instead of appreciating the way in which *Mississippi Burning* throws light on the horrors of racism and Klan-style terrorism, commentators were reduced to asking petty questions about details such as the color of the car that Schwerner and Chaney drove and who was really in the driver's seat.[41]

Zollo found Patrick Buchanan's complaint about the movie's ugly portrayal of Mississippi rednecks to be unfair. He stressed that key individuals in the Philadelphia crime story were very much as the movie had presented them—"truly creatures from the deep."[42] Zollo raised a legitimate point, for news photographs of the conspirators did indeed reveal them to be a frightening-looking bunch. Yet Buchanan, too, had raised a valid observation. Director Alan Parker had chosen many of the extras for the movie himself, seeking people with ugly, stereotypically redneck features. Virtually all the individuals representing common folk and segregationists in the movie reflect popular images of the southern "cracker." One of the few exceptions is the character of Mrs. Pell, the deputy sheriff's wife (played by Francis McDormand). In the movie she provides information to the FBI (the real informants were men). Mrs. Pell is supposed to represent the conscience of decent Mississippi moderates, but her singular presence in the story does not do enough to reveal that in the 1960s more than a few white Mississippians entertained thoughts of fairness and decency.

In general, Gerolmo, Parker, and Zollo raised some valid questions about the severity of the attacks heaped on *Mississippi Burning*. Often their movie was expected to be something other than what they intended. They had tried to examine a historical situation much as Shakespeare had portrayed Richard III. The drama was designed to be, as Zollo said, "reasonably true." Also, their movie was primarily about the FBI and the Klan, not about African Americans who struggled for justice or about the campaigns for civil rights.[43] Furthermore, advertising for *Mississippi Burning* created a mistaken impression about the subject of the story. The ads' attention to historical themes helped to excite public interest in the movie, but it also raised expectations that could not be realized.

Despite these problems, *Mississippi Burning* succeeded at the box office both in the United States and abroad, and it aroused the audiences' curiosity about an important subject from American history that had received very little attention from Hollywood. The motion picture reached many people who were not going to read about racial violence or watch *Eyes on the Prize* on PBS. *Mississippi Burning*'s powerful indictment of segregationist resistance stirred audiences to consider the history of race relations in the United States. It stimulated the movie viewer's interest in probing America's troubled past. Carolyn Goodman, the mother of the slain rights worker Andy Goodman, thought that the movie made a significant contribution to the thinking of many young people in the United States who were unaware of the history of the rights struggle in the South. Mrs. Goodman regretted the moviemakers' fictionalizing, and she was unhappy with their portrayal of the African Americans' role in the civil rights movement, but she recognized that a film like *Mississippi Burning* could raise the consciousness of the viewers.[44]

Ultimately, *Mississippi Burning* represents a lost opportunity. It successfully communicates a perspective on the southern tradition of violent vigilantism that had oppressed African Americans since the days of slavery, but many lost sight of that message when focusing attention on the debates about authenticity. The moviemakers took far too many liberties with the facts to win accolades for offering a powerful social comment to the public. In later years many remembered the movie better as a catalyst for a fiery debate about Hollywood's relationship with history than as a movie that effectively portrays an important problem in human relations.

If the filmmakers had based their motion picture vaguely on the generic qualities of white terrorism in Mississippi, they might have faced very little criticism about authenticity. In building their story around an actual event, however, they invited scrutiny over details and concern for the truth. By drawing so many parallels with the actual Philadelphia, Mississippi, case while also creating significant fictional elements, the movie appropriately generated controversy. Audiences as well as historians had good reason to complain that the filmmakers moved beyond the proper bounds of artistic license and manipulated the evidence excessively. *Mississippi Burning*'s treatment of the past is unfortunate, because where the movie reflects the record (particularly in the first half of the film), it projects vivid images of the racist South. Had the filmmakers followed the fascinating historical record to its conclusion, they could have produced riveting drama while escaping much criticism about the movie's interpretation. The real Mississippi story was so inherently theatrical that it did not need the degree of fictionalizing that Gerolmo, Zollo, and Parker applied to it.

2

JFK

"FACT. FICTION. AND SUPPOSITION"

Reporters question New Orleans district
attorney Jim Garrison (Kevin Costner), who
is investigating the assassination of President
Kennedy in *JFK*. Courtesy of the Museum
of Modern Art/Film Stills Archive.

*M*ore than any other Hollywood movie of the late twentieth century, Oliver Stone's production *JFK* (1991) provoked lively discussions about how far cinematic historians should go when exercising artistic license. Some praised Stone for using a variety of creative devices to arouse strong audience interest in significant historical questions. *JFK* mixes fact with fiction based on speculation, they maintained, and this blending helps to communicate broad "truths" about history. Others considered Stone's looseness with evidence to be appalling. Columnist George Will offered some of the most acidic responses. He called *JFK* "an act of execrable history" and said, "Stone falsifies so much that he may be an intellectual sociopath, indifferent to the truth."[1] Many others were bewildered by this debate. They were fascinated with the movie's bold suggestions but were not certain whether Stone had twisted historical facts to an extreme. With considerable interest they listened to the arguments on television, read about the disagreements in newspapers and magazines, and sought their own conclusions.

It was not surprising that so much commotion surrounded the motion picture, for *JFK* is electrifying in its thesis and its presentation. The movie suggests that the Warren Commission's investigation of President John F. Kennedy's assassination was a cover-up. *JFK* shows the workings of a vast conspiracy in and outside the U.S. government designed to eliminate President Kennedy because, according to the movie, he was liberalizing his position on the cold war and moving toward the removal of U.S. troops from Vietnam. *JFK* concludes that Kennedy's assassination represented a coup d'état. The movie tells this story in an innovative manner. It delivers a hard-hitting, fact-filled drama that bombards viewers with information for more than three hours. Borrowing techniques from television news broadcasting and music videos, Stone featured abundant brief clips of documentary-style evidence. Some of this material reproduces actual newsreel footage, and other segments present fabricated "evidence" that Stone invented to portray his interpretation of the events. The fictional footage appears so similar to actual news footage that many moviegoers could not discriminate between the real and the manufactured. The overall effect of this lengthy cinemagraphic stimulation was to raise significant doubts in the minds of viewers regarding the familiar claims that Lee Harvey Oswald had been the lone assassin of Present Kennedy.

Few movies have made as great an impact on public affairs as *JFK* did. Excitement about the motion picture led a number of individuals who had been public figures during the Kennedy years to speak out or write on the assassination case. More important, in Congress politicians tried to respond to their constituents' growing suspicion of the Warren Commission's report by demanding that all the remaining confidential papers from previous government investigations of the assassination be opened for public scrutiny. In the next few years Congress moved quickly on the matter, choosing to terminate the confidentiality of most of the documents. *JFK* sparked numerous demands for the U.S. government to revisit the tragic event in American history and attempt to answer many disturbing questions.

JFK owes much of its controversial character to the leadership of its gutsy creator. Oliver Stone not only designed the film project and served as the director; he became the movie's most active and ardent defender in the press and on television when it came under attack. Far more than most filmmakers, Stone stepped forward as a pugnacious public debater. He took on virtually every major challenge from the media, defending many details in his movie's interpretation and criticizing the theses of his critics. Stone's aggressive stand as an interpreter of history pushed the controversy about *JFK* from Main Street to the halls of Congress. His artistry and his actions helped to make *JFK* one of the most significant political movies of the twentieth century.

Stone had become intensely interested in politics and distrustful of the political establishment in large part because of his experiences in Vietnam. Stone first went to South Vietnam in 1965 after dropping out of Yale University at the end of his freshman year. At the time he was troubled by his parents' divorce a few years earlier and his father's revelation that the family business was deeply in debt and could no longer provide a life of wealth and privilege. At this point Stone took a variety of jobs. For a while he taught at a Chinese school in Saigon; then he chose to return to the United States by working on a tanker as a merchant seaman. Later Stone spent some time in Mexico and eventually found his way back to Yale. In New Haven Stone devoted much more time to writing a novel than to his courses, and before long, he dropped out of the university a second time. Hoping to find direction in his life, Stone joined the army and requested combat duty in Vietnam. He was ready to fight communism in the name of democracy. When Stone arrived in Vietnam for a second time, he quickly sensed how mistaken he had been. U.S. soldiers in the country seemed to be far more interested in returning home than in fighting a supposedly noble war for freedom. Now Stone sensed that U.S. policy in Southeast Asia was mistaken. While he tried to come to terms with these doubts, he witnessed the destruction of Vietnamese property and atrocities against the people of Vietnam. Stone received two wounds in action and won a Bronze Star and a Purple Heart with an Oak Leaf Cluster for his services in the war, but he came away with bitter memories.

Like many other U.S. veterans of the Vietnam War, Stone could not easily separate himself from his experiences in the war. Fortunately he soon discovered an effective outlet for his pent-up emotions. After drifting in inactivity and becoming involved with drugs, Stone found a career in moviemaking. He got his education at New York University's film school, received training from Martin Scorsese, and then began working as a screenwriter. With *Midnight Express* he won an Oscar in 1978 for best screenplay adaptation. For years he carried around his draft of *Platoon,* a story of a combat unit in Vietnam based in part on his own experiences, but he could not interest Hollywood in the screenplay. American audiences, he was told, did not want to watch movies about the Vietnam nightmare. In the mid-1980s Stone found an opportunity to express his discontent with U.S. foreign policy by directing *Salvador* (1986). This documentary-style drama, based on the experiences of a journalist friend in El Salvador, focuses on human rights violations by right-wing death squads linked to U.S.-backed governments.

Finally Stone got the financial backing he needed for *Platoon.* The movie was a splendid success, and Stone won Oscars for best director and best picture. The powerful 1986 drama builds its fiction around some of Stone's worst memories of the Vietnam War. It shows body bags and frightened U.S. soldiers, depicts the murder of an elderly Vietnamese woman in a village, and shows Americans setting Vietnamese homes on fire. With great emotional impact, *Platoon* suggests hard questions about the war's effect on the Americans and the Vietnamese. The film provided effective catharsis for Stone's frustrations, but his interest in addressing Vietnam themes in the movies was not satiated. In 1989 he released *Born on the Fourth of July,* which dramatizes the true story of Ron Kovik, a Vietnam veteran paralyzed from the mid-chest down because of a war injury suffered in Vietnam. The movie shows Kovik's personal transformation from confusion, anger, and near-suicidal behavior to a directed, committed life as an antiwar protester.

Stone had long been interested in the leadership of John F. Kennedy. He was only seventeen when the president died, and as it did for many Americans, the news of the assassination shocked him profoundly. As he watched his country's troubles grow in subsequent years, Stone came to believe that 1963 constituted an important watershed. During the thousand days of Kennedy's presidency, much seemed right about America; in the following years, much seemed wrong.

It was not until the late 1980s, when he was working on *Born on the Fourth of July,* that Stone became intensely curious about the story of the assassination. His interest grew after a woman gave him a copy of Jim Garrison's *On the Trail of the Assassins* in an elevator in Havana (Stone was in Cuba to receive an award for one of his movies). Jim Garrison was a New Orleans district attorney who unsuccessfully attempted to convict businessman Clay Shaw for involvement in a conspiracy to assassinate President Kennedy. Stone was fascinated with Garrison's account. He read though the book three times, arranged a personal meeting with Garrison, and began planning a movie about the man.

Recognizing that he needed assistance from someone knowledgeable about Garrison's activities, Stone soon brought Zachary Sklar into the project as the cowriter. Sklar's father had been an accomplished writer back in the 1950s and was blacklisted during the years of the Red Scare. Zachary Sklar held a master's degree in journalism and had taught as an adjunct professor in Columbia University's School of Journalism. He had served as editor at *The Nation* and as editor of *Juris Doctor,* a magazine of the legal profession. Sklar also had edited a variety of books written by former agents of the CIA. Most important, he had been effective in improving the manuscript that eventually became *On the Trail of the Assassins.* Garrison's original writing on the topic had the appearance of a scholarly account from an omniscient narrator, and it failed to satisfy Prentice-Hall's editors. Sheridan Square then took the project and assigned Sklar to the job of turning Garrison's writing into an attractive product. Sklar quickly sensed that Garrison was taking the wrong tack. He was trying to sound like an objective commentator on the assassination. Reminding Garrison that he had been a key player in the investigation of a possible conspiracy, Sklar proposed an account that placed Garrison at the center of the story. Sklar's adjustments helped to give *On the Trail of the Assassins* the appearance of an interesting detective story told from a personal perspective.[2]

Despite the improvements made by Sklar, *On the Trail of the Assassins* failed to attract much public attention. It would take an association with Oliver Stone to bring the story the huge audience that Garrison had sought.

When news became public that Stone was planning to make a film about the JFK murder, proponents of various assassination theories sought the director's attention. Several hoped to win lucrative contracts for sharing their information and ideas. One of the most successful in securing Stone's interest and money was Larry Howard, founder of the JFK Information Center in Dallas. Howard made elaborate claims about Kennedy's murder at the hands of "the real people who control the power base in the U.S.," but his assertions proved to be unsubstantiated. He succeeded, however, in collecting $80,000 for the services of his research center.[3]

A more important new acquaintance was L. Fletcher Prouty, a former United States Air Force colonel who had been an aide to the Joint Chiefs of Staff during the Kennedy administration. Prouty strengthened Stone's interest in the idea that representatives of the military-industrial complex wanted Kennedy eliminated because of his plans to withdraw troops from Vietnam. Prouty stressed the importance of National Security Action Memorandum 263, in which Kennedy endorsed a recommendation to take 1,000 advisers out of Vietnam by the end of 1963. Prouty also aroused Stone's interest in a memorandum that President Lyndon B. Johnson approved after Kennedy's death. The memorandum avoids mention of a withdrawal of U.S. military advisers and outlines preparations for possible future military actions in Vietnam. Stone considered these documents to be significant, for they give the assassination story a larger political meaning. They seem to support the idea that if Kennedy had lived, he would not have thrown American combat troops into action in Vietnam. Excited by this information, Stone assigned the colonel to the project as a technical adviser and created a "Mr. X" character in the story to articulate some of Prouty's ideas.

In time, however, Prouty became a liability. Stone's researchers discovered that Prouty had been associated recently with the Liberty Lobby, a racist and anti-Semitic organization known for publishing articles maintaining that the Holocaust never occurred. Further investigation revealed that Prouty contributed to the lobby's radio programs and newsletter, that he had been a featured speaker at the organization's annual convention, and that he had sold the rights to his book to the lobby's press. Nevertheless, Stone rejected recommendations that he drop Prouty from the post of technical adviser, and when debates about the value of Prouty's advice became public, Stone maintained that an individual can be right on some things and wrong on others.[4]

Fortunately for Stone, he located a new and more respected adviser around the time when Prouty's associations were causing trouble. This participant was John Newman, a scholar who was completing both a book and a Ph.D. dissertation about John F. Kennedy's plans for Vietnam. Newman was an officer in the military intelligence branch of the U.S. Army who was finishing his doctoral work at George Washington University, concentrating in the history of Soviet foreign policy and developments in modern East Asia. Newman also had been a Chinese-language specialist during his years of military service. When Stone learned about Newman's background and ideas, he invited him to California and proposed that he join the production effort. Newman had doubts about becoming involved, worrying that his new career as a scholar might abort quickly if he became associated with a controversial movie. Newman chose to join, however, hoping "to do something for the sake of history." His agreement to participate was contingent on the director's promise not to cite his military credentials as a means of giving authority to the movie. Stone agreed to the understanding. Newman then focused on the script's messages about Kennedy's Vietnam policies, recommending a number of adjustments. He also helped to write some of the scenes. Eventually Newman called into question several of Prouty's ideas about Kennedy's Vietnam policies, as well as his theories about an assassination conspiracy. Stone brought the two advisers into a room and listened to their perspectives. Prouty, upset by the criticisms of the junior officer, went into a tantrum. Stone tried to promote cooperation between the two, but after the confrontation he appeared to place greater trust in Newman and relied less on Prouty's advice.[5]

To coordinate much of the research effort, Stone hired a recent graduate of Yale University. Jane Rusconi consulted a number of assassination books and tried to sort out the evidence for a conspiracy. She found works such as Sylvia Meagher's *After the Fact*, Philip Melanson's *Spy Saga*, and Peter Dale Scott's *Dallas Conspiracy* particularly valuable in identifying leads for the drama.[6] Above all, she and others worked with Jim Marrs's massive book *Crossfire* (a recent publication that summarizes most of the important conspiracy arguments that emerged after 1963). Stone optioned *Crossfire* and employed many of its findings in the script.

In mapping out plans for a screenplay, Stone told Zachary Sklar, his cowriter, that he wanted the movie to borrow concepts from Constantin Costa-Gavras's *Z* and Akira Kurosawa's *Rashomon*. The movie would convey the sense of conspiracy in high places communicated in *Z* and challenge viewers to consider a variety of explanations for a crime, as *Rashomon* does. With regard to interpreting Garrison's activities, Stone decided to include information that came to light *after* the close of Garrison's prosecution of Clay Shaw (e.g., Garrison would know things in the movie that he did not know at the time of the trial).[7]

When *JFK* was ready for release, Newman appeared with him in some of the meetings with the press, and the major spoke publicly about various historical details in the movie.[8] Stone, in turn, actively promoted Newman's book, *Kennedy and Vietnam*, describing it to the press as an important breakthrough in the research on John F. Kennedy's Vietnam policies.

The movie that provoked many animated discussions beginning in late 1991 presents more than just a controversial interpretation of the Kennedy assassination. *JFK* also demonstrates a strong bias in interpreting other topics from recent American history. It suggests, for example, a strongly favorable assessment of the characters and leadership of John F. Kennedy and Jim Garrison. It also implies that President Kennedy intended to de-escalate the cold war and extricate the United States from the Vietnam conflict, and it suggests a dove's position on the larger question of the proper role of the United States in Vietnam's affairs.

JFK's highly romanticized picture of President Kennedy emanated partly from Stone's own positive personal memories of the Kennedy years. But there was also an important element of calculation behind Stone's promotion of the Kennedy mystique. The director understood that his case for an assassination plot would look more sinister if the victim appeared to be a heroic figure who offered the country much promise for a successful future. It would seem particularly tragic, then, that a fine man like Kennedy had been cut down before he had a chance to perform good deeds. Stone managed to convey this message not only in the suggestion that Kennedy would have kept the United

States out of a combat role in Vietnam and ended the cold war but also in the suggestions *JFK* makes about Kennedy's character. The movie shows news clips and home movie footage revealing a youthful, handsome, and vigorous president with an elegant wife and beautiful children. It gives the impression that Kennedy was a loving husband and a caring father, as well as a model statesman and peacemaker. Stone called his production company "Camelot Productions," and indeed, his movie promoted the legend of a once-happy society under the high-level leadership of John F. Kennedy, a popular president. This imagery begs the question: which evil people sought to destroy such a great person, and why?[9]

In painting a rosy picture of Kennedy's years in the White House, *JFK* avoids serious questions about the president's character and legacy. As critics pointed out, the movie shows nothing of John F. Kennedy's marital infidelities or the way in which he, his father, and his brothers were often ruthless in their quest for political power. *JFK*'s hints about Kennedy's successful management of the country's affairs contrast sharply with Kennedy's record on domestic legislation. The real Kennedy achieved very little of his legislative agenda, and for much of his administration's two and a half years in power, liberal and conservative elements in Congress remained deadlocked. Overall, Kennedy's accomplishments on the domestic front were quite mediocre. The movie's suggestions that Kennedy began to soften on the cold war shortly before his death also came under fire. Commentators pointed to the aggressive language Kennedy used toward the Soviet Union in his speeches from the time of his inaugural address, the great amount of money his administration injected into military spending (including the construction of nuclear missiles), and his dangerous nose-to-nose confrontation with Nikita Khrushchev in the Cuban Missile Crisis. Kennedy was very much a "cold warrior," they argued, and Stone greatly exaggerated the importance of the few Kennedy actions that gave small hint of a possible transformation in the president's foreign policy outlook.[10]

Stone recognized that Kennedy's achievements were debatable, but he preferred to emphasize the positive. For him, Kennedy's efforts toward a nuclear test ban treaty with the Soviets and his warnings about the dangers of war and need for coexistence expressed in an important speech delivered at American University signaled a change of course. These more sensitive responses to the problems of the cold war, along with Kennedy's recommendation to remove 1,000 advisers from Vietnam, showed that the president was prepared to reduce the tensions that had been threatening peace since the end of World War II, the director argued. Stone acknowledged that Kennedy had imperfections and that he had not been an immensely successful policymaker during his years in office. Americans lost the chance to see what he could have done, however, and another year and a half with Kennedy (and probably five and a half, assuming that he would have won a second term in 1964) would have benefited the American people. Historians could argue about the particulars of the Kennedy administration's record, Stone acknowledged, but "there is a larger issue at stake." Ultimately, the people on the Kennedy team "were good guys."[11]

Stone also encountered controversy because of the way he skewed his presentation of Jim Garrison in a strongly positive way. Stone made the New Orleans investigator (played by Hollywood star Kevin Costner) look like Jimmy Stewart in *Mr. Smith Goes to Washington*—a decent common man who tries to do right but is frustrated by powerful political scoundrels. *JFK*'s Garrison looks like he belongs in a Frank Capra movie. The film shows Garrison fighting a lonely battle. People ridicule him for pursuing what seems like a crazy idea about a conspiracy, and even his wife becomes irritated about his apparent obsession. Garrison remains steadfast, however, determined to discover the truth and bring the guilty to justice. He seems to be an impressive example of honesty and courage.

Critics maintained that this portrayal strays far from the record of the district attorney's life. The real Jim Garrison, they pointed out, conducted a very poor trial when he prosecuted Clay Shaw. Garrison faced allegations about bullying witnesses and suppressing evidence from a polygraph test. It appears that he bribed witnesses and lied in court. After a month-long trial the jury required only fifty-four minutes to acquit Shaw. Clearly Garrison had done a very poor job of making a case against Shaw. Furthermore, critics of the movie pointed out other evidence that should have alerted Stone to the dangers of trying to make a hero out of Jim Garrison. They noted Garrison's long-term associations with Mafia leaders and the efforts of criminals to pick up his gambling debts and help him to sell his home. They also drew attention to Garrison's later trial and acquittal following charges of bribery and conspiracy to protect illegal pinball gambling.[12]

As in the case with Kennedy, Stone acknowledged that he had romanticized the portrayal of Garrison for purposes of drawing attention to the evils of a conspiracy. "I made Garrison better than he is for a larger purpose," Stone explained.[13] Garrison served as a symbolic figure—the searcher for truth in a situation characterized by deception, cover-ups, and lies. Garrison's on-screen personality, reflecting genuineness and decency in the portrayal by Kevin Costner, effectively tied audiences to the district attorney's perspective, making them analyze the mystery through his eyes.

Stone's whitewashing in the Kennedy and Garrison portrayals could be defended in terms of the conventions of the cinema. Romantic depictions of protagonists are familiar features of motion pictures; directors frequently obscure questionable characteristics to convey a broad message about right and wrong. Just as Richard Attenborough's epic film *Gandhi* would have been a very different movie if the director had given considerable attention to reports about Mahatma Gandhi's personal shortcomings, Stone's film would have lost much of its punch if it had tried to convey both positive and negative pictures of Kennedy and Garrison.[14] To communicate his thesis about weaknesses in the Warren Commission's investigation, Stone felt he needed to treat the slain president and the lonely investigator as heroes.

In view of the historical record, Stone's portrayal seems better justified in Kennedy's case than in Garrison's. The screen time given to a retrospective on the life of President Kennedy is brief, and it is not surprising that the movie offers a favorable assessment in the few minutes of pictures and dialogue specifically about JFK. Like the authors of history books who give only a passing reference to an individual's record of presidential leadership, Stone chose to accent the positive in the limited footage available to him. Furthermore, all his major points about Kennedy's achievements as a leader had received detailed emphasis in works of scholarship. Various historians had commented on how Kennedy's intelligence and charisma made many Americans feel confident about the direction that their country was taking; some scholars had asserted that Kennedy was turning the corner on the cold war in his last year in office, and a number of scholars had supported the contention (really a guess) that, had JFK lived, he would have pursued a more peaceful course in Vietnam than Lyndon B. Johnson followed. In the context of this scholarship, Oliver Stone does not appear to be out of place in presenting Kennedy in a positive light. His movie's one-sided perspective effectively communicates a broad message that, in spirit if not in style, had foundations in historical writing. These written interpretations afforded more opportunities to include critical nuances, but many of them, like *JFK,* communicate a generally favorable assessment.

With respect to Stone's treatment of Jim Garrison, however, the romantic depiction appears to be much less acceptable. Far too much evidence had emerged raising serious questions about how Garrison conducted the trial of Clay Shaw. *JFK*'s tendency to portray Garrison as a man as honest and genuine as Jefferson Smith in *Mr. Smith Goes to Washington* contrasts glaringly with the district attorney's record in public office. Furthermore, Garrison offered one of the most discredited conspiracy theories to emerge in the decades following the Kennedy assassination. When Stone chose to pin his story on Jim Garrison's fight to prove the existence of an assassination conspiracy, he became the target of much of the ridicule that Garrison had received for his sloppy investigation.[15] Garrison's story of struggle made an appealing drama for a Hollywood screenplay, but it promised trouble once the movie came under scrutiny for its treatment of historical personalities and events. Stone gambled heavily in making Garrison's perspective the core of his story and left himself vulnerable to difficult questions.

In another respect, however, *JFK* made a useful contribution to the public's thinking about history. The movie gave new vigor to an old debate about John F. Kennedy's intentions in Vietnam. *JFK* suggests that Kennedy's 1963 plans for withdrawing 1,000 advisers from Vietnam as outlined in memorandum 263 reveal that the president wished to phase out U.S. military involvement in the country. The movie leads viewers to believe that the United States never would have plunged into a big war in Southeast Asia if Kennedy had lived.

A number of Kennedy administration veterans, as well as journalists and historians, gave support to this thesis when *JFK* stimulated public debate about Kennedy's policies in Vietnam. For example, Arthur Schlesinger Jr., a Pulitzer Prize–winning historian and former adviser to President Kennedy, articulated this case strongly in an article in the *Wall Street Journal* (although Schlesinger disagreed with Stone's assumption about an assassination conspiracy). Schlesinger said Kennedy continually opposed the military's recommendations that he send expeditionary forces into Vietnam to participate in the fighting there. The president planned on a phased withdrawal of U.S. military personnel, and he hoped that the Vietnamese would save themselves.[16]

Others were much more critical of these suggestions about Kennedy's plans for Southeast Asia. They thought that Stone built his assumptions about Kennedy's intentions in Vietnam on very shaky ground. Kennedy biographer James N. Giglio, for example, noted that the planned cutback of 1,000 men involved a construction battalion that largely had finished its work in Vietnam. Kennedy's own statements suggest that he intended no pullout after the 1964 election, and later interviews with his brother Robert, as well as documents later released in *Foreign Relations of the United States,* similarly support the view that no pullout was planned, said Giglio.[17] Ronald Steel, a foreign affairs specialist, also considered Stone's conclusions to be highly problematic. He noted that Kennedy had given a green light for South Vietnamese generals to overthrow their elected president, Ngo Dinh Diem, and Kennedy had created counterinsurgency forces to fight against communist threats in the Third World. Steel recalled also that Kennedy said, "I don't agree with those who say we should withdraw. That would be a great mistake."[18] The biographer of Lyndon B. Johnson, Robert Dallek, also joined the debate. He observed that Kennedy and his advisers were deeply concerned about the possibility of a communist takeover in Vietnam and that "Kennedy had no intention of 'losing' Vietnam." Moreover, said Dallek, Johnson agonized over the decision to escalate U.S. military involvement in Southeast Asia. He did not eagerly leap at the opportunity, as the movie suggests. Furthermore, Dallek reported confidently that information he obtained from the FBI under the Freedom of Information Act showed conclusively that Johnson had nothing to do with Kennedy's murder.[19] A year later Noam Chomsky offered a related perspective on the question of Vietnam policy. He said that even the dovish advisers who had worked for Kennedy told President Johnson that Kennedy's policy, as they understood it, was to resist a withdrawal without victory, and they urged Johnson to follow that course.[20]

JFK could not settle the important argument over Vietnam, but it did give the debate new energy. The airing of opinions in newspapers and on radio and television in the months following *JFK*'s release served a useful purpose. It stirred the public's thinking about how the United States entered its most frustrating war, and it demonstrated the difficulty of trying to interpret the motivation and actions of leaders such as John F. Kennedy and Lyndon B. Johnson. Stone's movie raised legitimate questions about the history of the cold war that had been the focus of attention by scholars and journalists for many years.

Furthermore, Stone challenged viewers to transcend the particular arguments about Kennedy's posture toward Vietnam (such as what, specifically, was intended by memorandum 263) and to consider a

broad question about how history might have been different if the tragedy of 22 November 1963 had not intervened. Stone argued that "the
Vietnam War as we know it would never have happened" if Kennedy
had lived. Although it is impossible to respond to this assertion with
certainty, it does seem likely that the American experience in Southeast Asia would have been different if Kennedy had enjoyed two terms
in the White House. It is difficult to believe that Kennedy would have
turned as quickly and extensively to placing U.S. combat troops in the
country as did his successor, Lyndon B. Johnson.[21] It is striking that in
less than a year after Kennedy's assassination Lyndon Johnson was
promoting misleading interpretations of reports from the Gulf of Tonkin
to win congressional justification for future military actions. Less than
two years after Kennedy's death Johnson was escalating American
combat involvement substantially and sending squadrons of planes to
bomb sites in both North and South Vietnam. In less than five years
after the assassination Johnson had committed over a half-million
American troops and billions of dollars in equipment to the U.S. effort in Vietnam.

Although it is true that many of the best and the brightest among
Kennedy's advisers served as architects of U.S. military action in Vietnam—men such as Robert MacNamara, Maxwell Taylor, Walt W. Rostow, Dean Rusk, and McGeorge Bundy—it is also true that during the
years of escalation a number of people who had been close to President Kennedy objected to Johnson's course of action. Among the
emerging critics were Kennedy's brother Bobby, the president's aide
Ken O'Donnell, his historian-adviser Arthur Schlesinger Jr., and his
speech writer Ken Sorenson. Even a "hawk" like Robert MacNamara
began to harbor doubts after a few years, and probably MacNamara
would have found a more receptive ear at that point if he could have
expressed his concerns in 1967 to President Kennedy instead of to
President Johnson.

Stone's provocative film stirred viewers to think about this important chapter from American history once again. Attempts to answer
the questions raised by *JFK* drew viewers into counterfactual history:
because the alternatives never occurred, audiences could never be sure
what would have happened had history taken a different path. Nonetheless, Stone's general observation seemed to be pregnant with meaning. The Vietnam War quite possibly would have followed a course
different from the one it took if the assassination had not taken place.

With respect to Stone's most important hypothesis, however (his assumptions about a conspiracy in the Kennedy assassination), the movie does not advance understanding much beyond the theories offered in hundreds of publications on the subject released since the 1960s. Stone suggested abundant questions about the Warren Commission's conclusions but presented no real answers. Like other individuals who proposed conspiracy theories, he demonstrated confidence in raising doubts about official explanations but pursued no counter-explanation to the point of a definitive conclusion. There might be much more to the story of the assassination than the Warren Commission discovered, but conspiracy buffs had not been able to make striking breakthroughs allowing students of Kennedy's murder to pursue a new line of thought successfully. Stone's movie simply helped to give popular expression to the many questions that lack answers.

JFK drew viewers' attention to a number of conspiracy theories that had been exciting public interest since the 1960s. The ideas presented in *JFK* had received detailed attention in hundreds of books and articles published on the subject in the three decades since Kennedy died. Many of the popular arguments about a conspiracy contained elements of the following claims: that representatives of the Mafia, the FBI, or the CIA were involved; that anti-Castro Cubans or agents of Fidel Castro had a hand in it; or that representatives of the "military-industrial complex" played a role. In terms of evidence, critics of the Warren Commission's report pointed particularly to questions about the timing and direction of the shots that struck Kennedy, to questions about the trajectory of the so-called magic bullet, and to information from the doctors who treated the president at a Dallas hospital.[22]

The possibility of Mafia involvement in an assassination plot had long been a subject of popular discussion. Authors who had pressed this interpretation emphasized that Kennedy's brother Robert had been pursuing an intensive war against professional criminals from his position as attorney general in the Kennedy administration. Robert was rather successful in making top Mafia figures nervous. Many of these criminal bosses spoke of their hatred for the Kennedys, and they issued threats against their lives. John F. Kennedy's own position in dealing with the Mafia was compromised by his sexual adventures, say the conspiracy theorists. Kennedy had an affair with Judith Exner, who had close ties to Mafia boss Sam Giancana. Giancana sent messages to Kennedy through Exner, they argue, and Giancana took actions that helped Kennedy to win his 1960 election campaign. Thus, the Kennedy administration's tough crackdown on the Mafia seemed to be a dou-

ble-cross in view of the valuable assistance Giancana provided earlier
to Kennedy.

JFK also implicated the FBI. The bureau maintained a variety of
contacts with Lee Harvey Oswald, argued the conspiracy theorists, and
Oswald probably served as an FBI informant. The FBI may not have
had a hand in the assassination, but possibly it obscured the evidence
about a conspiracy to hide its own association with Oswald. Supporters of this interpretation argue that the bureau suppressed and fabricated evidence in conducting an investigation of the Kennedy murder,
and this manipulation of the facts suggests the FBI's role in a cover-
up. Furthermore, these commentators note that the bureau's longtime
director, J. Edgar Hoover, harbored an intense dislike for the Kennedys.

JFK emphasizes CIA connections as well. For years critics of the
Warren Commission report had been drawn to the mounting evidence
of the CIA's involvement in covert operations designed to overthrow
foreign governments. Some of the CIA's leaders had even been plotting the assassination of foreign leaders. The agency, whose power had
grown tremendously in the cold war era, had been operating like a secret government, and leaders in the White House could not rein it in
adequately or keep fully abreast of its activities. During the early 1960s
CIA agents established contacts with a wide range of citizens, including
Clay Shaw, the man Jim Garrison accused of involvement in a conspiracy (important testimony about this association came out *after* Garrison's
unsuccessful trial of Shaw). Some suggest that Oswald was involved in
intelligence work for the agency, and they believe that a number of individuals who were in contact with Oswald were also maintaining contact with the CIA. Although the agency itself was probably not active in
the assassination plot, some of its renegade operatives who had participated in various political "dirty tricks" could have had a hand in the
assassination. If CIA leaders discovered that connection, they would have
had good motivation to conceal the evidence. Revelations about the
involvement of CIA figures in the president's murder could have laid the
agency open to attacks by its political enemies.

Anti-Castro Cubans had close contacts with the CIA, and they too
had good reason for killing Kennedy, as the movie suggests. Conspiracy theorists had been pointing out for years that many Cuban exiles
in the U.S. disliked Kennedy, because the president refused to commit American military power to the 1961 invasion of Cuba. The Bay
of Pigs assault was supposed to help free the Caribbean island from
Fidel Castro's grip. Instead, it was a fiasco. A number of anti-Castro

Cubans lost their lives or were imprisoned. Furthermore, as part of the understanding with the Soviets that settled the Cuban Missile Crisis, Kennedy agreed not to invade Cuba in the future. He also made efforts toward reconciliation with Castro after the Cuban Missile Crisis, trying to scale down the U.S. government's secret war against communist Cuba. These developments gave anti-Castro Cubans ample reason to hate Kennedy.

Another theory—not given much attention in the movie because it reveals an ugly aspect of policy in the Kennedy years—implicates Castro in the assassination plot. The Cuban communist leader would have had strong motivation to have Kennedy destroyed if he had discovered some of the details of the CIA's "Operation Mongoose," which aimed to create economic chaos in Cuba, or the CIA's plan to commit political assassination. Congressional investigations in the 1970s revealed that leaders in the CIA had enlisted help from the Mafia to try to eliminate Castro (some of the plans involved attempts to poison the Cuban leader). Evidence revealed later gave further details on the CIA's efforts to arrange Castro's liquidation with help from the organized crime figure Johnny Roselli, who in turn sought help from another Mafia figure, Santos Trafficante. Perhaps Kennedy ended up the victim in this dangerous game of international intrigue. A nation that promotes international sabotage and assassination jeopardizes the safety of its own leader.

Yet another motive can be found in the activities of the "military-industrial complex," and *JFK* makes much of this idea from the beginning, when it shows a clip of President Dwight D. Eisenhower warning specifically about the complex's power. Conspiracy theorists point out that military personnel were angered by President Kennedy's refusal to send U.S. military forces into the Bay of Pigs invasion and his refusal to accept his military advisers' recommendations to bomb Soviet missile sites during the Cuban Missile Crisis. They also note that military men were troubled by Kennedy's efforts to sign a nuclear test ban treaty with the Soviet Union. Above all, Vietnam figures prominently in this theorizing. Some military leaders, as well as representatives of arms industries holding big military contracts with the U.S. government, could have been very disturbed if they sensed that President Kennedy aimed to pull out of Vietnam.

To these prominent hypotheses investigators have added a number of other possible answers to the mysteries about Kennedy's death: that Vice President Lyndon B. Johnson could have had a hand in the plot (and, obviously, had much to gain from its success), that figures in New Orleans' homosexual underground may have played a role, that the Soviets worked closely with Oswald when he defected to the Soviet Union, or that representatives of the American news media went along with a cover-up. *JFK* gives brief screen attention to these ideas.

Investigators also focused sharply on newly discovered clues that they hoped would create a better understanding of the assassination, particularly insights about the origin of the shots that killed Kennedy. For instance, they made much of Abraham Zapruder's thirty seconds of 8-mm film shot from the grassy knoll in Dallas at the scene of the assassination.[23] The Zapruder film seems to offer striking evidence that Kennedy did not die only from a rifle used by Lee Harvey Oswald at the Texas School Book Depository Building. Its footage shows Kennedy's head falling backward violently, evidently from a shot coming from in front and to the right (in the direction of the grassy knoll). This impression stands in stark contrast to the Warren Commission's conclusion that the fatal shot came from the schoolbook depository building, which was to the rear. *JFK* gives much attention to the Zapruder film, playing it backward and forward in slow motion several times so that viewers can ponder its significance.

The matter of timing was also connected to the Zapruder film, and *JFK* makes reference to it. Many critics of the Warren Commission's version of the assassination claimed the Zapruder footage reveals that three shots were fired at Kennedy in just 5.6 seconds, not enough time for even the most expert marksman to handle effectively. Certainly 5.6 seconds was too little time for Oswald or his gun to accomplish the task from as far away as the depository building.

JFK also gives attention to claims made by eyewitnesses and earwitnesses who were present at the scene of the shooting. Various individuals believed, on the basis of what they saw or heard, that a second person was shooting from the grassy knoll, and some acoustic evidence appears to support their suspicion.

Moreover, *JFK* refers to a "magic bullet" that, according to Kevin Costner's derisive commentary in the movie, supposedly entered the president's back, headed downward, and then moved upward to leave from the front of his neck, where it waited 1.6 seconds, "presumably in mid-air"; after this pause it turned right, then left, and then penetrated Governor John Connally's body, going through his armpit and his rib and coming out through his chest, after which it reentered through his right wrist and then swung around and buried itself in his left thigh. Later the bullet presumably fell out and turned up, as Costner says, "in almost pristine condition in a corridor of Parkland Hospital."

The movie also raises suspicions about the handling of President Kennedy's body from the time doctors worked on it at the Dallas hospital to the time it appeared at a hospital in Bethesda, Maryland, for an autopsy. *JFK* refers to questions many authors raised about the possibility that someone could have tampered with the president's body, attempting to conceal evidence about the direction of the fatal shots.

Indeed, new testimony that came to light during the first months after *JFK* appeared in the theaters seems to give weight to this theory. A doctor who was a junior member of the team that operated on Kennedy in Dallas argued that he determined a bullet had struck the president from the front, but evidence of this seems to have been altered sometime before Kennedy's body arrived in Maryland.[24]

These "revelations" excited considerable discussion when they became public, but with the passage of time, as in the case of so many other supposed discoveries about the assassination, they came under serious questioning. It appeared that the Warren Commission's original conclusions about the direction of the shots that killed Kennedy were probably valid—unless better substantiated evidence could be introduced to dispute them.

For instance, physicians reported that the violent swing of Kennedy's head toward the rear developed out of the body's natural neurological reactions to a sudden shock. Indeed, nineteen of twenty medical experts who served over the years on four independent panels that examined the X rays and autopsy photos concluded that the president had been shot from the rear. Furthermore, the acoustic evidence that moved members of the House Select Committee on Assassinations to conclude that a second shooter had been involved in the assassination later came under serious challenge. The Committee on Ballistic Acoustics of the National Research Council found in 1982 that the theory had no scientific validity. Similarly, the theories about alteration of evidence regarding the president's wounds also proved to be shaky. The physician who suggested that someone had tampered with the body before it arrived in Maryland came under sharp challenge. In public statements two pathologists who performed the autopsy affirmed that the bullets that killed the president came from above and behind, and five doctors who treated Kennedy in the emergency room said that they observed nothing that contradicted the pathologists' conclusions.[25]

Other claims about additional shooters or gunshots also began to appear weak. On the question of timing, for instance, defenders of the Warren Commission pointed out that the Zapruder film does not indicate that three shots had to hit the president within 5.6 seconds. As Jacob Cohen explained in a response to *JFK* published in *Commentary,* "even assuming that two hits occurred 5.6 seconds apart, nothing in Zapruder indicates that a possible third shot, which missed, had to have come *between* the two shots. The Warren Commission concluded only that there were probably three shots and that the *two hits,* not the three shots, came within 5.6 seconds of each other." Additionally, it became clear that not one of the 692 people who were identified as being present at Dealey Plaza saw a gun on the grassy knoll, but six people did see what was apparently Oswald's rifle inside the sixth-floor window of the book depository.[26] Furthermore, defenders of the Warren Commission (and critics of Stone) were quick to point out that plenty of evidence from the scene of the murder clearly suggested Oswald was the culprit. The rifle in the book depository, which fired both the bullet found by the stretcher and two large fragments found in the car, had Oswald's fingerprint on it, and the House Assassination Committee, using enhancement techniques not available to the Warren Commission, proved that the rifle in Oswald's photographs was the same rifle that fired the shots.

As for the so-called magic bullet, the Warren Commission did not find what Costner/Garrison claimed in the movie. Governor John Connally's wounds, for example, were not remarkable. Connally heard a first shot and reacted by rotating his shoulders slightly, bringing his body into an alignment that made him vulnerable to the five wounds that he received. Indeed, in the twenty years before the appearance of *JFK,* several expert panels examined film, photo, and X-ray evidence and concluded that Kennedy and Connally were struck as the Warren Commission claimed. Furthermore, the bullet that turned up on the floor of Parkland Hospital was not in the pristine condition described by the movie's Garrison character. It lacked lead in the core, was flattened at one end, and was bent at its axis. There was nothing "magic" about the bullet.[27] Once again, supposedly striking new breakthroughs turned out to be poorly substantiated speculation.

In short, the many questions about what specifically happened in Dallas on 22 November 1963 remain just that—questions. *JFK*'s achievement was to pull the many examples of speculation into one story and to dramatize them in a clever mix of original and fictional documentation. Stone gave audiences a plethora of conspiracy theories to ponder. In just a little more than three hours his movie manages to touch most of the principal ideas outlined in Jim Marrs's 594-page book, *Crossfire*. Through creative docudrama, Stone provoked audiences with stimulating hints about the many possible sources of a conspiracy. He offered a hit-and-run approach to the subject. Stone struck each concept briefly and then moved on quickly to consider different explanations about who committed the crime and why. Near the end of the story Stone had the characters playing "Mr. X" and Jim Garrison try to sum up the supposed connections that tied the different theories together, but that effort could not demonstrate that *all* the ideas were valid and related. Clearly, Stone had amassed a great number of disparate concepts and tried to give them the appearance of a complex, interlocking plot. His "facts" about a conspiracy remained essentially guesses.

Despite all the public interest in *JFK*, theorizing about the Kennedy assassination did not advance in any significant way in the months following the movie's release. In fact, most of the speculation was notably undiscriminating. Conspiracy-minded investigators seemed to find a clue in every extraordinary statement made about the assassination. The enthusiastic interest in hundreds of different "leads" gave the impression that many viewers of *JFK* were so ready to accept the idea of a conspiracy that they would treat any loosely articulated idea as a potentially valuable key to unlocking the puzzle.

Despite the lack of important new evidence destroying the Warren Commission's conclusions, doubts remained strong. Before *JFK* reached the theaters, a poll showed that 56 percent of the American people believed that the assassination involved a conspiracy. Stone's movie probably pushed the percentage significantly higher. The number could continue to climb even though nothing significantly new had emerged to substantiate such an assumption.

In the absence of a breakthrough, Americans were left only with fascinating speculation. A strong case could be made for the involvement of the Mafia, the CIA, Cuban exiles, or others in the assassination. Because none of these ideas had been pursued to the point of validation, however, the Warren Commission's conclusion about a lone assassin remained—as of 1991—the best-supported theory. To be sure, years of investigation had revealed that the Warren Commission failed to probe adequately, and it relied too much on information supplied by the FBI (Americans learned later how much the bureau could not be trusted).

Nevertheless, recognizing the shortcomings of the Warren Commission's investigation does not necessarily mean that the commission was wrong in its essential findings. The criticisms that Oliver Stone leveled against the Warren Commission do not, in themselves, destroy the argument that Lee Harvey Oswald, acting alone, was the killer.[28] The best substantiated theory (not unassailable fact) about the assassination continued to be the conclusion that a psychologically troubled individual named Lee Harvey Oswald assassinated the president.[29]

For many people, this scenario appeared too random, too irrational to serve as an acceptable explanation. They found it difficult to conclude that Kennedy's assassination could represent a kind of "accident" in history that lacked great political meaning. As William Manchester noted, it was hard to believe that the president did not die for *"something."*[30] Many preferred to think that the president's murder resulted from a complex plot involving powerful and dangerous individuals who operated with specific goals in mind. Recent American history gave them good reason to become suspicious, of course. Revelations in the 1960s, 1970s, and 1980s about CIA-connected plots to assassinate foreign leaders and CIA overtures to Mafia figures for purposes of eliminating Fidel Castro stimulated the public's thinking about sinister webs of intrigue in government affairs. Still, in the absence of truly convincing evidence in the Kennedy case, the readiness of many people to accept *JFK*'s assumptions about a vast conspiracy raises questions. Did the images of conspiracy proposed by many critics of the Warren Commission resemble, in some ways, the perspectives of earlier conspiracy-minded individuals who pointed to the power of the Masonic order, the Catholic church, the international bankers, or the Elders of Zion? Was it worthwhile to reread Richard Hofstadter's book *The Paranoid Style in American Politics* to get a better understanding of some public reactions to the movie?[31]

As for *JFK*'s relationship to history, the issue became more controversial because of Oliver Stone's posture in defending his movie. Had Stone stuck to the concept that his film simply plays out a number of speculative scenarios about the assassination, he would not have provoked many people who insisted on a measure of authenticity in such a popular historical representation. When he insisted that he had made an important contribution to historical understanding, however, Stone invited heated debate.

On occasion Stone identified his role as a moviemaker in a defensible way, saying that he wanted to present a "countermyth" to the official "myth" of the Warren Commission report. The myth he wished to substitute was constructed through a "combination of hypothesis and fact."[32] Stone admitted that he had no smoking gun, that he did not know how or why Kennedy died. "I don't have all the facts," he explained. "The best I can do is to present a hypothesis which will hopefully encourage people to move away from the Warren Report and maybe read some books or at least to question the concept of our government's covert operations."[33] "I never had or claimed to have" the truth, Stone confessed.[34] The whole truth is "perhaps unknowable," so *JFK* presents "fragments of truth."[35] By suggesting a number of scenarios, the movie helps viewers to move well beyond the Warren report in imagining explanations. Stone reminded the press that he had used Akira Kurosawa's *Rashomon* as a model. *Rashomon* views a crime from multiple perspectives, Stone noted, and demonstrates the impossibility of arriving at a single truth. Thus, *JFK* is "not a true story per se" but "truth" at one moment and "art" in the next.[36]

By outlining his goals in this manner, Stone stood on firm ground. He did not promise more than he could deliver. The director identified his drama as a speculative analysis of the historical problem, one that presented a great variety of possible explanations for Kennedy's assassination. He hoped that many viewers would be sufficiently moved by the movie to demand that their government look more closely into the murder case. As such, *JFK* would serve as the beginning of a new understanding of Kennedy's assassination, not the end. It would offer questions, not answers.

Stone, however, was not willing to treat his movie only as an exercise in fiction designed to make audiences think about history. He also insisted on aggressively reviewing the historical evidence associated with the Kennedy assassination. Defending the details of his movie's interpretation of a conspiracy, he promised that, after seeing *JFK*, Americans would become more informed about their history. Stone announced proudly that he had done his "homework" and his research team "did a lot of fact-finding." Stone pointed out that he took much of the movie's dialogue "straight from the written record," thus "letting history speak for itself."[37] In an interview with the press he admitted to taking some creative liberties but said that he did not attempt many "because the material is very important and sacred to the public."[38]

When critics attacked the details of *JFK*'s interpretation of history, Stone eagerly defended his movie's treatment of the historical record. For example, in response to David Belin's and Gerald Ford's attack on

JFK's conspiracy argument published in the *Washington Post*, Stone published his own response, citing evidence about ballistics, the time Oswald had to shoot the president, the autopsy, and the role of Jack Ruby (the man who shot Oswald) that he claimed refuted Belin's and Ford's charges.[39] On another occasion Stone responded to the familiar criticism of his movie's thesis about the existence of a vast network of conspirators. The critics claimed that hundreds of people ranging from the Dallas police to the FBI could not have guarded a huge secret about their involvement in an assassination plot, but Stone maintained that the core of the conspiracy could have involved as few as five to nine people. "It's cellular," said Stone of the core group. The conspiracy to kill could have been very small, whereas the conspiracy to cover up could have been much larger. The plotters did not necessarily know each other, and they left nothing on paper, he explained. Responding to another familiar criticism—one about the movie's extraordinary suggestion that Vice President Lyndon B. Johnson had been part of the assassination plan—Stone said it was quite possible Johnson was involved, "but I never made that assertion." The movie shows Johnson involved only in the cover-up, the director argued.[40] Furthermore, Stone defended his movie's suggestion that the conspiracy extended beyond the matter of Kennedy's death. "There's no doubt," Stone concluded, that the three killings of John F. Kennedy, Robert F. Kennedy, and Martin Luther King Jr. "are linked."[41] Stone's claims about a conspiracy cabal, President Johnson's role in a cover-up, and connections between the killings of John F. Kennedy, Robert Kennedy, and King, of course, completely lack evidential support.

Stone was especially aggressive when addressing the question of who has responsibility for interpreting history to the public. Describing himself as a "cinematic historian," the director said that filmmakers have every right to contribute to historical understanding.[42] Stone asserted that *JFK* probably achieved a "higher truth" about the assassination than had many of the well-known journalists who had been writing about the subject for years.[43] Stone claimed that many members of the media were hostile toward his movie simply because they did not like to see art turn political, especially when the result contrasted with their own conclusions on an important subject.[44] Furthermore, a movie like *JFK* could embarrass members of the media who thought that they knew just about everything one could know about the assassination story. "I think the press blew it on the Kennedy assassination," Stone reported, "and I think a lot of people are angry that a filmmaker as artist tried to do some of the work they didn't do."[45] History is "too important to leave to newsmen" he said; artists have a right—even an obligation—to "step up and reinterpret the history of our times."[46]

While staking broad claims for the artist, Stone showed little tolerance for criticism. "You cannot tell an artist what to do," he said. "It's the First Amendment."[47] An artist's obligation is to his or her conscience only. Demands for "realism" and "social responsibility" (presumably responsibility for authenticating the movie's interpretation of history) smack of censorship and reminded him of the demands Soviet leaders had made of their artists. It is wrong to insist on socially and politically correct interpretations. In Stone's view artists have the right to interpret history as they see it. If an artist wishes to make a movie showing Hitler as a good guy, said Stone, that is acceptable.[48]

Because Stone would not simply promote his movie as a work of fiction and an exercise in speculation, he encountered much resistance. When he asserted that he was a "cinematic historian" and went on to denigrate the historical interpretations of those who disagreed with him and defend the fine points of his own interpretation of a conspiracy, he invited debate. In view of the director's ambitious claims for *JFK*, it is not surprising that the movie came under scrutiny for its presentation of the past. Stone encountered tough questions, because he openly advertised himself as a historian as well as an artist. Once he acknowledged his role as a cinematic historian, arguments about the validity of his movie's approach to the past were appropriate and relevant.

Stone's promotion of a "JFK Study Guide" further stimulated the debate he inspired about the filmmaker's role as historian. Warner Brothers distributed the guide to high school social studies departments and history departments in universities at the time of the movie's release. This action greatly antagonized individuals who saw themselves as guardians of integrity in the interpretation of history. One of the most outspoken critics of the study guide was David W. Belin, formal counsel to the Warren Commission and author of books and articles that defend the commission's principal conclusions. Belin said he was appalled that Warner Brothers would try to promote the movie's lies in America's classrooms through an advertising package thinly disguised as a study tool. He accused the moviemakers of spreading *JFK*'s "disinformation" into the public schools, "in effect brainwashing students through the power of commercial film and rewriting history the Hollywood way."[49]

Study guides were not new to the movie business; they had been published over many years in association with motion pictures that purported to throw light on history. In 1939, for example, a publication called *Young Mr. Lincoln: A Guide to the Study of the Historical Philosophy* appeared in connection with the popular movie starring Henry Fonda. By the 1980s television networks were releasing these documents to arouse teachers' interest in discussing docudramas with their students (for example, CBS sent thousands of booklets to schools and colleges to serve as ancillary readings for its miniseries *George Washington*). These booklets clearly suggest that the film under study is essentially true and that the documents can help students to gain a more informed understanding of the past.

By disseminating the study guide and by defending the film's claims as true in numerous articles and public appearances, Oliver Stone opened himself up to considerable criticism. Clearly, he had promoted *JFK* as an educational examination of a real historical problem. Instead of deflecting attacks by freely acknowledging his movie to be only a fictional exercise that tries to imagine (in extreme form) the possibilities for a conspiracy, Stone chose to defend his work aggressively as an incisive treatment of history. Whether he took this combative position because of genuinely felt personal beliefs or because he recognized the controversy over *JFK*'s historical interpretation could boost the marketing of his movie can be disputed. Whatever the case, in trying to present himself as a moviemaker-historian, Stone encountered hard questions about responsibility to the facts.

Not surprisingly, Stone's movie provoked a storm of criticism in newspapers and magazines. One of the earliest attacks came while the film was still in production. George Lardner Jr. of the *Washington Post* had been able to obtain a first draft of the screenplay with assistance from the longtime assassination researcher Harold Weisberg. Lardner had followed debates about the assassination for years, and he found the draft for the *JFK* script laden with factual errors and unsubstantiated speculation. Stone's attempt to promote *JFK* as history was shameful, Lardner argued in his article. The movie offers myth, not fact.[50] Soon other prominent columnists joined Lardner in criticizing Stone. Tom Wicker wrote in the *New York Times* that Stone treated "matters that are wholly speculative as fact and truth, in effect rewriting history," and the *Chicago Sun-Times* editorialized that *JFK* dishonored President Kennedy by presenting a "mush of fact, fiction, and supposition" that amounted to "clumsy fantasy."[51] With a touch of humor added to skepticism, Stanley Kauffmann of the *New Republic* warned that young audiences should not expect to learn about Kennedy's assassination from Stone's movie, just as they could not expect to learn about Mc-Carthyism by watching *My Son John* or learn about the Vietnam War by watching *The Green Berets* (both of those movies offer simple-minded theses about America's enemies).[52]

Edward Jay Epstein offered some of the most detailed charges of falsification in a biting article in *The Atlantic Monthly.* Epstein highlighted a number of distortions in the movie's portrayal of an interview with a gay soldier of fortune, David William Ferrie (actor Joe Pesci played Ferrie), the last before his death. In the real interview, said Epstein, Ferrie talked with *Washington Post* reporter George Lardner, Jr., but in the movie he confesses to Jim Garrison and his assistants. In the actual meeting Ferrie was at home and relaxed; the movie shows him in a state of panic in a hotel suite. Ferrie denied knowing Lee Harvey Oswald in Lardner's interview, reported Epstein; in the film Ferrie admits training Oswald. In the real interview Ferrie never mentioned Clay Shaw, whom Jim Garrison accused of complicity in the assassination, but *JFK* shows Ferrie admitting that Shaw controls him. Ferrie did not discuss the CIA with Lardner, yet *JFK* has him claiming a CIA connection. Ferrie denied knowing of an assassination plot, but the movie has him describing plot details, claiming that Oswald and Shaw are CIA affiliated, and talking about trained shooters. Finally, the authorities ruled Ferrie's death natural, but *JFK* identifies Ferrie as the victim of a Cuban associate of Shaw's. Such glaring contrasts with the facts led Epstein to conclude that Stone presented very poor history.[53]

The wave of criticism also included remarks from a number of people who had investigated the assassination. For instance, G. Robert Blakey, former chief counsel of the House Select Committee on Assassinations, complained that "as an artist, Stone has freedom of speech to say whatever he wants. But the Bible tells us that those who lie to the young should have a millstone tied around their necks and be thrown into the sea."[54] Former president Gerald Ford and David W. Belin, a counsel to the Warren Commission, were similarly appalled, saying that the film desecrated the memory not only of President Kennedy but also of the fine former chief justice of the Supreme Court, Earl Warren. Ford and Belin concluded that Stone gave "a fraudulent misrepresentation of the truth to the American public."[55]

Even those who had proposed conspiracy theories found the movie sorely lacking. For example, Mark Lane, one of the first to propose a conspiracy theory in a book-length analysis, considered the movie to be "very bad on the facts," and Harold Weisberg, the author of a number of books raising questions about the Warren report's conclusions, greeted Stone's work with hyperbole. Weisberg asked how anyone could "do a mishmash like this out of love for the victim and respect for history. . . . I think people who sell sex have more principle."[56]

Prominent Americans who had been in positions of political power at the time of the assassination also expressed disgust with Stone's movie. Former Texas governor John Connally, who had been wounded during the assassination attempt while traveling with the president, said that Stone's conspiracy theory was "so illogical and so unreasonable, it's hardly worthy of comment." Connally spoke nonetheless. He called the movie "a powerful propaganda piece. . . . It's fiction, . . . It's for sure not a documentary." Connally considered the movie "insulting" in the way it implicates the distinguished Warren Commission in a conspiracy without offering any proof to substantiate its charge, and he blasted Stone for making New Orleans district attorney Jim Garrison look like a hero when, in fact, his investigation of a supposed conspirator had been "a complete fiasco."[57] Jack Valenti, a former assistant to Lyndon Baines Johnson, also showed contempt for the movie's thesis. Valenti had tried not to make public statements about the film because of his sensitive position as president and chief executive of the Motion Picture Association of America. Five months after the movie's release, however, he broke his official silence. Valenti was outraged by *JFK*'s suggestion that the then vice president, Lyndon Baines Johnson, had played a role in the assassination. Valenti called the movie a "hoax," a "smear," and "pure fiction." He said that he could not live with himself if he stood by mutely and allowed a filmmaker like Stone to soil the memory of Lyndon B. Johnson. Valenti worried that the flawed movie would mesmerize America's youth in the way that Leni Riefenstahl's mixture of hoaxes and propaganda (*Triumph of the Will*) excited young Germans in the 1930s.[58]

A number of commentators were disturbed by the idea that young people would be particularly vulnerable to Stone's messages. They worried that youths would know little about the Kennedy assassination when they entered the theaters. What they saw on the screen was likely to seem like the truth. Moved by visual images even more than by words, these viewers would probably accept *JFK*'s version of the facts uncritically. "We live in a media age," *Newsweek*'s Leonard Maltin reminded readers. "If a television or theatrical movie can paint a vivid enough picture for young people, they'll believe that's the way it is."[59] Editors of the *New York Times* thought that young people would "swallow *JFK* whole." Children of the video age are easy targets for a filmmaker who wishes to manipulate history, they said, and American society lacks the power to police art for its inaccuracies. Anthony Lewis, also writing in the *New York Times*, concluded that a film as influential as *JFK* would "move a generation to believe that a conspiracy lay behind the assassination of Kennedy."[60]

Of course, not every critic who found serious fault with *JFK* was convinced the movie would do lasting damage to the public's perceptions of history. Some complained about Stone's errors but remained confident that many young audiences would recognize *JFK* for what it was—a product of the entertainment industry. *JFK* is "a travesty" as history, concluded Charles Krauthammer in the *Washington Post*, but it is nevertheless "harmless." Some children would accept its outrageous claims, but their beliefs would have little meaning. Anyone who thought that America was taken over by a fascist conspiracy in 1963 "should immediately sign up for the Red Brigades," commented Krauthammer. He thought that the American citizens were so overwhelmed by the media's cultural messages that they were anesthetized to them. The ideas of Stone and other dealers in "paranoia" were to many citizens "just another entertainment, another day at the movies."[61] Similarly historian Arthur Schlesinger Jr. considered much of *JFK*'s thesis to be implausible but saw little potential for serious damage. Schlesinger thought that young people had seen so much "hyped-up speculation, surmise and invention" in the media that they had learned to take pseudo-historical docudramas with a grain of salt. "History will survive," Schlesinger promised.[62]

Most individuals who raised criticisms about *JFK* were not so confident that history could survive undamaged from Stone's influence. They worried about the impact of a popular motion picture like *JFK*, recognizing that it could affect the way in which millions of viewers both in the United States and abroad perceived the workings of the U.S. government. They were disturbed to find that *JFK* made many poorly substantiated charges about the integrity of the Warren Commission, the practices of national security agencies such as the FBI and the CIA, the power of the "military-industrial complex," and Lyndon B. Johnson's role in a possible conspiracy. These critics wanted answers to the following questions: What were the limits to Stone's creative license? How far could he go in fictionalizing a story of the Kennedy assassination? Did

Stone face *any* obligation to present his case in an authentic way? Should viewers forgive the director for treating some speculation about the assassination as fact, since *JFK* is only a form of entertainment? Should a Hollywood movie such as *JFK* be regarded simply as fiction even though many viewers will interpret much of it as fact?

Oliver Stone had been angered by the attacks since when Lardner had criticized an early draft of the screenplay. He thought it outrageous that a journalist would launch an assault on his movie project based on a working document that was still taking shape in the period of research and scriptwriting.[63] Furthermore, his script had been grabbed surreptitiously from the production organization; it had not been released for public analysis. Stone and Sklar later spoke of the document as a "stolen draft." Sklar argued that Norman Mailer would not be happy if someone stole an early draft of one of his novels and then published a review of it. Additional criticisms from Tom Wicker, Dan Rather, and Anthony Lewis further angered Stone. He decided to answer every attack from the media quickly and aggressively. A strong offense would constitute a good defense.[64]

For several months Stone spent long hours each week at the word processor, hammering out detailed arguments about the fine points of *JFK*'s interpretation of history and attacking supposed weaknesses in the journalists' reasoning. He targeted the *Washington Post* and the *New York Times* at first, since he understood that their negative articles could influence other representatives of the media. Stone threatened to sue the *Post* for copyright infringement (referring to the *Post*'s acquisition of a confidential *JFK* script draft), and he threatened to take out an ad in the *New York Times* to protest that newspaper's negative reception for his movie. Both newspapers allowed Stone to write an article for their Op-Ed sections.[65] Stone used the opportunities to review evidence on the assassination and make point-by-point rejoinders to criticisms by columnists such as the *Post*'s George Lardner Jr. and the *Times*' Anthony Lewis, Tom Wicker, and Leslie Gelb. In these essays the director complained that spokespersons for the media establishment wanted to remain the "sole or privileged interpreters" of the nation's history, and they treated with contempt newcomers who tried "rewriting history." "History may be too important to leave to newsmen," said Stone, and he proudly described his own important role in reinterpreting it.[66] In the following weeks and months Stone granted numerous interviews to figures from the press and television, continuing his efforts to defend the picture's theses.

The director's struggle to gain respect and publicity for *JFK* got a boost in early 1992 when many Americans began demanding that all records on the Kennedy assassination be opened to public scrutiny. Their response came especially in reaction to a statement that appears on the screen near the end of *JFK*. The caption reminds viewers that some papers from U.S. government–sponsored investigations into the assassination were not to be made public until well into the twenty-first century (for instance, the House of Representatives' papers were not to be released until 2029). As Americans learned about this policy of confidentiality, they looked much more favorably on Stone's charges about conspiracy. If there was nothing to hide, they asked, why was there so much secrecy about the evidence accumulated in previous investigations? Did the public not have a right to know all that the government discovered in its research on the president's murder?[67]

Efforts by the Warren Commission and the House select committee to protect the confidentiality of some information were evidently not the result of a conspiracy to conceal shocking revelations about the assassination. Rather, they related to a variety of legal and moral considerations. Some of the papers involve personnel files, and in other cases they contain testimony given by individuals who spoke to investigators under the promise of confidentiality. The papers also contain information about intelligence-gathering methods and identify people who were sources of information—again matters that some wished to keep confidential. The very condition of confidentiality, however, strengthened the public's suspicions.

Outcries in favor of opening the files brought quick responses from politicians in early 1992. Many in Congress talked of passing legislation designed to make all the assassination records public. The advocates of openness included Louis Stokes, former chief of the House Select Committee on Assassinations. Thirteen former counsel and staff members of the Warren Commission also urged the release of all documents pertaining to the assassination, including the records of the FBI and the CIA. A spokesperson for these individuals expressed confidence that public disclosure would bear out the conclusions drawn by the Warren Commission. He believed the newly opened documents would show that popular assertions about a government cover-up were groundless.[68] Thus, both those who suspected foul play and those who believed the Warren Commission had conducted its work effectively joined in urging release of confidential data about JFK's assassination.

Oliver Stone's movie succeeded in creating a major public outcry in favor of disclosing historical evidence.

By the spring of 1992 Oliver Stone's counterattack on his critics, which was bolstered by the growing public interest in opening up records on the assassination case, appeared to enhance the public reception of *JFK* and give weight to the movie's thesis. A wave of pro-*JFK* writing began to appear in response to the bombardment of criticism the movie received in late 1991 and early 1992. This second, more positive wave came not only from film enthusiasts but also from some professional historians.

One of the strongest pro-Stone responses from the cinema studies community appeared in *Cineaste*. An issue of this publication featured several articles on *JFK* written by a variety of columnists, and it published Stone's remarks to the press, as well as a transcript from an interview with him. The forum included an article by Pat Dowell that compares *JFK* favorably with the movie classic *Citizen Kane* and one by George Michael Evica that notes similarities to Homer's *Iliad*. Evica observed that both *JFK* and *The Iliad* are tragic epics of great mythic importance to their audiences. Other contributors, such as Christopher Starrett, Dan Georgakas, and James Petras, reviewed the details of *JFK*'s treatment of historical issues, confirming that Oliver Stone raised valid questions about the possibility of a conspiracy. Published interviews with two key figures in *JFK*'s production, Zachary Sklar and Jane Rusconi, also suggested that the moviemakers had done their homework when dealing with the historical facts. In one of the few critical notes on the movie, contributors Roy Grundmann and Cynthia Lucia drew attention to the negative images of gays and women in *JFK*.[69]

Some historians also greeted the movie with applause. Particularly notable was the reaction of scholars in the April 1992 issue of the *American Historical Review,* the premier U.S.-based professional journal in the field of history. Marcus Raskin, cofounder of the Institute for Policy Studies, called the movie "a myth of tremendous dramatic proportions."[70] He said that Stone's purpose was to be disruptive to get at the truth. The U.S. government had covered up reprehensible activities, argued Raskin—from secret wars in Indochina, Angola, and Cambodia and CIA associations with gangsters and drug dealers to secret attempts to assassinate foreign leaders such as Fidel Castro and illegal wiretaps conducted by the FBI. Stone's fictionalizations symbolized real problems in recent American history, Raskin maintained, and the movie's contributions needed to be recognized. Historians would be wise not to be overly picayune in evaluating the picture, Raskin suggested. "It does no good to pick apart the rendering of an event by an artist. His or her purpose is not the particular but the general."[71] Similarly, Robert A. Rosenstone demonstrated tolerance for the director's attempt to deal creatively with historical evidence. Rosenstone noted that "the historical film will always include images that are at once invented and yet may still be considered true; true in that they symbolize, condense, or summarize."[72] Rosenstone thought that the overall meaning of Stone's theses could be "verified, documented, or reasonably argued," and he concluded that "*JFK* has to be among the most important works of American history ever to appear on the screen."[73]

The friendly reception that *JFK* received in *American Historical Review, Cineaste,* and other publications demonstrated that some observers were prepared to evaluate the movie with considerably more tolerance for symbolic interpretation than the critical reviewers in the *New York Times* and the *Washington Post*. These reviewers thought that the director communicated an important lesson to the public. Stone had used a dramatic format creatively to address doubts about the Warren Commission's conclusions, they said. *JFK* raised significant questions; it mattered less that the movie does not provide all the right answers. These figures applauded Stone for his success in giving new life to the old debate about the Kennedy assassination. They said that Stone showed the Establishment's explanations for Kennedy's death to be full of holes. The moviemaker made a strong case for the possibility of a conspiracy, and it was the task of society—not Oliver Stone—to investigate further and fill in the details about how that conspiracy could have operated.

If Oliver Stone had made these limited purposes clear from the beginning, journalists and historians probably would have given the movie's approach to portraying history a more positive reception. After all, Stone was engaging in a useful exercise when he attempted to speculate about what really happened on 22 November 1963 or to guess what Kennedy would have done had he lived on to direct the nation's course in Vietnam. In many respects, scholars have posed similar questions. They frequently have disputed popular conclusions about history and have posited alternative explanations. Some have engaged seriously in "counterfactual history," imagining what might have happened if a few critically important situations had turned out differently. In short, speculation is a legitimate exercise, and it can help to sharpen the public's thinking about history. Furthermore, as Stone noted, there are traditions in the cinema that provide a format for imagining distinct possibilities. The techniques of *Rashomon,* which many filmmakers borrowed and applied in a variety of ways to help viewers think of several different perspectives of the "truth," are relevant to what Stone was trying to do.

In advertising *JFK,* however, Oliver Stone miscast his product. He should have promoted his movie to the public as a work of fiction, as an imaginative study of alternative explanations to a troubling question. Stone could have presented *JFK* as an exciting story that dramatizes virtually every major conspiracy theory in current fashion about the Kennedy assassination. He could have tried to sell his motion picture as a drama with an only tangential relationship to history, as a movie that begins with the *fact* of a murder and then moves to bold *speculation* about the way a conspiracy could have been taken place. Instead, he used the film as the basis for a confident argument that a conspiracy actually existed. The certainty expressed in his conclusions forced *JFK* into a public test for historical authenticity, and it is not surprising that the movie failed that examination miserably.

Stone was wrong, too, in citing *Rashomon* as an example of what he wanted to accomplish. Akira Kurosawa had presented several conflicting perspectives of a murder in his Japanese classic; *JFK* provides only scenarios that lead to a broad conclusion about a conspiracy. If Stone had been truly guided by the spirit of *Rashomon,* he would have shown multiple dimensions of the controversy. This not only would have involved recognizing how some of the major conspiracy theories contradict each other; it would also have called for a presentation of the idea that no conspiracy really existed and that Lee Harvey Oswald could have been the lone killer of President Kennedy.

Stone's approach to the debate was unfortunate, because the controversies tended to diminish the credit he could receive for designing a truly innovative motion picture. Had Stone openly confessed to his goal of speculating about history with liberal mixtures of fact and fiction, his critics might have given him a warmer reception. Stone fudged the issue, however, claiming to be both a truth-seeking investigator and an artist who operated free of the standards that guide historical interpretation. Stone often switched hats according to the needs of the moment (when under attack for distorting history, he sometimes reached for the artist's cap). In playing this deceptive game Stone lost an opportunity to win broader applause for finding imaginative ways to stimulate the public's thinking about the past.

PART 2

DRAWING LESSONS

Making the Past Relevant to the Present

Sergeant York

"IF THAT IS PROPAGANDA, WE PLEAD GUILTY"

The usually wild Alvin C. York (Gary Cooper) acts
like a gentleman in his effort to court the lovely
Gracie Williams (Joan Leslie) in *Sergeant York*. Courtesy
of the Museum of Modern Art/Film Stills Archive.

*T*he international situation looked particularly frightening when Warner Brothers' production of *Sergeant York* had its premiere in New York City in early July 1941. In preceding years German and Italian fascism had become a monstrous problem for the European nations. Adolph Hitler was the biggest threat, bullying and beating countries that stood in his way. Hitler sent German troops into the Rhineland in 1936, marched troops into Austria in 1938, and frightened Western nations into allowing him to take control of German-speaking sections of Czechoslovakia. His demands on Poland led to the outbreak of war in 1939, and by 1940 he was overrunning Denmark, Norway, Holland, Belgium, and France. A little more than a week before the opening of *Sergeant York* in 1941, Hitler sent his German divisions into the Soviet Union for yet another shocking invasion. In the meantime the Japanese were making trouble in the Pacific. They had marched into China, were threatening to move into Indo-China, and had signed a three-power pact with fascist Germany and Italy promising that if any one of the three nations became involved in a war, all would fight together.

Against this backdrop, *Sergeant York* seemed to be good inspiration for a country considering involvement in a war it did not want. The film's story provided justification for Americans who sought a rationale to move away from the isolationist and noninterventionist sentiments that had been fashionable in the United States for two decades. The movie portrays the experiences of a real-life Tennessee farmer of strong religious principles who tried to get an exemption from military service as a conscientious objector when World War I broke out. Army officers persuaded York that fighting for his country and for freedom is a noble and moral thing to do, and once York agreed that it is permissible to kill for a good cause, he proved to be an extraordinary soldier. In the battle of Meuse-Argonne York killed twenty-five German machine gunners and brought 132 enemy prisoners to American lines. He became a national hero but walked away from many opportunities for fame and fortune to return to a simple life in the Tennessee mountain country. His story served as a powerful metaphor in 1941 for a nation that did not wish to engage in another foreign war but needed to convince itself that freedom was endangered and intervention necessary.[1]

Sergeant York contributed to the extraordinary transformation in public attitudes that took place between the outbreak of war in Europe in 1939 and American commitment to the fighting in December 1941. As late as the summer of 1941, when *Sergeant York* made its appearance in theaters across the country, many Americans were reluctant to see the United States become involved in a second world war (although for reasons different from Alvin York's Bible-based reservations against killing). The nation's experiences with World War I had left many Americans disillusioned. They thought that "The Great War" had not really been fought for the ideals that their leaders announced in wartime speeches and propaganda. Americans were disturbed when they learned about secret wartime agreements among the allies aimed at stripping Germany of its geographical and industrial resources. These revelations made it appear that the United States had assisted imperialist European nations in strengthening their own positions by weakening Germany. The hard bargaining of the victorious allies in the 1919 peace conference made President Woodrow Wilson's visionary statements about "Peace without Victory" appear to be a lie. Isolationist sentiment gained additional strength through the reports of a congressional investigation in the mid-1930s headed by Gerald P. Nye, a Republican senator from North Dakota. The committee's findings suggested that economic ties with the allies pulled the United States into World War I. Congressional investigators noted that U.S. manufacturers sold arms to the allies, and American bankers supplied them with loans. Evidence revealed by the committee suggested that by 1917 the United States could not allow Britain and France to lose the war; America had already invested too heavily in their future. The Nye committee's activities made a number of Americans angry about their country's commitments and apparent lack of neutrality in the previous world conflict. A 1937 Gallup poll reflected the growing discontent: it showed that two-thirds of the Americans interviewed believed that the United States had made a mistake by entering World War I.

By July 1941, however, the time of *Sergeant York*'s premiere, many Americans were reexamining these isolationist ideas. The fast pace of disturbing events in Europe and Asia made them wonder whether the

U.S. could keep a safe distance from international problems. Fascist and
Japanese aggression had increased at an alarming pace, and new assaults against various nations of the world seemed likely to occur soon.
Many believed that the United States could not afford to let much of
the globe fall to tyranny. They worried, too, that their own country
could someday fall victim. Taking action with these concerns in mind,
a number of prominent Americans organized the Committee to Defend
America by Aiding the Allies. Against this background of changing
sentiment, Hollywood's inspiring story of an American soldier who
overcame his doubts about participating in a world war promised to
add important weight to the internationalists' cause.

Although a motion picture about a World War I hero would have
obvious relevance to current events, the producers of *Sergeant York* were
at first reluctant to identify their film as a clear contribution to the debates about American intervention in the European war. They recognized that the symbolism in York's story carried messages relevant to
foreign policy issues of the day, and they hoped that the movie's timeliness would drive up sales, yet they also understood that partisan storytelling could backfire. The nation had long been badly divided on the
question of what to do about international aggression, and it appeared
that identification with a particular party in the dispute could alienate
many potential ticket purchasers. The producers were fearful that political controversy associated with the movie could have negative repercussions at the box office. Sensitive to the need to maximize profits,
they guarded their remarks about the movie very carefully, especially
while the movie was in production. *Sergeant York*'s Hollywood managers related their movie to politics only to the degree that the association could help sales. In the quickly changing political climate of 1940–
41, this meant altering their comments about the movie as the public
mood changed.

Interestingly, *Sergeant York*'s status as a political hot potato affected
the moviemakers' treatment of Alvin York's personal story. Because the
producers worried about alienating public sentiment in a period when
attitudes about the international crisis seemed particularly volatile and
unpredictable, they made a great effort to argue that the movie is an
objective, nonpartisan view of the war hero's life. The film's portrayal
is based in the facts, they insisted, representing a carefully researched
effort to tell the story of a famous American without hidden political
agendas. To cushion themselves against charges of bias, the producers
emphasized that they had given much attention to historical detail in

making the movie. They claimed to have carefully authenticated facts about Alvin York's life. The movie simply tells the truth about York, they boasted, and any political messages read from that realistic depiction are in the minds of the viewers, not the filmmakers.

This effort to evade controversy by focusing on the historical qualities of the story helped to keep the fabrications about Alvin York's career under a considerable degree of control. In their attempts to defend their production against claims of fictionalizing for political purposes, the producers worked hard to document the biographical treatment presented in their movie. They were also eager to please Alvin York, because they worried that they could lose audience support if the war hero expressed displeasure about Hollywood's rendition of his life. The attention to York's feelings created occasional tension for the production planners, but it did help to keep the dramatic flourishes from spinning out of control.[2] The film that emerged from this sensitive relationship between the moviemakers and their subject contains some exaggerations for dramatic effect, fictitious situations, and character distortions, but the fabrications are relatively mild in comparison to those seen in many later Hollywood productions that portray real-life personalities and events.

Alvin York's influence over the production developed in part from Hollywood's lack of experience producing films about living individuals. During the previous decade the industry had released a number of successful biographical dramas, but these movies usually dealt with famous persons from European history (English and French royalty, as well as heroic figures such as Louis Pasteur and Emile Zola). There had been little attempt to deal with the complicated legal questions associated with portraying contemporary personalities. In this poorly charted legal environment the producers of *Sergeant York* moved cautiously, and as a result, they gave their film's living subject far more authority over the screen's depiction of history than later producers of biographical movies would allow. Indeed, by the late twentieth century most moviemakers became convinced that living individuals who were the subject of a movie's story should not have any direct influence over the script. A buyout of rights (documented in a contract) usually gave producers complete freedom to interpret their stories without interference. In the years before World War II, however, such contractual arrangements were still in the nascent stages of development. Out of this ambiguity about the rules of the relationship, Alvin York was able to obtain a relatively powerful voice in the movie's design.

York also maintained leverage because of his status as a national hero and his reputation as an individualist who could not be "bought." The makers of *Sergeant York* knew that if they did not make the movie on Alvin York's terms, they could face a very troublesome antagonist.

The producers recalled that for many years, Alvin York had resisted efforts to make a movie about his life. They remembered that back in 1919, when York first appeared in the press as a national hero, he turned down lucrative movie offers. At the time York had returned from the war as a celebrity. After newspapers reported on his exploits against the Germans, American society greeted his return to the United States with parades and gala dinners. Then he received numerous business offers aimed at parlaying his new fame into commercial success. In addition to being offered book and movie contracts, York received invitations from a variety of manufacturers to endorse their products for handsome fees. One gun manufacturer promised $2,000 just for firing a single shot in front of a photographer. York turned down these bids. "Uncle Sam's uniform, it ain't for sale," he said when rejecting commercialism.

As he expressed his sentiments in 1919, York believed that he would compromise the high ideals he fought for in the war if he responded to the monetary overtures. Instead of basking in the glory of big city celebrations and milking public enthusiasm for thousands of dollars, York chose to return to a relatively quiet life in the land he loved, the mountain country of Tennessee. York did accept the gift of a Tennessee farm from the Nashville Rotary club and later used his name to raise money for the York Agricultural Institute and other educational and community projects in his region, but otherwise he rejected the opportunities to use his fame for the advancement of personal wealth.

York's independence from these appeals developed in large part out of his religious convictions. During the first months of American involvement in World War I York did not wish to participate in the fighting because of his fundamentalist commitment to the Bible's injunction against killing human beings. When the United States entered World War I, York went through a long period of soul-searching, agonizing over questions of faith and morality. He prayed a great deal. Eventually he convinced himself that service as a soldier was the right thing to do. His search for divine guidance may have looked like the simplistic behavior of an ignorant mountain man to some observers, but to York it was the necessary journey of a pious individual. Given this attitude, it was not difficult for York to dismiss appeals from businesspeople who wanted to exploit his success for profit after the war. York believed that the offers to endorse products and sell movie rights constituted a form of disrespect for the American flag. Just as he did not want to fight in the army without conviction that his action was proper, he was not going to exploit a uniform that, in his words, was not "for sale."

York's change of mind about working with a movie company developed in connection with his changing political sentiments. During the interwar period York, like many other Americans, expressed disillusionment over U.S. involvement in World War I. In the mid-1930s, for example, he told a visitor that he could not "see that we did any good" by fighting, and he expressed unhappiness over Wilson's use of the slogan "a war to end all wars." In the future, said York, the United States should let "those fellows fight their own battles and we'll fight ours when the time comes."[3] In the late 1930s, however, he began to reconsider his views. The growing threat of fascist aggression in Europe troubled York. Eventually he voiced support for military preparedness on the part of the United States and called for U.S. assistance to the British. It was during this time of disturbing foreign developments and York's reconsideration of America's role in international disputes that Hollywood producer Jesse L. Lasky approached York with an idea for a movie.

Years before, Lasky had been one of the most successful and famous movie producers in the country. He was the brother-in-law of Samuel Goldwyn and also had worked closely with other early moguls from Hollywood, such as Adolph Zukor and Cecil B. DeMille. Lasky maintained excellent connections with the major stars and directors and worked on a number of popular motion pictures. Back in 1919 Lasky had been one of the individuals who tried unsuccessfully to induce York to sign a movie contract. He tried again in the early 1930s, and in 1939 Lasky was ready for yet another effort. He still thought that the York story contained wonderful elements for movie drama, and he could see that world events were making the history of York's conversion to combat relevant to Americans who were pondering possible responses to the world's totalitarian aggressors. Lasky also needed to produce a successful motion picture, for he was badly stretched financially. In the early 1930s he had lost his entire personal fortune, including his home. Eventually he cleared his debts, but he remained short on cash. Alvin York represented an opportunity for economic redemption—if he would cooperate.[4]

Lasky approached York first with a letter but was unable to get a reaction. Then he tried another appeal, one designed to touch York's patriotic and political sentiments. The producer sent a telegram requesting a conference so that the two could discuss the making of "a historical document of vital importance to the country in these troubled times."[5] At last York agreed to a meeting. He talked with Lasky not only because of his interest in the international situation but because of his own financial needs back in Tennessee. York had been busy planning for the opening of an international Bible school in his state, but he lacked sufficient money to move the project forward. A movie contract promised a quick source of funds. Consequently, in March 1940 York met with Lasky in a Crossville, Tennessee, hotel to begin discussions.

After much negotiating and traveling back and forth, Lasky at last got his contract. York had held out for a much bigger cut than Lasky originally offered and was rewarded for his toughness.[6] Lasky then rushed to California to connect the project to a sponsor. Eventually he secured an agreement with Warner Brothers. The studio had a reputation for producing socially conscious films, and in the last few years before American intervention in World War II, it began to release some strongly anti-Nazi films, such as *Confessions of a Nazi Spy* (1939).

Lasky knew that international developments could fan public interest in his movie project, but he had to be careful about associating the film with politics. In early 1940 he could not be certain that the film would make a timely contribution to foreign policy debates in the United States at the time of its release the following year. Isolationist sentiment was still strong in early 1940, and many Hollywood executives worried about dragging their productions into political controversy. Presentation of a war picture that represented poorly disguised interventionist propaganda could attract negative reactions and damage audience appeal.[7] Lasky was in no position to weather such a storm; he had stretched his already precarious finances in the effort to sign a contract with York and to find a studio to sponsor the movie. His caution was evident in the way he publicized the project with journalists who covered the news of his agreement with York. Lasky underplayed the relevance of the story to political and diplomatic affairs. He emphasized that "this is in no sense a war picture," and he made a number of vague statements about making "a document for fundamental Americanism" and telling "a story that Americans need to be told today." Both Lasky and York emphasized that the movie would have a biographical focus (stressing York's personal growth and his work to bring education and modernization to the mountain people) rather than focusing exclusively on York's exploits in the Battle of Meuse-Argonne.[8]

Lasky was aware not only of the divided public sentiments regarding the European war but also of the antiwar messages projected in many Hollywood movies of the previous fifteen years. For example, *The Big Parade* (1925) conveys disillusionment with the wasteful and tragic loss of lives in the conflict of 1914–18. Particularly damning of war was *All Quiet on the Western Front* (1930), based on a popular novel that had been released in 1928. It shows young men enthusiastic over the prospect of glorious combat at the beginning of World War I and then portrays the ugliness of life in the trenches and senseless human slaughter on the front. By 1940, however, Lasky could also see evidence of a more interventionist outlook emanating in some Hollywood movies. One of the first to establish a bold antifascist position was *Blockade* (1938), which relates a story about an encircled coastal community in Spain being squeezed by Franco's fascists on the land and German and Italian submarines at sea. Another bold antifascist message appeared in *Confession of a Nazi Spy* (1939), which builds its story around the real-life indictment of spies working in the United States. These movies excited much public protest, however, from Americans who demanded neutrality (and many Catholics disliked the anti-Franco posture of *Blockade*).[9] Sensitive about profits and hoping not to alienate ticket purchasers, Lasky used very cautious language as he discussed his new movie project with the press in 1940.

As he moved forward in the development of *Sergeant York*, Lasky managed to assemble an extraordinarily talented production team. His coproducer was Hal Wallis, a close associate of Jack L. Warner and a producer of numerous successful films including *Little Caesar* (1930), *Gold Diggers of 1933* (1933), and *Captain Blood* (1935). After much searching, Lasky and Wallis signed Howard Hawks for the director's role (they had to borrow the accomplished filmmaker from Samuel Goldwyn for a considerable sum of money). For writers, Lasky and Wallis secured Howard Koch, an idealistic individual who had helped to write Orson Welles's famous radio script of *War of the Worlds* and would later cowrite the screenplay for *Casablanca,* and John Huston, the multitalented boxer, horseman, journalist, artist, actor, director, and screenwriter. Abem Finkel and Harry Chandlee also contributed to the screenwriting.[10]

Once production planning got underway, the movie developers faced complications dealing with principal figures in Alvin York's life. The filmmakers were treading on unfamiliar territory as they worked with living figures who were going to be depicted in the movie. A number of questions troubled them: What would the repercussions be if some became angry about the film's portrayals? Could the movie's advertisers succeed in their efforts to promote the film as authentic history if some of the real-life figures turned uncooperative? Might some of the Tennesseans try to sue the studio? Would Alvin York himself become disenchanted if many of his Tennessee friends were unhappy about the script? Could resistance from York undermine the entire project? The producers could not answer these questions confidently, and as they attempted to work with the living subjects, they agreed to compromise some of their original plans for the script.

Lasky and Wallis tried to get releases from each key individual in the story to prevent lawsuits or criticisms that could undermine the movie's claims to validity, but this proved to be more difficult than they expected. The so-called hillbillies were strong negotiators; they troubled the moviemakers over interpretive details, as well as over monetary compensation. A number of the Tennesseans insisted that the depictions remain faithful to the truth as they understood it, and some of them claimed that they would refuse to sign a release unless they were satisfied. A few of York's relatives and friends in Tennessee managed to hold out for agreements that brought $1,500 apiece. York's stepfather would not come to terms, and plans for the script had to be reworked to remove his role. Another figure, George Edward Buxton, who had been York's battalion commander, insisted that the writers place a Captain Tillman in several scenes. Buxton would not sign a contract until Tillman got "due credit."[11]

Pastor Rosier Pile, the minister who had counseled York when he struggled with his religious convictions in 1917, also created difficulties by demanding assurance in writing that he "would not be made to do or say anything that would be against his beliefs and his dignity." Pile became upset when he read a version of the script and saw himself portrayed as uncertain about whether York should accept the draft and go off to war and kill. Pile thought this depiction implied that he did not have the courage of his religious convictions. The filmmakers decided to bend to Pile's demands, because they became worried that a court might agree with the pastor and view the movie's portrayal of him as "an open and shut case of defamation of character."[12]

Even when the producers wished to please the Tennesseans, they discovered that complications could arise. Interpreting history required making choices about whose story they were going to believe. Some of the infantrymen who had served with York in World War I were particularly difficult. They disagreed about who was responsible for the wartime achievements, and some questioned Alvin York's role in the fighting. They would not sign releases unless they received credit for assisting York in his exploits. They wanted recognition of their heroism as described in affidavits and in the *Congressional Record*.[13] One in particular complained that York took too much of the credit for shooting and capturing the Germans at Meuse-Argonne. He said that York did not do the job single-handedly; rather, a number of men in the group contributed to the success. This individual, identified as Corporal Cutting, thought that York "hogged all the credit unjustifiably." Abem Finkel, one of the writers on the project, reported that Cutting claimed to be the individual who brought the prisoners back and said "that York pulled a fast one on him by bringing in these prisoners while Cutting was asleep in a shell hole." Alvin York was unhappy about these claims. He said that he had always acknowledged the contributions of others and had challenged reports that wrongly credited him with a one-man victory. The writers sided with the war hero, agreeing that "York has taken great pains to correct this impression." As the producers worked through this web of interpretations and demands, they decided that it was wise to try not to risk offending York or his buddies with highly fictionalized accounts of their activities. Writing to producer Hal Wallis, Abem Finkel said the writers "thought of a half dozen ways of playing the stuff more effectively or even inventing new incidents but discarded all of them because we felt it was safest to stick as closely as possible to the facts." Finkel warned Wallis to be on guard against "bright ideas" (fictional excesses) from the various people working with the script.[14]

Satisfying Alvin York, of course, was especially important to the producers. York did not make many demands about the particulars of the story, but the producers recognized that he could sabotage the whole project if he became disenchanted. They listened carefully when York expressed concerns. The producers took note, for example, of York's complaints about the way that the writers wanted to treat his early experiences with alcohol. The script showed York inebriated in 1916; York insisted he had broken away from alcohol two years earlier. York also worried that the script's attention to his romantic activities before his courtship with the woman he married (Gracie Williams) could reflect badly on Gracie. He insisted that, except for a few indiscretions in his youth, Gracie was the only woman in his life. York also made it clear that he did not want Gracie to appear in the movie as one of Hollywood's sexy bombshells or as a cigar-smoking lady of the hill country (indeed, the filmmakers had considered casting a "Jane Russell type" in the role). Given York's chivalrous concern about his wife, the producers anticipated problems with a proposed scene in the movie showing Gracie giving York the "come on." In this fictional episode Gracie would scratch York's face after receiving a kiss, and York would boast to his mother that the scratch revealed Gracie's true love for him. In his note to Hal Wallis, Finkel said, "even if this were not the tallest kind of corn, York would reach for his rifle gun and come a 'shootin.'" Finkel did not want to deal with an angry York. "You must remember," he wrote, "that York knocked off 25 German gunners and he wasn't even sore at them. Can you imagine if he really got mad." Finkel reminded Wallis that Lasky's contract with York guaranteed that the portrayal would "redound to his credit." It would be very unfortunate, said Finkel, if York, his lawyer, or York's friend, the governor of Tennessee, became angry and crusaded against the movie. It is "smarter to have him for us then [sic] against us," said Finkel.[15]

In their efforts to focus on historical details and promote their movie as an authentic, nonpartisan examination of a war hero's experiences, the moviemakers conducted more research into the background of their story than was typical of Hollywood productions at the time. For example, the filmmakers made a considerable effort to re-create the Tennessee mountain environment and culture, as well as the particulars of York's life. For written material on York, they depended heavily on two books that had been published in the 1920s: Samuel K. Cowan's *Sergeant York and His People* (1922) and Thomas Skeyhill's *Sergeant York: His Own Life Story and War Diary* (1928), which was a collaborative work that Skeyhill helped York to write in autobiographical style. The writers, producers, and director also turned to the *Congressional Record* for information about York's exploits in the war. An on-site investigation in Tennessee helped to provide information that could add dimension to the storytelling. Shortly after Lasky got his contract, he sent a cameraman along with Julian Josephson and writer Harry Chandlee to York's little community of Pall Mall, Tennessee. The visitors interviewed local people, made notes about the geography and architecture of the region, and learned as much as they could about York, Rosier Pile, York's mother, and other principal figures in York's

Tennessee experiences. The cameraman took sixty pictures of the mountaineers and their houses to assist the set designers back in Hollywood.[16] The Californians were particularly enthusiastic about signing on a "technical adviser" who seemed to be a genuine example of backwoods Tennessee wisdom. He was Donoho Hall, a Cumberlands native who had been illiterate until age seventeen. Hall was "realistic enough to make a houn' dog go 'round smellin' for coon tracks," one of the Hollywood visitors boasted.[17] Meanwhile, back in California, researchers dug for details about York's experience in the army. They learned, for example, the exact date York entered the front lines, established the design of his regiment's flag, learned the correct bugle call for medal-awarding ceremonies, and gathered details on the procedure for awarding the French Croix de Guerre.[18]

In planning the design of the set the producers put the most money in re-creating the environment of Tennessee and designing a battlefield for the war scenes. The production crew built a forty-foot "Appalachian" mountain made of timber, cloth, plaster, rock, soil, and 121 live trees. They mounted the various materials on a large turntable and were able to swivel the landscape around for a variety of camera angles. For the battlefield, they turned to an eighty-acre site forty miles from Hollywood. With 300 workers laboring for three weeks, they transformed beautiful California fields into a war-blasted wasteland. The effort required five tons of dynamite, 400 denuded tree trunks and stumps, and 5,200 gallons of paint, which were used to spray the trunks and stumps black.[19]

In discussing the design of the script the writers and producers revealed their concerns about the political implications of York's story. They were sensitive to the debates taking place at the time regarding the appropriate role for the United States in the European and Asian crisis, worrying that some viewers might consider *Sergeant York* to be a "war picture." That kind of identification could alienate isolationists in the audience and possibly excite the anger of some members of Congress. Josephson and Chandlee told Lasky the movie "should not be interpretable as either propaganda for or against war." They were particularly concerned that the movie's treatment of York's exploits at Meuse-Argonne might "have the flavor of war story material" (seeming to be pro-war). To get around the problem, the writers recommended handling the army episodes from York's point of view. The military aspects of the film thus would seem to be an aspect of York's personal story rather than a partisan commentary supporting U.S. intervention in the war.[20]

Josephson and Chandlee also worried that the depiction of York's religious activities could make him look like a simple-minded "religious fanatic" and thereby "lose heavily in audience understanding and sympathy." To avoid this problem, the writers tried to ascribe a number of motives to York's actions, explanations that went beyond the issue of religious convictions. The need for showing multiple causes of behavior seemed to be especially important when dealing with York's belief that divine intervention would protect him from being killed in France. If York's bravery in destroying and disarming gangs of German soldiers could be attributed to blind religious faith, his heroism would seem diminished, thought Josephson and Chandlee. In this and other instances the writers tried to apply more mundane explanations for York's behavior while retaining some understanding of his spiritual nature.[21]

The writers also wondered whether the saga of a southerner from the mountain country would appeal to the millions of moviegoers who lived in America's cities. As a "foil to increase human interest," they decided to add a "Brooklynite or East Sider who [had] never been out of the city." This would provide an opportunity for the two representative figures to describe their home environments to each other. York could promise to take the city fellow coon hunting after the war, and the fictitious character could promise to take the Tennessean for a ride on the New York subway. The filmmakers thus could explain York's real-life request for a ride on the New York subway when he was honored as a war hero.[22]

The *Sergeant York* that moviegoers saw in the theaters, for all its fictional excesses, came reasonably close (for a popular motion picture) to a realistic rendition of the man and the people around him. The pressures brought on the moviemakers by principals in the story, as well as the moviemakers' own concerns about presenting a relatively true picture of a living figure, helped to bring considerable attention to detail. Gary Cooper (thirty-nine years old at the time of the filming) and actress Joan Leslie (age fifteen), who played Gracie, nicely reflected a significant age gap (in the real case York was twenty-eight, and his wife to be, fifteen). Actress Margaret Wycherly, with her sad, drawn face and simple clothes, looked very much like the real Mama York. The movie's Tennessee scenes showed a number of real aspects of York's life: York drinking at a bar perfectly placed on the Kentucky-Tennessee border so that locals could drink in a neighboring state without violating their own state laws; York dissipating his energies on drinking, fighting, and shooting sprees; and York's lack of knowledge about world affairs and the factors behind U.S. involvement in the war. Some information conveyed about York in the movie may have appeared to audiences to be colorful examples of movie fiction, but the presentation was based on fact. For example, the movie shows York killing Germans by using a trick he applied when shooting birds. Rather than aim at the lead bird, York shot the one to the back of the flock so that the others were less likely to become aware of the danger. York applied this technique very effectively against the Germans at Meuse-Argonne.[23]

In a variety of small ways the writers also invented scenes from York's life. Some of this fictionalizing related to the familiar magic making of Hollywood productions. For instance, the writers dramatized York's religious conversion by showing him riding off to kill a man who cheated him. Then a lightning bolt knocks York to the ground and destroys his rifle. The scene communicates York's desire to be "saved" from his uncivilized ways, showing a religious basis for his rejection of violence. Not surprisingly, Alvin York maintained that his religious conversion involved more serious thought and conviction than the movie suggests, and he claimed that he had changed from a drinking, brawling, card-playing man to a churchgoing citizen especially to satisfy Miss Gracie. Nonetheless, York posed no serious objections to the movie's attempt to associate his personal transformation to a divinely inspired lightning bolt from the heavens. "A bolt of lightning was the nearest to such a thing that Hollywood could think up," he said.[24] The movie also shows York receiving free acreage, a new house, and an abundance of farm animals for his heroism (he actually received undeveloped acres with a mortgage attached; the debt gave him considerable trouble in later years).

A number of the film's efforts at fictionalization were identified specifically by Harry Chandlee in a letter that he wrote to Jesse L. Lasky more than a year after release of the movie. Apparently angry because he was not receiving proper credit for his contributions to the story, Chandlee pointed out that he was the one responsible for imagining many of the dramatically appealing elements in the story. Chandlee noted that York never participated in a turkey shoot specifically to win money to buy a farm, and there had been no double-crossing in the sale of a farm by a man named Nate Watson. Furthermore, York did not shock military officers with constant bull's-eyes on the military rifle range, and the scene in which York discusses lessons from the Bible with his officers and considers balancing the Bible's messages with lessons from an American history book was largely Chandlee's inven-tion.[25] Still, none of these fictional flourishes jeopardized the overall presentation of York's life, and the final product did a relatively effec-tive job of portraying the main biographical points.

The movie traces the steps in York's life pretty much as they actu-ally happened. As the movie shows, Alvin York seemed to be a fun-loving but directionless young man through his early years. Until the age of twenty-seven York drank heavily, indulged in long hours of card playing, got into drunken brawls, and sometimes, while inebriated, participated in shooting sprees. Then, as the movie shows, he began to sense that he was not making much of his life, and he took more seriously his mother's constant appeals to find salvation in the church. York's affection for young Gracie Williams also altered his behavior; Gracie would not agree to marry him if he did not change his ways. After finding inspiration at the prayer meeting of a traveling evange-list, York acknowledged that he was a sinner and asked God for par-don and assistance. He soon joined a small fundamentalist sect. He gave up his roughhouse manner and accepted his church's exhortations against violence. The former mountain ruffian with a reputation as a sharpshooter turned to singing in the church choir and teaching Sun-day School.[26]

After the United States entered World War I, York received notice to report for military training. Remembering the injunction against killing in the Ten Commandments, he was reluctant to serve in the armed forc-es. York spent several nights wandering in the mountains as he contem-plated his decision. His pastor, Rosier Pile, who was a trusted adviser, counseled him to appeal as a conscientious objector. York followed the pastor's advice, but the army turned down his appeal. On beginning army training, York demonstrated his skills with a rifle, but his doubts about killing remained. Both a company commander and a battalion commander recognized his dilemma and tried to convince him that some of the Bible's teachings could be interpreted as sanctions for war. See-ing that York acknowledged the validity of their arguments but that he was still deeply troubled about his decision, they allowed him to return to Tennessee for a period of ten days to think about his choices. They told York that he could have a noncombat assignment when he returned if he wanted it. During the furlough York spent a whole day and night on a mountain praying for guidance. York then experienced a second conversion. He believed that God granted him approval to fight and thought that he would return unharmed. (The film, of course, gives much dramatic flourish to York's conversion experiences. It does not accentuate the notion that God would protect York from harm, however, because the idea could have reduced the audience's sense of tension when watching the scenes of York in military action in France.) York then returned to the base, ready for military service and confident that he would have good fortune in Europe.[27]

York joined the "All-American" Division in Europe, which included soldiers from around the country. In the important battle of Meuse-Argonne he performed the feats that made him famous. Of course, the German soldiers were war-weary at the time; their country had been engaged in four painful and frustrating years of fighting by 1918, and their prospects looked gloomy in view of the growing American presence in the war (the movie reveals nothing about the low morale and pessimism of the German soldiers). Still, York's accomplishments were extraordinary. His group took heavy casualties. Half his patrol lay killed or wounded, and York lost his best friend in the shooting. In the face of heavy fire he managed to slip away from the spraying German bullets. He then killed a number of the enemy by shooting as their heads popped up (much as he had shot at turkeys back in Tennessee). York got behind nests of machine gunners on a hill and managed to wipe them out and force many to surrender. In all, he (along with the men who assisted him) captured 128 enlisted soldiers and four officers and put thirty-five machine guns out of order. Alvin York was behind enemy lines at the time of this success and had to get his prisoners back to American lines with help from his tattered group. Only seven able-bodied men were available to assist him.[28]

Stories about York's achievements soon appeared in newspapers and magazines, and York quickly emerged as a national hero. In New York he enjoyed a ticker-tape parade and received a room at the Waldorf Astoria. An appearance at the House of Representatives brought a standing ovation. The governor of Tennessee officiated at his wedding. Lucrative offers appeared, enticing him to promote products and allow movies to be made about his life, but York chose to return to the familiar scene of the Tennessee mountains.

Sergeant York renders this story rather authentically, framing its biography in a melodramatic tale that suggests the virtues of the common man. The emphasis on York's humble origins and sincere convictions resembles a message that appeared in a variety of motion pictures in the late 1930s and early 1940s, such as *Meet John Doe, Mr. Smith Goes to Washington, Mr. Deeds Goes to Town*, and *The Grapes of Wrath. Sergeant*

York presents its subject as a descendant of the hearty pioneers who, through common sense rather than formal learning, helped to create a vibrant agrarian society in America. The York portrayed in the film displays the old-fashioned decency of the mountain folk, particularly their individualism, interest in community, respect for hard work, and closeness to nature.[29]

These themes were appealing when the movie appeared in theaters in the summer of 1941, but by that time, the film's relationship to American foreign policy assumed new importance. In the year of the motion picture's premiere the war in Europe took an ominous turn. German armies had swept through the Netherlands, Belgium, Luxembourg, and Norway, and Americans were shocked to learn about the quick fall of France and the Luftwaffe's subsequent air bombardment of London. The Germans' sea and air blockade made the British heavily dependent on food, arms, and raw materials from the United States. In March 1941 President Roosevelt requested and received from Congress support for the Lend-Lease Act, which provided the British much-needed military aid. Another important development came just a few weeks before the film's premiere. Americans learned that the Germans had invaded the Soviet Union and that President Roosevelt had responded by promising the Russians significant U.S. aid. After these developments a growing number of Americans believed that the United States' direct involvement in the war was just a matter of time. *Sergeant York* carried an upbeat message in this tense period. It reminded Americans that they had done a good job when Europe came under threat in 1917 and suggested that, if necessary, they could return to the scene of trouble and accomplish the task a second time.

When Alvin York went to New York City to participate in the gala events celebrating the opening of the movie about his life, he readily commented on the film's political message for America's troubled times. York said he hoped that the film would contribute to "national unity in this hour of danger" when "millions of Americans like myself, must be facing the same question, the same uncertainties, which we faced and I believed resolved some twenty-four years ago."[30] In a speech to the Veterans of Foreign Wars at the time of the film's release, York noted that America fought the previous war to make the world safe for democracy, "and it did—for a while." Liberty, freedom, and democracy "are so very precious that you do not fight to win them once— and then stop," he said. York criticized the isolationists strongly, called for all-out aid to Britain, and said that if Americans stopped fighting for the right to be free, "then we owe the memory of George Washington an apology, for if we have stopped, then he wasted his time at Valley Forge."[31] President Franklin D. Roosevelt deeply appreciated York's remarks. The president also understood that the movie could arouse sympathy for his policies supporting national preparedness and aid for the Allies. FDR met with the war hero for ten minutes and was pleased to hear York say that the people of Tennessee stood behind his diplomacy.

The premiere in New York was a gala affair that nicely served the interventionists' cause. In attendance were the first lady, Eleanor Roosevelt, World War I commander of the American "doughboys," General John "Black Jack" Pershing, and the selective service director, General Lewis B. Hersey. The Astor Theatre featured a four-story caricature of the hero: 15,000 flashing red, white, and blue lights changed the image of York from a hunter with a squirrel gun to a soldier carrying a rifle.[32]

Sergeant York fared well with the commentators and the public. *Newsweek*'s reviewer said it "ranks with the best screen biographies turned out by Warners, or anyone else," and the *Catholic World*'s critic called it "a record of American life which is worth many pages of written history."[33] *Commonweal*'s reviewer claimed that the movie "shines like a bright light and stands with 'Citizen Kane' as one of the year's best movies."[34] While praising *Sergeant York*'s creators for their artistry, commentators also complemented the filmmakers for handling a highly controversial subject with subtlety. "If we are to have patriotic movies . . . and the times indicate that we are in for many of them," said *Commonweal*'s reviewer, "let them be like *Sergeant York*—inspiring, sincere, unpretentious, and without maudlinism."[35] *Time* also found a political message evident but noted that it was subdued and responsible. *Sergeant York* did not glorify war, said the reviewer, and it did not try to "horn in on the United States and World War II." At the same time, by showing that Alvin York found something worth fighting for during World War I, "it becomes Hollywood's first solid contribution to the national defense."[36] Moviegoers responded to such positive reviews by rushing to the theaters, and they were pleased with the entertainment they saw. Tickets sold briskly, and *Sergeant York* became one of Warner Brothers' biggest hits of the early 1940s.

The isolationists were not pleased to see that a Hollywood film could add fuel to the national debate about international commitments. They were growing increasingly suspicious of the moviemaker's motives. A number of them suggested that Hollywood producers were interventionist partisans, and some pointed the blame especially at the Jewish producers and directors. Senator Gerald P. Nye, the isolationist-minded politician who had led the congressional investigations into U.S. involvement in World War I, complained that "the movies were created to be an instrument of entertainment." Nye suggested that films "have been operating as war propaganda machines almost as if directed from a single bureau."[37] He asked, "Are you ready to send your boys to bleed and die in Europe to make the world safe for this industry and its financial backers?"[38] In the late summer of 1941 a subcommittee of the Senate Interstate Commerce Committee began to investigate claims that some movies served as highly partisan prowar and anti-Nazi publicity. The subcommittee examined films such as *Sergeant York* and Charlie Chaplin's *Great Dictator* and lashed out at the Hollywood "monopoly," which was supposedly controlled by foreign-born producers (meaning Jews).

The movie industry hired the recently defeated presidential candidate Wendell Willkie for the job of defending its interests, and Willkie performed magnificently. He brought Hollywood leaders to testify openly that they opposed the Hitler regime. Industry spokespersons said that their movies were not instruments of propaganda; rather, they told the painful truth about the horrors of Nazi leadership. As for *Sergeant York,* studio mogul Harry Warner claimed it to be "a factual portrait of the life of one of the great heroes of the last war." Warner concluded, "If that is propaganda, we plead guilty."[39]

Warner stressed the word *accurate* many times in his testimony before the Senate subcommittee. He claimed that his studio's only sin was "accurately recording on the screen the world as it is or as it has been." Warner Brothers was interested in the "facts" and making pictures that were "true to life." The studio was "attempting to record history in the making," because movie patrons wanted to see "accurate stories of the world in which they lived." Recalling the long-term efforts of Jesse Lasky to get York's approval to make the movie and Warner Brothers' efforts to let York watch over the production and obtain his approval of the script, Warner told the senators, "I cannot conceive how anyone can claim that the picture Sergeant York is not accurate."[40]

Wendell Willkie cleverly associated the studios' freedom to make movies without interference with freedom from press censorship. His efforts to discredit Hollywood's attackers were assisted by Senator Nye himself, who quickly lost ground when quotations from his emotional diatribes appeared in the press. Nye's speeches revealed that he was ill-informed about the movies and tolerant of anti-Semitic and pro-Hitler ideas. Congressional hearings adjourned in late September 1941, and they closed completely after the bombing of Pearl Harbor in early December. Once the United States joined the war, it was no longer fashionable to criticize Hollywood for making interventionist films.

Sergeant York served as a powerful metaphor, showing how one young man's experience could represent a model for a nation struggling to decide what it should do about a serious international problem. Yet it did not make its case through transparent interventionist propaganda. Created during 1940, a period when the United States was still deeply divided about the issue of sending its soldiers abroad to fight, the filmmakers moved cautiously in developing their theme. They tried to anticipate partisan criticism and avoid giving their motion picture the appearance of a controversial prowar document. When promoting the movie with the press, they stressed the point, claiming that *Sergeant York* offered a balanced perspective that was not "political." It was, they said, an "accurate" portrayal of one American's experiences. Consequently, in advertising the movie the filmmakers concentrated on the historical material. They promoted their story as a drama that many could enjoy simply as interesting history. At the same time, they recognized fully that other viewers would see *Sergeant York* as a sanction for intervention in the world war. The filmmakers tried to please both camps, and consequently, their movie reflects a fair degree of integrity in relating the experiences of Alvin York.

Sergeant York also treats the historical evidence fairly responsibly, because its creators feared antagonizing the famous hero of World War I. Jesse Lasky had worked a small miracle getting York to authorize the movie. The Tennessean had resisted Hollywood's offers for years, and Lasky had to promise York more authority over the script than most filmmakers have allowed when designing a story about a living person. As a result, York was able to prevent attempts to sensationalize the characterizations of himself, his wife, and his preacher. His influence over the film's treatment of history ensured greater respect for the record than would be evident in many later biographical movies from Hollywood, productions that did not give the individuals being portrayed as much authority over the presentation of their stories.

4

Missing

"AN ASSAULT ON THE INTEGRITY OF THE U.S. GOVERNMENT, THE FOREIGN SERVICE AND THE MILITARY"

In a scene from *Missing*, Beth (Sissy Spacek) and Ed (Jack Lemmon) search for Charles in a stadium filled with political prisoners. Courtesy of the Museum of Modern Art/Film Stills Archive.

When the Hollywood film *Missing* had a special opening-night performance in Washington, D.C., in 1982 for members of Congress and other dignitaries, Ed Horman attended the event and felt tremendous emotional satisfaction after years of intense frustration. The movie tells the story of his search for his missing son, Charles, in the frightening days of Chile's right-wing military coup of 1973. Ed Horman's investigations led him to believe that the U.S. State Department had not been forthcoming in what it knew about Charles's experiences, and Ed Horman suspected that U.S. representatives in Chile were implicated in Charles's disappearance. After Ed Horman learned that his son was executed and he recovered his son's body, he sued U.S. officials associated with the case. These legal efforts were unsuccessful. Horman's attorneys pointed to their inability to obtain critically important CIA documents as a principal problem in prosecuting the case. In view of the absence of this vital information, Ed Horman withdrew his suit in 1981. His family suffered a terrible personal tragedy, and they failed to win satisfaction in the courts, but the movie, *Missing*, turned out to be a fulfilling consolation prize. The motion picture's gripping message about conspiracy and injustice gave Mr. Horman and his wife, Elizabeth, solace. *Missing* provided a forum to tell the Hormans' story to millions. It could embarrass officials who evidently did wrong, and it might make an impact on the way government officials practiced U.S. foreign policy in the future.[1]

On the other hand, *Missing* rubbed salt on an old wound for Nathaniel Davis, the United States' ambassador to Chile at the time of the 1973 coup. Davis had been troubled by the Horman case for years. When news about Charles Horman's disappearance turned up in major newspapers in the weeks and months after the Chilean coup, discussion drew attention to Davis's role as ambassador, and later, when an attorney named Thomas Hauser published a book about Horman's death, Davis and some of his associates in Chile were implicated in the tragedy. Now Davis was being portrayed in the Hollywood motion picture as an insensitive ambassador who demonstrated more interest in caring for United States business interests in Chile than in protecting United States citizens who were living in the country.[2] "The thrust of the movie essentially is that we were complicit in telling the Chileans to murder Charles Horman," said Davis. He believed *Missing* suggests that he and his associates were involved "in conspiracy to murder an innocent young citizen of our own country." Davis considered the proposition absurd. Since 1947 he had been proud of his career as a foreign service officer. Now it seemed that all he had accomplished was being eclipsed by *Missing*'s critical message. The movie could make a much bigger impact on his reputation than the critical newspaper articles about him or Hauser's book, and the film could cut much deeper emotional scars. Seeking redress of his grievances, Davis, like Ed Horman, turned to the courts. He searched out two other former U.S. officials who had received negative characterizations in the movie and got them to join him in a $150 million lawsuit against the movie studio, the filmmakers, and Thomas Hauser, the author of the book on which *Missing* was based. Davis did not include the Hormans in the suit. "Whatever grief they've given me, they've suffered more," he explained.[3]

The issue did not go all the way to the courtroom, but the questions raised by Davis's challenge deserve consideration. Who was right? Does *Missing* relate the evidence in the Horman case fairly and accurately? Does it tell the truth about the United States' role in Chile's affairs? Were Americans partly responsible for the military coup in Chile, as the film suggests? Did U.S. government officials in Chile, including Ambassador Davis, have foreknowledge of Charles Horman's execution and possibly order it?

These questions concern the specific events in Chile in 1973, and they do not, in themselves, convey the larger significance of *Missing*'s message to its audiences. The director wanted his story to illustrate the kind of surreptitious U.S. intervention in foreign affairs that occurred in a variety of developing countries during the cold war years. Using this historical test case for instruction, he hoped to alert audiences to the broader problem of U.S. covert operations around the world and the tragic consequences they sometimes created. *Missing*, by suggestion, draws attention to the record of American attempts to overthrow foreign governments in the 1950s, 1960s, and 1970s. It gave a useful reminder to Americans in the 1980s of the ethical questions stimulated by these practices. The movie delivered a worthwhile message for the age, for Ronald Reagan's administration sanctioned a variety of covert and morally questionable activities in El Salvador, Nicaragua, and other countries in the years following *Missing*'s release. It is important, then, to ask the following questions: Did the filmmaker's messages rest on a sophisticated reading of the specific historical case in Chile? Did the director draw lessons for the present on the basis of a valid and fair reading of the past? This is the broad issue concerning the uses of history that troubled some of *Missing*'s critics.

To address both the specific questions about Charles Horman's experiences in Chile and the larger questions about implications for U.S. foreign policy, it is helpful to trace the manner in which this film project took shape. Its production history reveals how filmmakers obtained evidence, fashioned it into a screenplay, and attempted to use information to suggest an argument for Americans in the 1980s.

The genesis of *Missing* came when Ed Horman was seeking ways to channel his anger over his son's tragedy in a constructive way. He was contemplating a suit against a number of people. During this time he encountered a Wall Street attorney, Thomas Hauser, who knew a friend of Charles Horman's wife, Joyce. The lawyer had assisted other aggrieved parents in suits against government officials, including Arthur and Doris Krause, who lost a daughter in the shootings at Kent State University in 1970. Hauser told Ed Horman that such suits consumed many years, were very difficult to win, and often dominated the lives of the people who engaged in them. A more fruitful approach, Hauser thought, would be to help in the preparation of a book that Hauser could write about Charles Horman's tragedy. Ed Horman rejected this offer at first, but after making little progress in three and a half years of effort with the courts, the Congress, and the news media, Horman agreed to the attorney's proposal.[4] Thomas Hauser then took a leave of absence from his law practice to research and write *The Execution of Charles Horman* (published in 1978). The experience led him away from his career in law. He became a full-time author, and by 1992 he had written fifteen books on a wide variety of subjects.

Hauser's book describes both the historical events in Chile and Charles Horman's particular experience there. The publication assembles evidence that seems to link U.S. officials to Horman's problems. Hauser constructed his argument from public records, historical texts, and documents obtained from the Department of State through the Freedom of Information Act. He also developed his thesis from interviews with various people who met Charles Horman in Chile, as well as from discussions with Horman's wife, parents, and friends.

During this time a husband-and-wife team of Hollywood producers had been working on plans for a movie about the Horman case. After seeing stories about Horman's death in the newspapers, Eddie and Mildred Lewis (the producers of numerous films, including *Spartacus*) prepared drafts for a screenplay. When they learned that Hauser was completing a detailed investigation of the subject, they bought the rights to his book. The Lewises also met Ed and Elizabeth Horman to learn more about their perspective and to win their confidence. They needed to obtain a signed statement from the Hormans allowing them complete liberty to tell the story as they wished. Without such an agreement in hand, their project was not likely to be supported by a Hollywood studio. Eventually they secured an agreement with the Hormans, obtained a contract with MCA/Universal Studios, and hired Donald E. Stewart to write the script along with a director, Constantin Costa-Gavras.[5] Both Costa-Gavras's and Stewart's names appeared on the screen as the writers.

For the critical role of director, the Lewises chose someone with an impressive reputation for making movies about government oppression and the horrors of state-sponsored terrorism. Constantin Costa-Gavras, a Greek-born filmmaker, was no stranger to controversial films. Several of his earlier movies had delivered stinging criticisms of injustice. *Z* (1969) examines the assassination of Gregorios Lambrakis, a liberal member of Greece's parliament; *The Confession* (1970) looks at political trials in Czechoslovakia; and *State of Siege* (1973) suggests that Daniel Mitrione, a representative of the United States Agency for International Development in Uruguay, was really an undercover specialist in police state intimidation and torture. Costa-Gavras had a solid reputation for creating fast-paced movies with a leftist perspective that expose the dark, frightening faces of political repression.

The director was born into a middle-class Greek family. His father, who held a boring post in the government bureaucracy, became a Greek resistance fighter. His mother, an intensely religious woman, steeped him in the teachings of Greek Orthodox Catholicism. At the age of eighteen Costa-Gavras left his homeland and took up residence in Paris. He gained entry to the Sorbonne, obtained a degree in literature, and then studied filmmaking at the Institut des Hautes Etudes Cinématographiques. Michele Ray then came into his life, a beautiful journalist who had worked as a fashion model with the House of Chanel. Ray had attracted considerable attention in the international press when she was captured by the Viet Cong in 1967 and later sent out dispatches describing the Vietnamese guerrillas in sympathetic terms. Costa-Gavras and Ray shared a deep distrust of the United States' role in international affairs, pointing to the country's overt activities in Vietnam and to its covert activities in Uruguay. By the 1970s Constantin Costa-Gavras had established an international reputation for making movies with political messages. As he explained after releasing Z, "I always meant the film as a political act."[6]

Eddie and Mildred Lewis contacted Costa-Gavras at a time when the director had been searching for a screen story that could dramatize the horrible examples of political repression that had scarred Latin American society in the late 1970s. Costa-Gavras had his eyes on the Argentine case in particular. The army takeover in that South American country had led to a broad assault against leftist groups. Thousands of young idealists were arrested; many were tortured and murdered. Mothers of these "disappeared" victims marched in the streets of Buenos Aires in protest. The Argentine army's violations of human rights had received worldwide attention, and this story seemed to offer rich material for a movie script. But Costa-Gavras could not easily move from the general to the specific. He knew about the way in which thousands had suffered, but to create an interesting docudrama he needed to obtain a great deal of evidence about one person's experiences. The details in Thomas Hauser's book satisfied this need. Costa-Gavras could switch from the Argentine story to the Chilean one and achieve the same goal. The case of Charles Horman would illustrate the horrors of political repression that were troubling many Latin American countries. Moreover, the Horman story had the attraction of dealing with an American victim. It could help moviegoers in the United States to identify with the victim.[7]

Costa-Gavras was also familiar with the recent history of Chile. He had met Chileans in Europe, individuals who had fled the repressive regime of General Augusto Pinochet in the 1970s, and he learned about the tragic disappearances of friends, neighbors, and children. The director had also met Salvador Allende, the socialist president of Chile who died during the 1973 military coup. Costa-Gavras considered Allende to have been "a nice, sweet man," a "provincial doctor" who wanted to feed hungry children and bring significant change to his country. The director believed that Allende had good intentions, but the Chilean president's task had become more difficult when he "was pushed by the extreme left-wing movement."[8]

As Costa-Gavras went to work on turning the Charles Horman story into a movie, he discovered that his arrangement with the Lewises provided the basis for a project more ambitious than his previous films. *Missing* was his first Hollywood production, and it came with an attractive budget. MCA/Universal's financing enabled Costa-Gavras to hire famous actors and spend a greater amount of money on cinematography than in his earlier work. MCA/Universal also provided the marketing clout necessary to promote the movie actively in the United States and abroad. Costa-Gavras's associations with Hollywood led to an adjustment in his storytelling style, as well. Hollywood wanted less emphasis on politics and more concentration on the personalities and emotional experiences of the leading characters.

The drama that Costa-Gavras fashioned from the book on Charles Horman created an image of a fascistic regime viciously imposing its will on vulnerable citizens. *Missing* shows Charles Horman and his wife caught up in a violent Latin American coup. Gunshots ring out in the streets, sirens blare, and uniformed soldiers aggressively shout out orders. Bodies litter the pavements. "Don't worry, they can't hurt us. We're Americans," Charles tells his wife, Beth (her real name was Joyce). It is a naive statement, of course, and uniformed soldiers soon enter the couple's home and take Charles away, along with boxes of his papers. Back in the United States, Ed Horman learns of his son's disappearance in Chile, and he decides to travel to Latin American to investigate.

The movie suggests that the United States was closely involved in the coup, that members of the Chilean military executed Charles Horman, that U.S. officials in Chile were deceptive in telling the Horman family what they knew, and that U.S. agents in Chile played a role in the events that led to Charles's death. The force of this conclusion strikes hard at the end of the movie when a U.S. naval attaché tells Ed Horman, "Your son was a bit of a snoop. He poked his nose into a lot of places he didn't belong. If you keep on playing with fire, you get burned."

Costa-Gavras's film leads the audience in this manner by showing Ed Horman arriving at his conclusions through a deductive process. Horman (Jack Lemmon) first appears in the movie as a conservative businessman who believes the confident explanations of U.S. government officials. In the screenplay Ed Horman's contempt for his son's idealism and liberalism receives much stronger emphasis than in Hauser's book. By accentuating Ed Horman's conservatism, Stewart and Costa-Gavras made the story credible to viewers who might be reluctant at first to accept the idea that the U.S. government was at fault in the case. Ed Horman's reactions to the growing evidence of deception resembles the initial reactions of many Americans to revelations about the Watergate scandals. At first Horman cannot believe that a conspiracy exists. He assumes that those who make accusations about wrongdoing (particularly his daughter-in-law) must be politically biased. Nixon's portrait appears several times in the scenes representing the U.S. State Department and the U.S. embassy, hinting that the empty promises of U.S. officials in Chile were similar to the confident assurances President Nixon gave the nation about his innocence in the Watergate affair.

In many ways *Missing* is a love story as well as a docudrama about international politics. This quality helps to make the drama attractive to audiences seeking entertainment rather than political messages. The film portrays not only the love between Charles Horman and his wife (Sissy Spacek) but also the growth of Ed Horman's understanding of and respect for his son and daughter-in-law. When first visiting Chile, Ed Horman displays anger. He assumes that his son got into trouble because of his idealistic enthusiasm for the leadership of socialist president Salvador Allende and that his daughter-in-law was partly responsible, because she supported her husband's interests. "I don't want to hear any of your anti-establishment paranoia," he tells Beth. "If [Charles] had settled down where he belongs, this couldn't have happened in the first place." He asks her, "What stupid thing did Charles do to cause this arrest or make him go into hiding?" In the course of searching for his son, Ed learns much about the kind of decent young idealist he was, and as the evidence of duplicity from U.S. officials grows, he develops a new appreciation for Charles and Beth. Eventually Ed Horman comes around to accepting his daughter-in-law's point of view. He begins to appreciate her disgust for Chile's counterrevolutionaries and the people representing the U.S. State Department and the U.S. military. When someone tells him that military men in the country would not order the disappearance of an American citizen without consulting the Americans first, he becomes deeply suspicious. Eventually he learns of his son's death, and he confronts the American ambassador and his associates with the evidence. Horman suggests that members of the diplomatic corps knew all along that Charles was dead. The ambassador denies involvement, and he insists that the United States was neutral at the time of the coup. He explains that he has had many responsibilities besides looking for Charles Horman, including the protection of 3,000 business firms. "I'm concerned with preservation of a way of life," he explains. Horman later offers a final gesture of anger by informing U.S. officials that he intends to sue them.

In the course of telling the story of a personal tragedy, Costa-Gavras also threw light on the larger tragedy of Chilean society. His portrayal of the environment of terrorism is especially memorable. Throughout the movie, viewers see frightening examples of violence and intimidation. Automobiles burn in the streets and bodies stretch across the pavement or float down a river. Soldiers are seen setting fire to books and ripping the pants off a woman while telling her to wear skirts in the new Chile. All these scenes actually occurred in the ugly days after the army coup of 11 September 1973. Costa-Gavras portrays the excesses of uncontrolled violence with poignant symbolism when he shows soldiers in a jeep joyfully chasing a white horse through the city streets, keeping the animal in flight by firing their rifles into the air. Virtue is on the run in this disturbing picture of fascist-style oppression in Latin America.

Does *Missing* present an authentic picture of Charles Horman's death and the backdrop of counterrevolution in Chile? A statement that appears at the beginning of the film suggests that it does. The crawl says, "This film is based on a true story. The incidents and facts are documented. Some of the names have been changed to protect the innocent and also to protect the film."

In various interviews Costa-Gavras affirmed his confidence in the validity of his presentation. He claimed that he "personally verified everything we said and showed in this film." Costa-Gavras maintained, "The story is true and is based on true facts."[9] He said that he had an obligation not to manipulate characters or elements in the story to slant the depictions in one direction. Costa-Gavras explained that he "could have cast Jack Palance as the American ambassador and prejudiced him from the start, which is what casting is used for a lot."[10]

When public debates broke out over the veracity of the film, Costa-Gavras came under attack for slanting the evidence to produce the conclusions he desired. One of the most critical statements came from Flora Lewis of the *New York Times*, who said that the director should not have made bold claims about presenting a true picture of history. Costa-Gavras's approach represents one point of view—Ed Horman's—

said Lewis, and it "raises serious ethical, moral and political as well as artistic questions." She pointed out that Costa-Gavras worked closely with the Horman family but made no effort to speak with the government officials he portrayed. He also failed to consult the records of the Senate Intelligence Committee, which issued a report entitled *Covert Action in Chile: 1963–1973* in the mid-1970s. Although Flora Lewis acknowledged that U.S. agents worked to prevent Allende's ascension to power at the time of Chile's 1970 presidential elections, she maintained that the United States' role after 1971 was limited to channeling funds to political parties, press, and radio stations. U.S. representatives tried to stay away from right-wing extremists and military plots in Allende's last years, Lewis maintained, and U.S. ambassador Nathaniel Davis lacked knowledge of any serious wrongdoing by U.S. agents during the period of his leadership. She also pointed out that Seymour Hersh, the *New York Times* reporter who wrote important news-breaking articles about CIA activities in Chile in 1970, found no evidence of U.S. involvement in either Horman's death or the military coup. In short, Costa-Gavras lacked complete evidence to support his hunches.[11]

The director, in turn, defended his approach to the story. He claimed that he could not go into small details and present contradictory evidence because a film "is not a court." Critics should not ask a film director to be a political technician, Costa-Gavras argued. "Either you give two points of view or you say: 'Here is what I think. I draw my conclusion.'"[12] Lewis, of course, was not satisfied with this explanation. "Is an artist's conviction a reality?" she asked. Lewis insisted that a director should make distinctions between "fact and verisimilitude, proof and suspicion."[13]

New York Times entertainment critic Vincent Canby joined Lewis in questioning Costa-Gavras's claims about telling the "truth," although Canby praised the director for his achievement in crafting a good drama. Canby said Costa-Gavras "knows better than anybody else that every film is fiction. . . . To pretend that 'Missing' is 'truth' is a cheap, unnecessary hype." The *Times* critic observed that Ambassador Charles S. Whitehouse, president of the American Foreign Service, was "outraged and saddened" by the film. Canby gave weight to Whitehouse's remarks by expressing concern that *Missing* "gives the impression that our fellows around the world are not helpful to American citizens, and are, in fact, contemptible."[14]

A number of other commentators in the press joined Lewis and Canby in berating Costa-Gavras for applying political bias to his evidence. Jeffrey Hart, writing in the *Los Angeles Herald-Examiner,* claimed that no real evidence existed to prove that any of the story was true. He denounced as "rubbish" Costa-Gavras's claim that artistic license gave him the right to present whatever interpretation he wanted.[15] Peter Rainer argued that Costa-Gavras should have made a psychodrama about Ed Horman's mental agony, which could have explained how a father, not knowing why his son died, single-mindedly pinned the blame on the American government.[16] Although several of the criticisms came from the political right wing, few could match the intensely conservative perspective of columnist Patrick Buchanan. He lambasted Costa-Gavras for telling a story that was not supported by the facts uncovered in the Senate investigations. Buchanan concluded, "If you want to know what really happened during the coup in Chile, don't see 'Missing.'"[17]

The claim that Costa-Gavras's movie lacks a balanced perspective contains some merit, although it would have been difficult for the director effectively to make a two-hour dramatic film presenting two viewpoints of the reforms in Allende's Chile or the causes of Charles Horman's death. Actually, *Missing* deserves some credit for applying a *Rashomon* technique: it shows more than one version of eyewitness reports about how Charles Horman disappeared (to reflect the reality of conflicting reports).[18] The movie does not, however, attempt to show multiple perspectives in a broad sense. To reveal conflicting viewpoints of the Chilean revolution, the United States' role in it, or possible explanations for Horman's death would have changed the nature of the film radically. Such a film would not have resembled the hard-hitting partisan political drama that was Costa-Gavras's trademark. It was certainly appropriate for Costa-Gavras, in his role as a filmmaker, to select a highly controversial topic, make personal judgments about the facts, and work the evidence into an emotionally charged interpretation. Nevertheless, the important questions remain: Did he work responsibly with the evidence? Were the movie's principal conclusions justified?

In considering these questions, it is helpful to move from the general to the specific. A review of the way in which Costa-Gavras and his associates portrayed conditions in Chile provides a useful context for examining the sophistication of his particular description of U.S. policy in Chile. An assessment of the manner in which Costa-Gavras portrayed actions by representatives of the United States in Chile, in turn, throws light on his handling of questions about Charles Horman's relationship to Chilean politics and the possibility of the complicity of agents of the United States in his death.

In reviewing these questions it is important to note that Thomas Hauser's book served as the primary source of information for the film-makers. Although Donald E. Stewart and Constantin Costa-Gavras supplemented their research with interviews involving the Horman family and their friends, and they sought some details from the Senate hearings, they did not read widely about Chilean history, politics, and economics, study the record of U.S. foreign policy in Chile in considerable detail, or probe deeply into the findings of the U.S. Senate's Select Committee on Intelligence or the work of the Senate Foreign Relations Committee. In many respects the strengths and weaknesses evident in the movie's portrayal relate to the strengths and weaknesses of Thomas Hauser's book.

The basis for much of *Missing*'s one-sided perspective on Chile's problems can be found in *The Execution of Charles Horman*. Hauser's account informed the movie's point of view on the political conflicts in Chile and, in turn, affected the movie's explanation of Charles Horman's actions and of the motivation behind U.S. policy in Chile. Generally, *The Execution of Charles Horman* describes the policies of Salvador Allende in glowing terms and blames most of Allende's problems on U.S. intervention in Chile's affairs. Hauser's book claims that Allende's government established an excellent record in improving the Gross National Product and reducing inflation and unemployment in his first year and a half in office.[19] Then the book describes the Nixon administration's long pursuit of "a policy of economic strangulation of Chile." The United States' "economic squeeze" forced cuts in loans from the Inter-American Development Bank and other lending sources, Hauser explained. The shortages of food, industrial materials, and consumer goods that occurred in the days of Allende's leadership were the result of these foreign pressures. Shortages also developed because Chile's poor people achieved greater purchasing power under Allende and at last could afford to participate in the economy as active consumers. People in the slums of Santiago and the rural farms of Chile continued to support the Marxist president, says Hauser, but the United States worked effectively to bring him down. Street demonstrations were "organized by the CIA." The United States financed labor and trade groups, funneled money to support strikes, bankrolled the anti-Allende newspapers, infiltrated the upper echelons of Chile's Socialist party, and even paid government employees to make deliberate errors on the job so that they could contribute to the economic chaos. These policies succeeded in weakening Allende's leadership and building support for the coup.

There is a significant degree of truth in Hauser's claims, of course. The United States' record in Chile in the early 1970s constitutes one of the ugliest examples of U.S. interference in another nation's affairs. The Nixon administration, worried about U.S. investments in Chile and fearing that Allende's style of socialism could spread to other Latin American nations, made extraordinary efforts to prevent Allende from taking office. The U.S. tried to bolster Allende's political opponents in the 1970 presidential elections and possibly encouraged actions that led to the assassination of General Rene Schneider, the important military leader who pledged to stand by Chile's constitution and allow Allende to take office. Then the United States hurt Chile badly by discouraging international financial institutions from providing loans to the country, and the CIA evidently bankrolled Chilean copper workers in their major strike at the important El Teniente mines. Furthermore, as the book and the movie contend, the United States maintained a close relationship with the Chilean military, training officers at a U.S. base in the Panama Canal Zone and participating in joint maneuvers with the Chilean armed forces.[20]

The report of the Senate's Select Committee to Study Government Operations with Respect to Intelligence Activities, published in 1975, describes a variety of covert actions in Chile that involved CIA-led manipulation of the Chilean press, large-scale support of political parties, and efforts to "foment" a military coup. The Senate report shows that representatives of the United States tried to "make the economy scream" by cutting credit and the sale of manufactured parts to Chile, and they tried to excite resistance to Allende by spreading false information about the plans and activities of his administration. The CIA spent $8 million to secure Allende's overthrow (worth about $40 million at the time in Chile's black market).[21]

Secret contacts with a number of Chilean military men were particularly disturbing to the Senate investigators. In several instances during the 1970–73 period U.S. military and intelligence officers met with members of the Chilean armed forces. Although it was not clear that these discussions involved direct U.S. cooperation in the coup, the investigators did conclude that "penetration" of the Chilean military contributed to a climate of intrigue. Even though the greatest evidence of U.S. communications with the Chilean armed forces related to the period before 1973, it is clear that Chilean officers were aware in September 1973 of the Americans' positive attitude toward extralegal measures to get rid of Allende. Senate investigators could not easily "draw a firm line between monitoring coup plotting and becoming involved," but evidently the clandestine contacts sent an important message about American enthusiasm for military action.[22]

The sorry record of U.S. mischief making gives weight to some of the criticisms of U.S. foreign policy suggested in *Missing,* but U.S. covert actions in themselves do not provide a complete explanation for Allende's downfall. The history of Allende's problems is not as strikingly one-sided as Thomas Hauser maintained in his book. Even the Senate report is far from comprehensive in its explanation, for it focuses on U.S. clandestine activities and gives only limited attention to other developments in Chilean society.

Despite the very serious efforts of U.S. conspirators to sabotage Chile's socialist experiment, the policies and actions of Salvador Allende's government also contributed to the failure of the revolution. Many of Allende's difficulties related to the actions of left-wing political groups in Chile. Leftists in Chile disregarded Allende's appeals for political caution and compromise. The powerful MIR (Movement of the Revolutionary Left) was especially troublesome to the president. Its members invaded privately held land and buildings, threatened violence, and provoked armed confrontations. The MIR's activities helped to polarize Chilean politics. The book and movie give almost no hint of this side of the story.[23] In fact, *Missing*'s single statement suggesting an assessment of Allende's experiment appears when a character in the story says, "They were trying to do something new here." In the context of the screenplay, these words suggest that the "new" things Allende gave the Chilean people were effective and almost universally welcomed.

Actually, Allende's revolution began to encounter tremendous resistance from the Chilean population in its last two years. Whatever the role of U.S. influence, Allende's days in power seemed limited by the second half of 1973. The Marxist president had alienated many of his compatriots through his policy of nationalizing private property. His government took control of banks and industries and expropriated much of the privately owned farmland. The critically important copper industry, which had already come under considerable government control in the previous administration, was nationalized, and the government also took control of the production of cement, steel, and electricity and began nationalizing the telephone services. Throughout his period in office, Allende lacked a clear mandate for radical reorganization of the economy. He won only 36.3 percent of the vote in the 1970 presidential elections. Nevertheless, after this "victory" his administration moved forcefully to change Chilean economic life in fundamental ways. Then, in March 1973, the pro-Allende Popular Unity Party garnered 43.4 percent of the vote. Despite this gain, Allende's supporters still fell short of a majority, and their election totals hardly could be interpreted as authority for a massive assault on private property.

Discontent with Allende's leadership also related to the rapidly deteriorating economic situation. By 1973 productivity in Chile's farming and industrial sectors had dropped precipitously, and inflation climbed to 32.3 percent. Then Chile's truck drivers, fearful of a government takeover of their industry, began a series of devastating strikes and held up shipments of milk, sugar, and other important food staples. Gasoline was in limited supply during the strike, and alternative transportation dried up as bus and taxi drivers also stopped their work in protest against Allende. Chile's middle-class women also made a contribution to the resistance: back in 1971 they had drawn attention to their difficulties by banging on empty pots and pans in marches through city streets.[24]

The polarization of Chilean society made the military increasingly nervous, and the evidence that some leftist groups were stockpiling weapons brought pressure on the army to intervene before the country exploded in a civil war. Allende recognized that the actions of the leftist groups could provoke a counterrevolution and wreck his dreams, but he discovered that there was little he could do to control the situation. Members of the MIR led peasants in illegal takeovers of farmlands and apartment buildings, and they encouraged their followers to obtain weapons. Chile seemed to be turning into an armed camp after the middle of 1973 as forces of the Left and Right distributed firearms and prepared for a violent conflict. A nation that had boasted a proud record of relatively peaceful and constitutional rule over many decades seemed about to break into civil war.[25] Under the circumstances, a coup was likely. The prospect was on the minds of many Chileans in September 1973, and certainly Charles Horman must have been aware that the military was going to attempt a takeover.

It is difficult to measure the influence of the U.S. covert operations in this time of turmoil. Probably the CIA's most important role was funneling money to Chilean trade unionists. The unionists, in turn, participated in various work stoppages that badly hurt the Chilean economy. Strikes and delays in the delivery of vital goods and services intensified the Chilean people's sense of frustration. The disruptions helped to polarize Chile's working and middle classes and contributed significantly to the military's decision to stage the coup in September 1973.[26] It is wrong, however, to assume that without the CIA's intervention the coup could not have occurred. Allende's policies challenged private property directly and polarized millions. Demonstrations and strikes were to a substantial degree natural outbursts against the government's controversial policies. Henry Kissinger exonerated U.S. actions too greatly when he wrote that they "played no role whatever" in the conception, planning, and execution of the coup, but he was correct in stressing that it was opposition within Chile that especially triggered the overthrow.[27] A more balanced assessment comes from a longtime student of U.S. relations with Chile, Paul E. Sigmund. He maintained that U.S. activities made a psychological difference, "contributing to the polarization that led to a bloody coup and repression," but "CIA or embassy involvement seems unlikely to have changed the outcome." It is doubtful, says Sigmund, that the covert activities were "a necessary or a sufficient cause of the Chilean opposition to Allende."[28]

In view of the broad economic and political problems troubling Chile in the last year of Allende's rule, it is a mistake to lay almost all the blame for Allende's fall on the United States, as Hauser did in his book (and Costa-Gavras did in the movie by implication). The United States intervened in Chile's affairs significantly, but Allende's regime was being pulled so hard by the forces of both the Left and the Right in 1973 that it did not need tugging from the United States to complete its disintegration.[29]

More specifically, what was Charles Horman's relationship to the events in Chile? Why was he taken away by Chilean soldiers? Did representatives of the United States play a role in his disappearance? The book and the movie suggest answers to these questions. In view of the controversies surrounding *Missing*'s presentation of history, the writer's and filmmaker's handling of the evidence merits consideration.

The movie's perspective on Charles Horman comes largely from Hauser's book. In *The Execution of Charles Horman* Hauser describes the tragedy of an attractive young American idealist who got caught up in a revolution. After studies at Harvard and work with public television and a federal poverty program, Horman began a long trip through Latin America with his wife. Eventually he settled in Chile, helped the poor in his neighborhood, and worked with a nonprofit magazine, *FIN.* Edited by Americans, the publication described U.S. activities in Chile and generally attributed the Latin American country's problems to the United States' mischief making. The magazine also featured articles from American publications that were critical of U.S. involvement in Vietnam.[30]

According to the book, Horman was visiting the coastal resort city of Viña del Mar when the military coup began, and during the crisis he engaged in conversations with U.S. military agents. In these discussions his acquaintances seemed to reveal that the American military cooperated with the anti-Allende forces and perhaps even assisted in planning the coup. One of the most telling conversations occurred with a retired naval engineer on special assignment who told Charles, "I'm here with the U.S. Navy. *We came to do a job and it's done"* (emphasis in the original). Charles Horman probed for details in these discussions, and his inquisitiveness may have raised some suspicions. A few days later, after he returned to Santiago, a group of Chilean soldiers went into his home. Twenty minutes later they emerged with Horman as their prisoner and a box of his books and papers. They took Horman to the National Stadium, where troops had placed thousands of prisoners marked for detainment, torture, or murder.[31]

As Hauser explained in the book, Ed Horman arrived in Chile to help Joyce Horman search for her missing husband. The two received friendly receptions from U.S. officials but not significant help in their quest to find Charles. Sometimes the officials appeared to give them misleading information. After much searching, they located Charles's body. Chilean representatives claimed that it had been found on a street by a passing military patrol (an apparent lie). Enrique Guzmán of the Chilean Foreign Ministry argued that Charles had been deeply involved in leftist activities and perhaps had been shot by his own comrades for "betraying the cause" (another apparent lie).[32] A comment made by a Chilean intelligence agent about Charles's death seemed to the Hormans to offer a more plausible explanation. The agent said that Charles had to disappear because he knew too much. The man also asserted that the Chilean military authorities would never risk murdering an American without approval from the United States government.

Ed Horman's frustrating experience trying to discover what had happened to his son in Chile led him to ask three important questions (according to Hauser's book): (1) Did members of the Chilean military kill Charles? (2) Did the U.S. government knowingly seek to cover up facts surrounding Charles's death? (3) Did the U.S. government have foreknowledge of or possibly even order Charles's execution?[33] *The Execution of Charles Horman* leaves the impression that all these questions are answerable in the affirmative, and the movie reinforces the same message.

Neither Hauser nor anyone else has produced conclusive proof, however, identifying a connection between Charles Horman's disappearance and the activities of people representing the U.S. government. To this day the reasons for Charles Horman's difficulties with the Chilean soldiers remain obscure. Former ambassador Nathaniel Davis cannot attribute a reason for the behavior with certainty, but he speculates that Horman may have been writing about the plot to assassinate General Rene Schneider back in 1970 and that documents about this subject taken from his home at the time he was apprehended could have placed him in jeopardy.[34] Thomas Hauser offers another explanation. He points out that the soldiers came specifically for Horman, and they treated him differently from other Americans by taking him directly to the national stadium for interrogation rather than to a *caribineros* station, where other Americans were first held. At the stadium soldiers kept Horman apart from other Americans, another unique situation. Hauser believes that representatives of the Chilean military treated Horman differently from the other Americans because Horman heard comments suggesting U.S. involvement in Chile's affairs, particularly the words of the retired navy engineer.[35] Nathaniel Davis disputes this interpretation. He contends that the individual who spoke those words or said something similar was in Chile to repair fire extinguishers for the Chilean navy. The man was referring to the completion of his business assignment, not to U.S. covert operations. In fact, says Davis, the individual testified to this explanation in a sworn deposition.[36]

Could Charles Horman's activities in Chile have placed him at risk at the time of the coup? The book and the movie do not give much weight to this possibility, but a different description of his role may be valid. Charles Horman's friendships with pro-Allende Chileans and especially his editorial work with *FIN* may have put him at risk. Recognizing this vulnerability does not represent an effort simply to "blame the victim." No evidence has come to light linking Charles Horman with revolutionary activity. He has not been identified as a dangerous conspirator plotting to defend Allende militarily or to destroy his opponents. It is useful to recognize, however, that in a time of polemical politics and bloody confrontations, an idealistic foreigner who takes sides through his writing can find himself treated as a serious partisan. Charles Horman may have suffered in the manner that numerous Chileans suffered for sympathizing with the Left. Many of them paid dearly for the simple act of writing an essay or attending a meeting. For their interest in Chilean politics, they experienced arrest, torture, and in some cases, "disappearance." Thousands of these Chileans became victims of the repression that attended the 1973 coup. There can be no complete body count; some reports suggest that as many as 20,000 or 30,000 Allende supporters died in the wave of violence associated with General Augusto Pinochet's ascension to power. It seems clear that many of these individuals were selected with little forethought. Rumors or suspicions sufficed to mark a victim. In the chaotic days of violent activity, common soldiers were encouraged to search out and destroy the "enemy," and they sometimes acted with no more curiosity about the guilt or innocence of their victims than U.S. soldiers displayed toward the Vietnamese population they slaughtered at My Lai.

The record of Chile's bloody Thermidor in September 1973 reveals much of this sort of undiscriminating, gratuitous violence rather than a coherently organized, thoughtful campaign to round up radical opponents deemed dangerous to the new order. In failing to clarify this distinction Costa-Gavras misled his audiences. The movie's focus on deceptive statements by U.S. representatives accentuates the idea that Charles's disappearance was probably the result of an ugly conspiracy involving some highly placed Chilean and American figures. *Missing* fails to give much weight to the more likely possibility that Horman became a victim of the wild, uncontrolled violence of a counterrevolution that harmed and sometimes destroyed many decent people. His death takes on special meaning not because he was treated more unfairly than other victims but because he was an American. As such, his case drew international attention and eventually became the subject of a book and a movie. By seeing what can happen to a young man whose only "crime" was to visit another nation, observe its politics, and write about what he saw in a committed manner, viewers gain a profound sense of the enormity of the injustices that occurred in Chile. Charles Horman's case reminds audiences of the tragedy of thousands of Chileans whose names are not well known but whose experiences should not be forgotten.

With regard to the depiction of Charles Horman's goals and motives, the cowriter of the screenplay, Donald E. Stewart, did not agree fully with the depiction Costa-Gavras had in mind. Stewart wanted to give Charles Horman a stronger personality in the story and show that he had a partisan interest in Chilean politics. Charles Horman "was definitely on the list for a reason, and he was picked up for a reason," Stewart assumed. Horman evidently "had ambitions for a more active role in the things that were going on" in Chile. He was not just "the innocent American snatched up on the streets," said Stewart. In the early versions of the script Stewart tried to show Horman doing things that would help to explain his demise. Costa-Gavras preferred the image of an innocent victim, however, choosing a portrayal that did not risk alienating audience sympathy for Charles Horman. He and the producers brought another writer into the project, one who, among other things, was to "soften" Horman's character.[37]

Stewart also had other reservations about the movie's handling of the facts in the case. For example, in planning the drama Costa-Gavras placed Charles Horman in the anteroom of a high official at the Chilean Ministry of Justice. "I was taken aback by that," said Stewart. The individual who reported seeing Charles Horman at the ministry was not reliable, Stewart observed; he made conflicting reports to other people. In view of this shaky evidence Stewart preferred not to make firm claims concerning critically important questions about Charles Horman's whereabouts. Stewart also noted that Ed Horman did not go to see his son's body in Santiago, Chile, as the movie depicts in a dramatic scene. Ed Horman was a Christian Scientist, and he declined the opportunity for religious reasons.

Despite these concerns, Stewart was pleased with the powerful, emotional force of Costa-Gavras's movie and sensed that it raised important questions for audiences to consider and made an impact on the foreign policy establishment. "Movies have a tendency to really heat up the emotions," he commented. Hauser's book had aroused only a limited debate about Charles Horman's death and U.S. policy in Chile. *Missing*, on the other hand, provoked a lawsuit from some of the principals in the story and excited a discussion about many related issues in the national media.[38]

The movie certainly did stir interest in the United States' role in foreign affairs. During the week before its official release, a number of officials in Washington, D.C., viewed closed screenings of *Missing*. State Department employees in the nation's capital participated in lively discussions about the movie's thesis, and references to the film came up quickly in hearings of the Senate Foreign Relations Committee. The

State Department took an unusual position, releasing an official three-page statement about the movie. This statement noted that the U.S. government had made a substantial effort to investigate Charles Horman's disappearance over many years and had tried hard to assist the Horman family. The document noted that, despite these extensive efforts, no light could be thrown on the reasons for the disappearance, and the culprits had never been discovered.[39]

Nathaniel Davis continued to believe that *Missing* makes an "appalling accusation" about his role in the Horman case, as well as that of other U.S. public officers who had served in Chile. Davis believed that the movie is "corrosive of any confidence in our government abroad," and said that it touches "at the heart of the integrity of the United States foreign service."[40] Davis regretted that his costly lawsuit against the filmmakers was unsuccessful, remarking, "The message to public servants appears evident. Don't sue, even if you believe you have been accused of murder, accused without supporting evidence of any kind."[41] Davis received a number of donations from members of the American Foreign Service Association and the American Association of Foreign Service Women to support his legal challenge. When his suit came to a close and some money remained in the bank account from contributions, he donated the proceeds to a scholarship fund.[42]

It remains difficult to weigh the diverse claims of Nathaniel Davis, Constantin Costa-Gavras, Thomas Hauser, the Hormans, and several others who took a strong interest in *Missing* because of their personal stakes in the disputes. Even complete access to CIA files or opportunities to interview Chilean leaders would probably fail to uncover a smoking pistol. It is likely that the American public will never know exactly why Charles Horman died or whether anyone connected with the U.S. government had foreknowledge of the danger he faced or played a role in his death. On the broader question of U.S. involvement in Chile's affairs in the period leading up to Allende's overthrow, greater insight may be gained as foreign policy documents are opened for public examination in future years. Enough information has already come to light to suggest that U.S. activity in Chile in 1970–73 was in violation of many of the nation's stated principles.

In view of the clouded condition of much of the evidence, it seems fair to say that the makers of *Missing* adopted a controversial thesis when they chose to dramatize the material in Hauser's book. To tell a comprehensible and shocking story, they had to assume that several of Hauser's debatable conclusions about Charles Horman's case were true. Costa-Gavras stated his position bluntly when he said candidly, "Here is what I think; I draw my conclusion."[43] The director intended to show his understanding of the events in highly dramatic, emotional form. He was not going to apply much subtlety to his presentation of good and evil. His depictions of Ambassador Davis and other figures associated with the U.S. government are not as controlled and objective as he suggested in his comments to the press. The U.S. officials and agents in *Missing* demonstrate considerable deception. The actors who portray them play the part of phony, sugar-sweet bureaucrats who do not intend to reveal to Ed Horman everything that they know and think about his son.

When Costa-Gavras came under criticism for making assumptions about the Horman case without sufficient evidence, the director defended himself by saying that his movie was not intended to be a specific study of events in Chile. Costa-Gavras did not want audiences to dismiss the examples of repression as just another tale about troubles in a remote South American country, he explained. Rather, he hoped that the generic quality of the scenes would suggest messages applicable to many contemporary situations associated with the problems of dictatorship. Costa-Gavras's goal was noble, but *Missing* contains too many elements specific to Chile and the case of Charles Horman to make it invulnerable to questions about authenticity.[44] The director succeeded in providing a chilling lesson on the horrors of a police state and the possibilities for doing wrong through American covert operations in foreign countries. In this respect he used a story about the past to convey an important message for the present. Costa-Gavras effectively reminded Americans that their nation must no longer try to overthrow revolutionary governments and bolster right-wing military dictatorships. Costa-Gavras's use of evidence in delivering this instruction was problematic, however; because important documentation about the U.S. role in the Chilean coup and in the murder of Charles Horman was lacking, Ambassador Davis appears to be correct in his claims that the movie represented "an assault on the integrity of the U.S. government, the Foreign Service and the military" without sufficient justification.[45]

PART 3

REFLECTING THE PRESENT

Revealing Current Controversy in Portrayals of the Past

5

Bonnie and Clyde

"VIOLENCE OF A MOST GRISLY SORT"

Clyde Barrow (Warren Beatty) and
Bonnie Parker (Faye Dunaway), bloodied
but still resistant, face the lawmen in
Bonnie and Clyde. Courtesy of the Museum
of Modern Art/Film Stills Archive.

*B*onnie and Clyde, a 1967 Warner Brothers picture about a roman-tic pair of gangsters that terrorized the Great Plains in the 1930s, became an instant success in the United States and abroad. Many reviewers praised *Bonnie and Clyde* for its innovations (*Time* called it a watershed picture, saying that it signaled a new trend in movie-making, much as *Citizen Kane, Stagecoach,* and *Psycho* had in previous years). Those who criticized it strongly soon appeared to be out of step with the masses, since long lines of eager patrons were forming at the theaters, helping to make the movie one of the box office leaders of 1967. Public enthusiasm for *Bonnie and Clyde* became so great that Warner Brothers was unprepared to cash in fully on the market for ancillary materials. The studio did not have in place a large collection of songs for the film, releasing only an album of the movie's banjo music by Lester Flatt and Earl Scruggs. Others responded to the de-mand, however. English songwriters quickly released the "Ballad of Bonnie and Clyde," a tune that climbed to first place in the British charts. The French banned this "ballad" because it contains symbols of gangster life in the form of sirens and gunshots, but then various French composers wrote seven more acceptable musical versions of their own about the outlaw couple. Meanwhile, clothing designers in the United States and Europe discovered a lively market for Bonnie and Clyde fashions. Wide-lapelled pin-striped suits for men with "Clyde fe-doras" became popular, as did Bonnie-style maxidresses.[1]

Bonnie and Clyde became tremendously successful because it offers a stylish picture of cultural rebels in the 1930s that appealed to audi-ences experiencing the cultural revolution of the 1960s. The movie suggested familiar themes to individuals who were questioning con-ventional ideals about the promise of American society and the author-ity of the "Establishment." Audiences warmed to the movie's images of economic inequality (*Bonnie and Clyde* portrays hard times in the Depression Era and shows poor people feeling contemptuous toward the rich, particularly the bankers). The film spoke meaningfully to viewers who were experiencing disillusionment and a "generation gap." It presents a somewhat appealing portrait of two independent-minded and troubled young people who rebel against mainstream society and impulsively display their emotions. The creators of *Bonnie and Clyde* succinctly identified what they hoped would be their movie's attraction to audiences of the 1960s when they put their plans on paper: "If Bonnie and Clyde were here today, they would be hip. Their values have been assimilated in much of our culture—not robbing banks and killing people, of course, but their style, their sexuality, their bravado, their delicacy, their cultivated arrogance, their narcissistic insecurity, their curious ambition have relevance to the way we live now."[2]

As it turned out, the matter of robbing banks and killing people also had relevance to the way Americans lived in the 1960s, and that association provoked a good deal of controversy. A number of people complained about the film's graphic depictions of violent crime; they also objected to what they considered to be a sympathetic treatment of the 1930s outlaws. These critics worried that the fascinating action scenes in *Bonnie and Clyde* and the romanticized vision of gangster life might encourage the criminal behavior of some viewers. They lambasted the moviemakers for appealing to the audience's base interest in seeing blood on the screen. *Bonnie and Clyde*'s glamorized violence could excite imitation from some moviegoers, they warned.

Many other Hollywood productions had depicted violence. *Bonnie and Clyde* provoked such strong reactions, however, at least partly because of the movie's panache in exhibiting violent acts. Portrayals of bloodshed are central to the movie's innovative style. *Bonnie and Clyde* shows injury and death in shocking fashion (often following immediately on humorous scenes). The horror of the violent experience appears in graphic detail. Body parts split apart. Skin flies away in pieces. Blood spurts. Victims do not perform quick falls, as in many previous Hollywood movies; viewers get to see their gaping and painful wounds. In this respect *Bonnie and Clyde* makes a significant impact as the cinema of violence. It presents realistic and horrible bloodshed in a manner that many other filmmakers later copied.

The movie also excited strong reactions because it appeared at a time when Americans were growing particularly sensitive to the problem of violence. By 1967 America was engaged in a bloody conflict in Vietnam, and at home the society was troubled by aggressive antiwar protests,

growing militancy among African Americans, ghetto riots, and the assassination of prominent figures such as John F. Kennedy and Malcolm
X. All these factors made the subject of violence troubling, but the problem of violent crime in the 1960s seemed to be the most relevant of all.
Critics worried about a surge in assaults, robberies, and murders, and
they wondered whether a motion picture like *Bonnie and Clyde*, which
seems to glamorize the life of violent gangsters, could have an unfortunate effect on behavior. These critics worried especially about the effect
on youths of little sophistication, impressionable individuals who might
model their behavior on actions they saw in the movie.

Reactions to *Bonnie and Clyde* brought into conflict the interests of
art and the broader interests of society. As a creative attempt to portray a historical episode with imaginative use of new techniques and
fashions of the cinema, the movie was a stunning achievement. *Bonnie and Clyde* won accolades from a number of cinema aficionados who
recognized that it could become a watershed picture that would be well
remembered for its artistry and flair and for setting trends in the motion picture industry. Yet this very accomplishment made the movie
an object of intense controversy. *Bonnie and Clyde*'s popularity revealed
the power of art in exciting viewers' feelings about a troubling subject. By presenting innovative depictions of violence in 1967, the movie
excited criticism. It served as an emotional lightning rod, drawing bolts
of protest from many who were upset about the growing danger of life
in America. Debates had been building in previous years about the possible role of television and film in contributing to the escalation of violent crime; in this context the complaints about *Bonnie and Clyde* symbolized a larger public criticism of the media's impact on attitudes and
behavior.

The movie's story had a basis in fact—at least in general terms.
During the early 1930s Clyde Barrow and Bonnie Parker went on a
two-year binge of robbery and murder in the Southwest and Midwest.
Barrow, a small-time thief, met Parker in 1932, and together they held
up stores and banks and ran constantly from the growing number of
law enforcement officials trying to capture them. They picked up some
associates along the way, including a seventeen-year-old car thief and
Barrow's brother and sister-in-law. The small gang killed between
twelve and fifteen people (reports on the numbers varied) until May
1934, when a former Texas Ranger named Frank Hamer led a group
that ambushed them along a Louisiana highway. Clyde Barrow and
Bonnie Parker fell dead in a hail of gunfire.

Bonnie and Clyde follows the rough outlines of this history. The story begins with the meeting of Bonnie and Clyde (Faye Dunaway and Warren Beatty), showing the two demonstrating a need for each other. They casually fall into a life of crime, beginning a spree of petty robberies. The couple then picks up the young thief, C. W. (Michael J. Pollard), and Clyde's brother, Buck, and sister-in-law, Blanche (Gene Hackman and Estelle Parsons). Complications in interpersonal relationships soon emerge. Clyde is sexually impotent, and in a Freudian touch the movie suggests that Clyde views shooting a gun as a symbolic form of ejaculation. Bonnie considers Clyde's squeamish and self-righteous sister-in-law to be offensive, and she pleads with Clyde to dump both Blanche and Buck. When the outlaws' cabins are raided, the gang makes an extraordinary breakaway. A short time later, however, they are ambushed in a field. Buck is mortally wounded, and Blanche, now hysterical, stays behind and is captured. Bonnie, Clyde, and C. W. make their escape, and Bonnie indicates a yearning to see her mother. Later her relationship with Clyde grows particularly warm when Bonnie reads a poem she has written about Clyde and their adventures. This moment of psychic fulfillment helps Clyde to overcome his sexual inadequacies. Bonnie and Clyde become lovers for the first time. Clyde takes Bonnie to her mother in Texas, and C. W.'s father makes a deal with the police to save his son from the gang. The lawmen then stage an attack on the two in Louisiana.

Violent scenes in the movie appear suddenly and unexpectedly. Clyde kills a butcher who comes at him with a meat cleaver, the gang shoots a pursuer in the face after a bank robbery, and when the group is under assault, Blanche's eye is shot out and Buck's head blows apart. The last shootout comes after several hints of a bloody finish. Eventually lawmen succeed in pumping several rounds of bullets into Bonnie and Clyde. The two die in slow motion as machine gun fire rips across their shaking bodies.

The criticisms of *Bonnie and Clyde* came at a time when evidence appeared of a significant growth in violent crime in the United States. The problem of widespread crime seemed to be new to America in the 1960s, and in fact, it was a relatively new experience for many Americans. Since the mid-1930s the incidence of criminal violence in the United States had declined dramatically. The streets of American cities were relatively quiet from the 1940s to the early 1960s.[3] Then came a surge in robberies, muggings, and murders (the statistics showed a particularly sharp rise beginning in 1964). Americans grew fearful about their safety, especially those who lived in urban environments. Many added locks to their doors, installed alarm systems, cut back on their leisurely activities in the streets and parks, and remained in their homes after dark. A number purchased firearms for protection. Criminals also bought guns, and the firearms race escalated. Fear of urban crime contributed to the large-scale migration of middle-class families to suburbia in the 1960s (the general migration to the suburbs had already been growing, of course, since the end of World War II). In the 1960s millions sought security in planned neighborhoods, and those who could afford premium comfort moved into communities that featured walled perimeters, guarded entrances, and security patrols.[4]

Published data revealed an extraordinary escalation of crime. Rates for assault, armed robbery, and manslaughter climbed significantly. FBI *Uniform Crime Reports* released at the end of the decade revealed an overall increase of 156 percent in violent crimes in the 1960s.[5] Many argued that the FBI's reports underestimated the breadth of the problem, because the bureau's data reflected only crimes reported to the police (many victims, out of fear, frustration, or disillusionment over the police's failure to solve cases, did not report their encounters with criminals). Data also showed that increasing numbers of these cases in the 1960s involved strangers (criminals attacking people they did not know personally). An element of viciousness was also becoming evident. More and more crimes involved gratuitous violence, actions that showed no obvious functional purpose for the criminal. Attackers shot or slashed their victims out of a vague sense of anger or apparently for the thrill of bringing injury or pain to the victim. All these developments aroused emotion in the United States.[6] Americans in 1967 realized that the tranquility of their city streets had been broken dramatically in just a few years, and they wondered what had caused the sudden change.

Many explanations came under consideration as the public, politicians, and social scientists offered theories about the causes of the growing violence. Theorists pointed to the increasing popularity of guns in youth gangs, complained about a breakdown of law and order, and worried about declining family and community values. Some said that the violent activity was not really new to American life; they explained that it had been deeply ingrained in American culture from the time of the frontier experience.[7] Others investigated human nature and reported that humans are part of the animal kingdom and therefore practice violent aggression as a means of survival.[8] These and many other explanations were the focus of lively public discussions, but the one that applied most interestingly to Hollywood's *Bonnie and Clyde* was the contention that popular entertainment could make an impact on impressionable viewers and, perhaps, influence some to commit anti-social acts.

Well before *Bonnie and Clyde* made its appearance in American theaters, the public had debated questions about the influence of movies on criminal behavior. Back in 1930s movies such as *Public Enemy* (1931) and *Scarface* (1932) aroused controversy because they seemed to glorify the life of the violent gangster.[9] During the 1950s some began to wonder whether examples of violence involving youth gangs had some relationship to the depictions of rebellious youngsters seen in the movies. Disputes particularly centered on three Hollywood productions: *The Wild One* (1953), starring Marlon Brando; *Rebel without a Cause* (1955), featuring James Dean; and *The Blackboard Jungle* (1955), which features Glenn Ford and Sidney Poiter. Then, in 1960, an Alfred Hitchcock movie helped to inject new energy into debates about the social impact of violence in the movies. *Psycho* contains a shocking scene in which a mad killer (Tony Perkins) knifes a woman in her shower (Janet Leigh). The movie follows the action graphically, finishing with a disturbing view of the woman's blood swirling down the shower drain. Some criticized Hitchcock for capitalizing on the public's interest in gore, yet *Psycho* proved to be a critical and box office success. Within a few years a number of filmmakers were imitating Hitchcock's style, and the bloodletting in *Psycho* no longer seemed unique. In films such as *The Good, the Bad, and the Ugly* (1967), *The Dirty Dozen* (1967), and *The Wild Bunch* (1969), directors concentrated on the excitement of violent action and featured graphic scenes of bloodshed.

Bonnie and Clyde was not necessarily *more* violent than other movies of the 1960s, but it represented a stylistic advancement in the way it *portrays* bloodshed. The movie leaves its viewers off-balance from start to finish. At various places in the story the picture amuses and then horrifies. *Bonnie and Clyde* makes viewers laugh at the criminals' behavior, elicits a sense of pathos, and also excites feelings of disgust. Viewers sometimes feel these contradictory impulses within a period of a few seconds. The movie shocks and confuses by closely juxtaposing contrasts. Scenes suggesting romance or comedy are broken abruptly by vicious acts of violence and then followed by more amusement (such as rapid car chases accompanied by the lively banjo music of Earl Scruggs and his Foggy Mountain Boys).

Bonnie and Clyde also applies a fascinating artistic touch to its study of the violent couple that made it seem innovative and memorable to its audiences. In the final scenes, when law enforcement officers catch up with Bonnie and Clyde along a Louisiana highway, the couple's eyes meet, communicating an awareness of the terrible climax that is about to take place. There is an explosion of bullets, and their bodies bounce, shake, and roll in slow motion. A piece of Clyde's head flies in the air in the manner of the documentary film footage showing John F. Kennedy's assassination. The outlaws' deaths take on the appearance of a cinematic ballet, choreographed intelligently to stretch the emotional payoff of the movie's last images. Audiences frequently talked about this moment in the movie; they treated it much as Alfred Hitchcock's audiences remembered *Psycho* for its shower scene.

Bonnie and Clyde's concentration on bloodshed and its graphic depictions of injury and death excited a strong negative reaction from a number of critics. Some of the angriest and most influential words came from Bosley Crowther, a longtime and influential movie reviewer for the *New York Times*. Crowther called the motion picture a "blending of farce with brutal killings" and complained that it contains abundant "blotches of violence of the most grisly sort."[10] He also expressed disgust with the movie's romantic perspective on the 1930s criminals Bonnie Parker and Clyde Barrow. Crowther noted that 1934 newspaper reports about Bonnie and Clyde described them as ugly and evil desperadoes. He blasted the filmmakers for distorting history and pandering to the public's appetite for bloodshed at the cinema.

Andrew Sarris and Pauline Kael, two popular New York–based film commentators, criticized Crowther strongly for making an issue of the film's depiction of violence. Sarris accused Crowther of trying to link violence in the movies with violence in society and of flirting with ideas about censorship when condemning the movie so harshly. Crowther's "inflammatory diatribes" against violence on the screen were "downright mischievous," said Sarris; they could incite the forces of repression. He said that it was easy for writers to blame the movies for criminal violence rather than to deal with the real causes of the trouble, such as poverty in the slums.[11] Pauline Kael objected to demands that the filmmakers reduce the violence. "*Bonnie and Clyde* needs violence, violence is its meaning," she said. Kael insisted that filmmakers must be free to use violence if they considered it to be essential to their drama, and she warned that society needs to keep at bay the so-called guardians of morality who would try to determine for others what is acceptable entertainment. Like Sarris, she disputed the notion that violence in film can make a substantial impact on human behavior. Kael said that a movie cannot encourage people to go out and commit a violent crime "any more than seeing an ivory hunter shoot an elephant makes us want to shoot one." In fact, movie violence can have exactly the opposite impact from the one imagined by people like Crowther, she argued. It can sensitize viewers to the ugliness of violent crime. Furthermore, someone viewing *Bonnie and Clyde* could easily leave the movie theater concluding that violent crime does not pay. After all, she noted, the movie reveals that Bonnie Parker and Clyde Barrow met a violent finish because of their crime spree.[12]

Several letter writers to the *New York Times* also reacted strongly to Crowther's attacks on the movie. Some argued that the film makes important statements about violence in America in the 1960s. "To a generation seeking to bring new and real meaning to life in a decade characterized by brutal, senseless violence, such a film is emphatically of special relevance," said one reader. Another applauded the filmmakers for giving audiences a valuable lesson about the modern-day problem of violence. He said that the makers of *Bonnie and Clyde* cleverly drew viewers into the same trap that attracted the real Bonnie Parker and Clyde Barrow. In the first part of the film violence appears to be a successful way for the criminal couple to deal with their personal problems. By the end of the picture, however, it becomes clear that the members of the Barrow gang have created a nightmare for themselves. The movie, said the writer, reveals that people can easily be duped into believing in the mythical efficacy of violence. Hence, *Bonnie and Clyde* provided a valuable lesson for Americans in the troubled 1960s.[13]

Reviewers for the prominent news magazines *Time* and *Newsweek* initially took the same critical stand as Crowther, ridiculing the movie's sometimes light and humorous approach to violence, but within a very brief period, more favorable perspectives appeared. *Time* assigned a new reviewer to the film, one who gave an assessment that contrasted dramatically with the tone of *Time*'s first judgment. The reviewer applauded *Bonnie and Clyde*'s director, Arthur Penn, for presenting an exciting perspective on both the 1930s and the 1960s. He maintained that *Bonnie and Clyde* is both an important "commentary on the mindless violence of the American Sixties and an esthetic evocation of the past."[14] In the case of *Newsweek* the turnaround was more extraordinary, because it involved the same reviewer who had criticized *Bonnie and Clyde* just a short time before. Whether *Newsweek*'s Joseph Morganstern truly had discovered a personal appreciation of the film after a second viewing or came under editorial pressure to change his assessment is not clear. He may have felt embarrassed about heaping criticism on a movie that was quickly becoming a popular sensation and winning acclaim for its artistry. Perhaps, too, Morganstern worried about seeing himself perceived as an ally of the forces of censorship. Whatever the reason, he offered an unusual apology. Morganstern explained that he had become "so surfeited and preoccupied by violence in daily life" that he had overreacted to the film. It was unfair to blame a movie for the problems in American society, he reasoned. "Violent movies are an inevitable consequence of violent life." Morganstern acknowledged that some films may "transmit the violent virus" but concluded that they "do not breed it any more than Los Angeles television stations caused the Watts riots" (by broadcasting news about the urban turmoil). Morganstern congratulated Penn for displaying "dazzling artistry" and for showing that a movie could serve as "an ideal laboratory for the study of violence, a subject in which we are all matriculating these days."[15]

Inevitably, these questions about the movie's impact on its viewers came around to Arthur Penn. In a number of discussions conducted both in the weeks after the film's release and in the months and years to follow, interviewers asked the director why his movie portrays bloodshed so graphically and inquired about his reaction to criticisms such as Crowther's.

Penn maintained that the film does not glorify crime. He said that it shows "the squalor, the isolation, the terrible boredom" of Bonnie and Clyde and their gang. These outlaws were in constant flight, argued Penn, and they did not achieve much in monetary rewards for their efforts.[16] Furthermore, Penn pointed out, the death scenes in the movie carry a terrible shock effect. In fact, the murders in the movie become less and less funny and more impersonal as the plot develops. Penn also stressed that he did not invent the violence in the story or try to present American society in an unrepresentative way. The real Bonnie and Clyde were a dangerous pair, and the United States has, in many respects, a violent tradition. Violence was a characteristic of the gangsters of the 1920s and 1930s, he noted, and it was also prevalent on the American frontier. Indeed, America was still a "violent society," he said, because it was deeply engaged in a "ridiculous war" in Vietnam. Penn reflected on American history and concluded that "we have not been out of a war for any period of time in my life-time.

Gangsters were flourishing in my youth, I was at war at age 18, then came Korea, now comes Vietnam. We have a violent society." He observed that "America is a country of people who act out their views in violent ways" and claimed that the country lacks "a strong tradition of persuasion, of ideation, and of law."[17]

When confronted with questions about the danger of violence in the media, Penn compared Crowther's concentration on violent content with the concern of other critics about the depiction of sexuality or juvenile delinquency in the movies. People who became excited about such depictions were often disturbed about problems in society, he explained, and they were looking for a single-cause explanation. Film might be a factor in influencing violent behavior, Penn admitted, but it is only one of many causes and certainly "one of the least pernicious."[18] Violence in the movies could stimulate a viewer, he acknowledged, "but some people are also turned on by music." It would be foolish to try to censor or control such depictions. The question is not even one of good art versus bad art. Even a bad artist—a director who employs violence in an isolated or arbitrary way just to excite viewers—does not deserve censorship.[19]

Penn exaggerated Crowther's criticisms for effect, of course. The *New York Times* writer had not claimed movie violence to be the single cause of contemporary urban problems, and he had not called for censorship of the movie industry. Crowther was expressing his emotional reactions to the motion picture in relation to the modern problem of criminal violence, which was a particular preoccupation of people living in New York City in 1967.

Crowther's other worry—that movies like *Bonnie and Clyde* might inspire copycat behavior—could not be assessed easily. In the years after 1967 social scientists devoted considerable time trying to prove or disprove the theory in terms of its broad applications for violence in film and on television. With respect to television, by 1993 congressional investigators had concluded that research evidence from hundreds of studies had generally supported the conclusion that violent entertainment programs could influence violent personal behavior. As for *Bonnie and Clyde*, certainly most viewers were not going to go out and commit crimes after seeing the movie. In an audience of millions, however, some individuals could be impressionable. Evidently a few viewers did model themselves on the figures they saw on the screen. Shortly after *Bonnie and Clyde* reached Westport, Connecticut, for example, a group of teenagers dressed in 1930s-style clothing brandished a snub-nosed revolver at an armored car outside a bank. They had watched the movie enthusiastically and then went out on a "lark." Unfortunately for the youngsters, their adventure ended when the police arrived, confiscated the gun (a toy pistol), and arrested them.[20] Reports also came in from Atlantic City and the Bronx indicating that women were participating in bank robberies shortly after the movie's appearance at local theaters.[21] The movie also seemed to be implicated in the case of Yancey Morris. After seeing the film, Morris imitated the robbery scenes in thirty-four separate crimes. He liked to think of himself as "Clyde," and he called his girlfriend "Bonnie." Morris received a sentence of thirty years in prison for his modeling efforts.[22] Still more serious was the case of an eighteen year old who was similarly impressed with the movie. Just one-half hour after leaving the theater, he killed the owner of a drive-in grocery store. Apparently he was imitating the activities of Bonnie and Clyde. A leading citizen of the town described the crime as a "senseless murder."[23]

If *Bonnie and Clyde* had not touched so many sensitive nerves in the portrayal of criminal violence, less attention would have been given to its handling of the history of the 1930s couple. Many critics would have accepted the filmmaker's mixture of fact and fiction as allowable exercises of artistic license. In this case, however, the issue of authenticity became integrally tied up with the issue of public accountability. Individuals who were deeply concerned about the new waves of violent crime in the United States worried that a glamorous depiction of the 1930s outlaws would suggest to audiences that armed robbery is worthwhile and murder is emotionally fulfilling. They complained that the movie mixes comedy with tragedy and develops a romantic view of the outlaw pair as heroes of the Depression era. In this disturbingly false account, said the critics, *Bonnie and Clyde* turns violent desperadoes into beautiful lovers and makes an orgy of murder look like a lark.

One of the loudest voices of protest concerning the movie's treatment of history was Bosley Crowther, the same *New York Times* reviewer who claimed that *Bonnie and Clyde* panders violence to its audiences. In three separate articles published in the *New York Times* Crowther expressed outrage over the movie's depictions. He complained that the promoters of *Bonnie and Clyde* hinted in their press releases that the movie offers a faithful representation of the careers of Clyde Barrow and Bonnie Parker. The picture does nothing of the kind, he protested. Crowther called the film a "cheap piece of bald-faced slapstick comedy that treats the hideous depredations of that sleazy, moronic pair as though they were as full of fun and frolic." He considered the blending of farce with brutal killings to be pointless and lacking in taste. Crowther claimed that the picture makes no valid commentary on the truth and amounts to nothing more than "strangely antique, sentimental claptrap."[24]

Crowther's assault and related criticisms about the movie's treatment of history from other reviewers drew attention to questions about authenticity and forced director Arthur Penn to address the issue when he promoted *Bonnie and Clyde* with the press. Penn took an evasive path in his public remarks, sometimes pointing to the lessons his film offers about the American past and sometimes claiming that his picture does not have much to do with history.

Penn made a number of statements that advertised the production's attention to historical detail. In an interview with *Variety,* for example, he claimed that there is no major incident in the picture that did not actually happen.[25] In various other interviews Penn spoke of Bonnie and Clyde as "a product of their times," and he said that he wanted to view them "as historical figures in the social-political situation in which they found themselves."[26] Penn also elaborated on the movie's messages about life in the Southwest during the 1930s. He talked about the local culture that bred figures like Bonnie and Clyde, explained the causes of the crime wave of the early 1930s, and commented on how the automobile had replaced the horse as the principal means of mobility for outlaws. Penn pointed out that Texans in the 1930s were churchgoing, highly moralistic, and "puritanical" people. Whereas outwardly they seemed religious and respectable, inwardly they believed in the morality of violence against other human beings, he claimed. Penn also promoted the notion that Bonnie and Clyde served as folk heroes for poor Americans in the era of the Great Depression.[27]

At other moments in his public discussions, however, Penn seemed eager to distance himself from claims about historical authenticity. In these discussions he referred to *Bonnie and Clyde* as mythology, not an exercise in historical interpretation. At a Montreal press conference in 1967, for instance, Penn said that he had hung his movie on the historical characters of Bonnie Parker and Clyde Barrow but did not "confine" the movie to them. "This is not a case study of Bonnie and Clyde," Penn argued. "We did not go into them in any depth."[28] When Vincent Canby of the *New York Times* asked about the movie's historical accuracy (referring, essentially, to Crowther's criticisms), Penn bristled. He said that the film might be accurate in small details "but not in the big one." Penn observed that "we weren't making a documentary, any more than Shakespeare was writing documentaries in his chronicle plays." He confessed to fabricating aspects of Bonnie and Clyde's life, particularly with regard to their sexual relationships. This was all right, he argued, because the film deals with the "mythic aspects of their lives."[29]

If Penn had not come under criticism from Bosley Crowther and others regarding the film's treatment of historical evidence, he might have continued promoting *Bonnie and Clyde* as a revealing study of a problem in the history of American life. Instead, the excited negative reviews that focused on historical details apparently led Penn to retreat to the role of the artist. Instead of advertising the movie as an informed perspective on the past, he promoted its "mythic aspects."

Although Penn could not completely separate history from myth, many film critics concluded that historical accuracy was not really important. They recognized that the movie's version of Bonnie and Clyde's story probably clashed with the historical record on a number of counts, but they insisted that the film had not been designed as a reflection of reality in the first place. *Bonnie and Clyde* deals "with legend, not life," said Robert Hatch in *The Nation*, and Judith Crist, commenting in *Vogue*, argued that "where the fact ends and fiction begins is no longer decipherable or very relevant."[30] Similarly, a reviewer in *Time* declared efforts to compare the fictional and the real Bonnie and Clyde to be "a totally irrelevant exercise."[31] Richard Gilman of the *New Republic* offered a related point of view, saying that the director had every right to use the sordid lives of the historical Bonnie and Clyde "as pretexts for an imaginative work that is interested in something other than historical truth."[32]

Although a number of prominent reviewers preferred to declare questions about historical authenticity irrelevant, the matter could not be put to rest. Throughout 1967 and in various publications in later years, arguments about the movie's relationship to the real case of Bonnie and Clyde continued to emerge. The controversy would not go away, because *Bonnie and Clyde* contains abundant references to the real case of the Barrow gang, as well as to the physical and social environment in America in 1930s. The movie contains so many links to history that it cannot be treated simply as a work of fiction.

The complex nature of *Bonnie and Clyde*'s relationship to American history can be seen in the record of the movie's production. The men who carried the project forward from conception to production were interested in history, and they traced their inspiration for the motion picture to their reading of a popular book about violent crime in the 1930s. These filmmakers tried to build the framework of their story around the facts in the real case of Bonnie and Clyde. Although they conducted considerable research to ground their story in historical evidence, they did not intend to create a completely authentic docu-drama. Indeed, the filmmakers wanted to include a number of highly interpretive avant-garde elements that would distinguish their movie as a unique work of art.

The idea of making the movie developed from the fertile imagina-tions of David Newman (an editor) and Robert Benton (an art direc-tor) at *Esquire* magazine. Newman came across the story of Bonnie Parker and Clyde Barrow in John Toland's popular narrative about Depression-era gangsters, *The Dillinger Days* (1963). He was fascinated with the reporting on the "bizarre, aberrant" behavior of the criminal couple. Newman observed that Bonnie Parker and Clyde Barrow were famous in their day but largely unknown to Americans in the 1960s. When he came on Bonnie Parker's poetry in Toland's book and learned that the 1930s criminal liked to send her poems to the newspapers, Newman sensed that the characters' history would make an attractive subject for a Hollywood movie. Benton agreed (he was especially in-terested because he had grown up in Texas and recalled hearing sto-ries about Bonnie and Clyde in his youth). The two *Esquire* executives then enthusiastically followed up on their hunch. They began search-ing for additional information about the Barrow gang, looking through old books, newspapers, and detective magazines of the 1930s. New-man and Benton also made a trip to Dallas to speak with people who had known either Bonnie or Clyde and to gather details about the region and its culture.[33] They carried a tape recorder to assist them in studying the Texas speech patterns so that they could create a dialogue that reflected the local culture with "absolute accuracy." Newman and Benton then designed a treatment for the movie's story (a general description of the characters, the scenes, and the story's significance).[34]

Their proposal called for an imaginative approach to filmmaking that would mix a realistic portrayal of the past with artistic innovation. Newman and Benton associated their style with what they called the "New Sentimentality." In an article in *Esquire* they described the con-cept and hinted at the approach they would take in shaping their movie. They described the work of British director Alfred Hitchcock as an exemplar of the New Sentimentality. Hitchcock represented "the manipulation of the audience, the humor of horror, cynical control; tension as art," they wrote. Similarly, in television fare, *The Untouchables* captured the spirit of the New Sentimentality. The television gangsters "are the Real Idea of Television," said Newman and Benton: "the violence; love gets in the way and ruins the scheme; Ness as cynical do-gooder; The Rotten Twenties; the Cult of the Criminal; Kicks for art's sake."[35]

Throughout the development of *Bonnie and Clyde* Newman and Benton thought of contemporary concerns. They tried to design a movie that would offer reflections on life in America in the 1960s as well as the in 1930s.[36] *Bonnie and Clyde* is about "style and people who have style," Newman and Benton wrote after completing the movie. Just as American culture was creating instant celebrities in the 1960s, during the 1930s it produced people like Bonnie and Clyde. But there were differences. When Bonnie and Clyde made headlines in the 1930s, they seemed unusual in comparison to "the general run of society." By the 1960s; explained Newman and Benton, aspects of Bonnie and Clyde's values had become integrated into mainstream American culture. The attitudes and behavior were familiar features in the United States in the later 1960s. Bonnie and Clyde were "wildly aberrant" in their time, yet they "would have been right at home in the Sixties," Newman later explained. Thus, *Bonnie and Clyde* is not only about historical figures; it is also "about what's going on now." The movie allowed them to "use the past to talk about the present."[37]

In addition to giving their film contemporary flavor, Newman and Benton wished to root its story in history. They intended to stay reasonably close (by Hollywood standards) to the real-life saga of Bonnie Parker and Clyde Barrow, and they wanted to incorporate a variety of background materials that would convey to audiences a sense of what life in America was like in the particular setting and time. Newman and Benton's accent on time and place appears clearly in the essay they wrote as a preface to their treatment. In "A Few Notes about This Movie" they described conditions in the American Southwest and Midwest in the early 1930s, discussed the impact Bonnie and Clyde made on people in the region, and pointed out the importance of automobiles in the careers of criminals such as the Barrow gang. Their projected film, then, was to be an imaginative blend of historical and modern perspectives.[38]

Although Newman and Benton created the film project, they could not serve as its producers. They had designed an attractive *concept* for movie but were not in a position to *make* the picture. To attract financial backing for their project in Hollywood, they needed to enlist the services of a producer with impressive credits to his name. Newman and Benton first sought François Truffaut, the respected French moviemaker who produced films that displayed some of the spirit of the New Sentimentality. Truffaut met with Newman and Benton, but he was too busy to take on the project. Later Truffaut told actor Warren Beatty about the proposal in France. Beatty jumped at the opportunity.[39]

Newman and Benton were fortunate in finding a young and dynamic producer who understood their product's potential and would use his influence in Hollywood to the fullest to get the film developed. Warren Beatty, the son of a Virginia school superintendent, was a Northwestern University dropout who had established a fast-rising career as a handsome movie actor. Despite his popularity, in the mid-1960s Beatty was restless, looking for a new venue to test his talents. He searched for a script that could launch his new career as a producer (he intended to act in his own movies), and he found what he was looking for in the document Truffaut brought to his attention. When Beatty returned to New York, he quickly called Robert Benton and arranged to meet with the surprised author within a half-hour. Beatty later explained his tremendous enthusiasm for the Newman and Benton outline by noting the story's relevance to American life in the 1960s. "I guess it was appealing then to see a film about a time when the banks were foreclosing on people," he said. "The unfairness of our society was something that people were becoming aware of in the middle sixties. There was a lot of racial unrest, and the war in Vietnam had eased up to the point where the unfairness of it all was pretty obvious."[40] Convinced of the story's potential for designing an attractive and innovative motion picture, he appealed for support from Columbia Pictures and Universal Pictures. These efforts were unsuccessful. Then he made a strong personal claim with Jack Warner. The actor reportedly got on the floor to beg for funds, saying "Please do what I say. I won't waste your money." Warner replied, "Get up off the floor, kid; you're embarrassing me." Warner provided the needed funds, and Beatty secured 40 percent ownership for the project. Beatty then asked Arthur Penn to serve as the director. Beatty had worked with Penn before and admired his work, especially his skills in crafting a tale about people on the run.

Once Penn came on as director, Newman and Benton saw their control over the project quickly slipping away. They learned that in the movie business, "once there is a director, he is the boss. The absolute boss. . . . Ultimately, his vision becomes the primary one."[41] Penn reworked the script, giving emphasis to aspects that aroused his interest and applying his own imagination to the movie's explanation of Bonnie and Clyde's behavior. Penn also turned to screenwriter Robert Towne, a friend of his, for assistance with the rewriting. Penn found the advice of his neighbor, a Hollywood professional, to be more useful on a day-to-day basis than the counsel of two New York writers who could visit him only occasionally.[42] Consequently, the movie took on features that Newman and Benton had not anticipated when they wrote their original treatment. Some of the artistic flourishes incorporated by Penn and Towne contributed to the story's dramatic appeal, but they strained the movie's connections to history even more than Newman and Benton had done in their original creative design. This flourish helped to make *Bonnie and Clyde* a memorable motion picture, but it also made it more controversial as a statement on violence and as a reflection of the past.

One of the issues that particularly irritated critics who claimed that *Bonnie and Clyde* glamorizes the life of violent gangsters (thereby providing unfortunate role models for movie audiences) concerns the film's messages about the Barrow gang's legendary status. Critics disagreed with the movie's suggestion that Americans in the 1930s viewed the notorious couple as folk heroes. They argued that the filmmaker had blown out of proportion the idea of Bonnie and Clyde's popularity.

The folk hero concept had originated with Newman and Benton. They had pointed out in their notes that America's dispossessed took vicarious pleasure in learning about how Bonnie and Clyde frustrated law enforcement officers. Newman and Benton explained that officers "busted strikes, pushed bread lines, ticketed caravans and, in general, seemed to represent oppressive authority at a time when everything was tough for everyone." Bonnie and Clyde's audacity in embarrassing these lawmen made them "folk heroes" who were followed with interest by millions. Families even sent their children to parties dressed as Bonnie and Clyde and attributed many murders and robberies to them that they did not actually commit, Newman and Benton commented.[43]

Arthur Penn found this historical note so fascinating that he expanded on it and made the concept central to his film. He accented the idea that conditions in the Great Depression made the outlaw couple popular with America's common people. As Penn explained the concept to reporters when promoting the movie, during the hard times of the early 1930s, banks were foreclosing mortgages and folding without reimbursing their depositors. People began to resent these institutions, and bank robbers like Bonnie Parker and Clyde Barrow were sometimes treated as "enormous folk heroes." The times were "out of joint," explained Penn, and people created their "own myths and heroes." Bonnie and Clyde, two dangerous criminals, were unusual heroes, he admitted, but "that is a clue to the times."[44] Robert Towne, who rewrote much of the script for Penn in California, stressed this thesis, too, when speaking to the press. Towne said that the Great Depression was critically important for understanding *Bonnie and Clyde*. Poor, frustrated Americans of the early 1930s resented the "system," he noted. During those hard times, a bank robber might look like Robin Hood to a farmer who was threatened with bankruptcy. Popular outlaws like Bonnie and Clyde "served a very great end," Towne maintained, "by calling attention to grave injustice."[45]

In this manner a note concerning historical background mentioned by the project's originators emerged as one of the dominant themes in the movie's perspective on two criminals. In Penn's eyes, especially, Bonnie and Clyde exhibited heroic qualities, because they tried to attack institutions that symbolized power at a time when many poor Americans blamed those institutions for their troubles. This theme gave the outlaws a degree of audience appeal; the movie seems to say that Bonnie and Clyde were dangerous criminals, but their bold acts expressed the legitimate frustrations of many underprivileged Americans.

Critics of the movie who expressed a concern for historical authenticity found this thesis troubling. To view the two gangsters as folk heroes was to invent an interpretation, they said. *Bonnie and Clyde* contains many fictional excesses designed to convey the message about folk heroes. Much of the material designed to endear audiences to Bonnie and Clyde really came from the history of other gangsters. Critics noted, for example, that the movie shows Bonnie and Clyde refusing to rob an obviously poor customer during a bank robbery (a scene designed to demonstrate that the gangsters preferred to take money from institutions rather than poor people). The producers took this incident from John Toland's book *The Dillinger Days,* said the critics, and the behavior concerned John Dillinger, not Bonnie Parker and Clyde Barrow. Critics noted also that other important scenes in the movie are fictional. For instance, the movie shows Clyde Barrow giving a gun to an impoverished farmer who has lost his home to a bank. The farmer then shows his delight in shooting holes in the bank's foreclosure sign and shooting out the windows of the home that is no longer his. This never happened; it was invented by the filmmakers. In another example of Hollywood's imagination, homeless people who look like extras from *The Grapes of Wrath* try to feed Bonnie and Clyde when they are fugitives. This, too, was Hollywood's invention, said the critics. The scene was designed to suggest that America's dispossessed showed sympathy for the famous gangsters because they had boldly attacked the hated symbols of financial power. As such, said the critics, the movie seems to justify Bonnie and Clyde's behavior.[46]

The critics raised a valid point. In promoting the picture in this fashion, Penn and Towne greatly exaggerated the Robin Hood image. Although some Americans in the 1930s may have been thrilled about Bonnie and Clyde's successes in embarrassing the Establishment, that was not the key factor behind the American people's interest in them. The public's curiosity related especially to Bonnie and Clyde's extraordinary success in evading the law, their reliance on speedy cars to outrun the authorities, their penchant for newspaper publicity, the publication of their homemade photographs in the newspapers (including the famous one showing Bonnie smoking a cigar), their reputation for kidnapping a number of people, including lawmen, and the string of murders they committed without getting caught across several midwestern and southwestern states. People were fascinated with the news about the outlaws, because they wondered how long the gang could continue on its rampage while evading the law. Public curiosity also related to Bonnie's status as a criminal. Famous outlaws of the early 1930s were predominantly male; this case involving a female gunslinger who sent homemade poetry and pictures of herself to the newspapers naturally excited interest. All these qualities made the pair notorious even though they never brought in as much cash as other famous criminals of the era. Bonnie and Clyde never obtained more than a few thousand dollars in any of their bank robberies. In terms of arousing public interest, though, they seemed as important as Al Capone, "Baby Face" Nelson, and "Machine Gun" Kelly.

Arthur Penn's treatment of Bonnie and Clyde subordinated these considerations to the image of Bonnie and Clyde as folk heroes of the Great Depression. Penn accentuated this thesis, evidently sensing that it would have considerable appeal with the disenchanted younger generations of the 1960s. This emphasis helped to make the characters appealing and the story intriguing. It made *Bonnie and Clyde* into something more than just a story about ugly, violent, and vicious criminals.

Penn's interest in treating Bonnie and Clyde as legends in their time affected the characterizations that he developed in the story, and these alterations, too, aroused protests from the critics. Some of the most lively controversy related to the portrayal of Clyde Barrow. When Penn saw Newman and Benton's original document revealing that Clyde had homosexual as well as heterosexual tendencies, he decided to alter the script. Newman and Benton had established this profile from the historical evidence, which contained claims that Clyde had a sexual relationship not only with Bonnie but also with some of the male gang members and probably participated in a *ménage à trois* with Bonnie. Penn believed that it would be difficult to attract audience sympathy for Clyde and excite interest in his romance with Bonnie if the movie concentrated on Clyde's bisexuality. To avoid a "dreary story," Penn fabricated a new sexual characterization for Clyde, one that fascinated movie viewers and contributed to the film's artistic success.[47] He applied a Freudian interpretation to Clyde's personality. Penn made Clyde impotent, the apparent victim of low self-esteem. The film suggests that Clyde was fascinated with guns because he viewed them as phallic symbols. It communicates this concept early in the story, showing Bonnie caressing Clyde's pistol tenderly while he excitedly jerks the match in his mouth up and down. Later in the movie (in scenes fashioned largely by Penn), it becomes clear that, to Clyde, robbery and violence are substitutes for the excitement of sexual intercourse. Near the end of the story Clyde experiences a self-discovery. When Bonnie writes a poem in his honor, suddenly Clyde feels confident. He appreciates the prominence Bonnie has bestowed on him ("You made me somebody they're gonna remember," he says). At last he is able to consummate sexual intercourse.[48]

Penn, building on ideas suggested in the original Newman and Benton materials, accentuated other psychological themes as well to appeal to audiences of the 1960s. He gave Bonnie what he called an "identity crisis," showing her seeking to be "somebody" and fearful of anonymity. Penn's characterization was filled with irony, revealing that Bonnie yearned not only for adventure with Clyde but also for a family life and respectability.[49] With regard to the rebelliousness of the two, Penn (with Newman and Benton) left the explanation hazy, reflecting some of the complexity of rebellious youth behavior in the 1960s. Sometimes Bonnie and Clyde's activities seem to represent an assault against cruel and faceless institutions, sometimes they look like a revolt against authority, and sometimes they appear to be related to emotional fulfillment (the criminals seem to rob and kill just for the thrill of the moment).

Although these personality characteristics of the leading characters made intriguing entertainment, critics complained that the movie fails to reveal adequately the ugliness and viciousness of the real Bonnie and Clyde. They said that the picture presents the outlaw couple as an attractive and interesting romantic pair. Worried that a film like *Bonnie and Clyde* could inspire imitation and contribute to the problem of criminal violence, they argued that the filmmakers should have revealed the true character of the historical figures.[50]

Critics noted, for example, that the real Clyde Barrow was not as attractive and lovable as the figure played by Warren Beatty. The real Barrow had a weak chin and pixie ears, they said. He displayed a sadistic streak in his childhood and enjoyed torturing animals (Clyde loved to break birds' necks and wings). As an adult criminal Clyde was unusually vicious, murdering law officers and civilians at the slightest provocation. John Dillinger described him as "kill crazy," saying that he gave decent bank robbers a bad name.[51]

Critics also pointed out that the real Bonnie Parker did not resemble the tall, striking, and blonde Faye Dunaway. They observed that Parker was less than five feet tall and boyishly slender. She was a hard-faced woman who wore a tattoo on her thigh in honor of her marriage to a man who was in the penitentiary when she met Clyde. During her speeding highway escapades with Clyde, Bonnie suffered bad burns and almost lost her right leg when their car ran out of control and crashed. Local farmers came to their aid, and Bonnie later shot one of the assisting women in the hand. The movie makes no mention of these incidents, and although it shows Bonnie firing guns along with Clyde, the picture does not portray her to be as violent as she actually was.[52]

In short, these critics argued that *Bonnie and Clyde* makes a romantic hero and heroine out of people who were reprehensible criminals. Essentially they supported the conclusions of Bosley Crowther, the *New York Times* film reviewer who described the team as "ruthless killers" and "human rats" and claimed that the filmmakers were "cheating with the bare and ugly truth" when they made the gangsters glamorous.[53] Support for Crowther's assaults came quickly from writers associated with the *Los Angeles Times*. Columns by Robert Joseph and Phil Casey quoted John Toland's *Dillinger Days* to point out the disgusting qualities of the real Bonnie and Clyde. Casey referred to Toland's description of Clyde as "altogether unheroic in physical appearance," and Joseph claimed Clyde to have been a "murderer who killed without giving his victims a chance to draw."[54] Another article in the *Los Angeles Times*, this one by Mike Royko, details the tragic stories of real families that suffered at the hands of Bonnie and Clyde. Royko described the cases of two men who were struggling to make a living during the difficult days of the Great Depression. They had taken jobs as law officers to make enough money to care for their families. Both were killed by Bonnie and Clyde, Royko noted, leaving five children as orphans in one case and a wife with three children and no insurance in the second case.[55]

Critics of the movie were particularly upset about the portrayal of Frank Hamer, the law enforcement officer who helped to trap Bonnie and Clyde in Louisiana. The movie shows the gang capturing Hamer and humiliating him. In the film Hamer is disgusted by the treatment he receives, and he spits in Bonnie's face. Later he seeks revenge by leading the hunt for the Barrow gang. Hamer appears cold, mean, and ruthless. He is dressed in black at the time of Bonnie and Clyde's massacre and generally looks like a stereotypical Hollywood villain. Hamer symbolizes law and order, but he also represents the forces that will ultimately destroy the colorful subjects of the story.

Critics pointed out that the real Frank Hamer never met Bonnie and Clyde until the day of the final confrontation along a road in Louisiana. Hamer was one of the greatest Texas Rangers in history, they observed, having shot and killed a number of desperadoes and coming close to death himself on several occasions (historian Walter Prescott Webb gave a glowing account of his exploits in *The Texas Rangers*). When the head of the Texas prison system invited Hamer to help find the Barrow gang, Hamer was earning a comfortable $500 a month with a Houston oil company. If he had died in the effort to track down Bonnie and Clyde, he would have left his family with severe economic difficulties, the commentators pointed out. Hamer took the assignment out of a sense of duty, and he followed the Barrow gang's trail assiduously for 102 days. Hamer learned as much as he could about the gang members—their eating and drinking habits, their preferences in clothing, their means of communicating with their families, and other information that might assist the efforts. Although Hamer did not crack the case single-handedly (he had assistance from the FBI, state authorities, and others), his efforts were critically important in stopping the desperadoes. Hamer could have been a hero in the movie, said the critics; instead he is portrayed as a humorless, hate-filled, sinister-looking lawman. Detractors of *Bonnie and Clyde* held up this example as proof that the filmmakers approached history with a warped perspective. Too much romantic attention had been given to the outlaws, they argued, and too little consideration had been given to the real heroes like Hamer who fought for justice.[56]

At first glance these complaints about a popular movie's handling of historical evidence may seem like the carping of fact-oriented observers who failed to recognize that they were commenting on a film designed for entertainment, not education. Perhaps their criticisms were irrelevant, because they applied standards of judgment about authenticity that the Hollywood filmmakers never intended to achieve. A closer examination of the movie, however, reveals that the story remained closely tied to the historical record. Despite the many fictional elements added by the filmmakers, *Bonnie and Clyde* faithfully followed the main outlines of the real case of Bonnie Parker and Clyde Barrow. Too much of the factual evidence that Newman and Benton had discovered in their original research was retained in the final script to let the movie escape evaluation for its treatment of history.

The story line of *Bonnie and Clyde* follows the activities of the Barrow gang in many essential details. From its first moments the picture hints of a documentary foundation to its design. Nineteen-thirties-style photographs and brief biography cards appear on the screen to identify Bonnie Parker and Clyde Barrow. The information is correct regarding their dates of birth, where they lived, and what they did before they met each other. The film then shows Bonnie and Clyde meeting in the Dallas, Texas, area, which is where they first encountered each other, and in their first conversations Clyde reveals correct information about his career, including the incident in which he had two of his toes cut off so that he could get off a prison work detail. The movie also accurately portrays the circumstances of Clyde's robbery of a small grocery store and murder of the owner (the real crime took place in Hillsboro, Texas, in 1932 against a proprietor named J. W. Bucher). Just as the real Bonnie and Clyde did, the film's pair travel hundreds of miles to rob, kill, and slip away from the police.

At a filling station they find C. W. Moss. Believing that his mechanical skills might be valuable in their activities on the road, they convince Moss to join them. The details in this segment reflect the historical situation, except the name of the seventeen-year-old person was Daniel Jones. (Later, when in the hands of the police, Jones claimed that he had been forced to join the Barrow gang, and he begged for police protection).

Clyde's brother, Buck (Gene Hackman), soon joins the gang along with his wife, Blanche (played by Estelle Parsons). Both characters are drawn directly from the historical record, including their names. The real Blanche was given to fits of hysteria, just as Parsons plays her. Eventually law enforcement authorities find the gang in a cabin at a motel (this actually happened in 1933 in Platte City, Missouri, and the name of the town appears on a sign in the movie). Buck suffers mortal wounds during a shootout, after which Blanche comes apart emotionally over their troubles (a photograph of the real moment shows Blanche with arms extended, crying in anguish). The movie also shows Blanche blinded in one eye during the shootout (this actually occurred after flying glass hit her in the face during a gunfight).

Toward the end of the movie audiences see that the outlaws, for all their transient living and antisocial behavior, have family attachments. The interest is especially strong in Bonnie's case; she desires to see her mother again. The real Bonnie displayed similar concerns about making connections with her family. The movie also reveals Bonnie's interest in the way that the newspapers reported on their exploits, and it shows her hunger for fame and her attempts to write poetry. All these touches are authentic, including the words of the poem that Faye Dunaway's character reads to Clyde ("Someday they'll go down together / They'll bury them side by side / To a few it'll be grief / To the Law a relief / But it's death to Bonnie and Clyde").

In the final scenes Bonnie and Clyde meet their death very much in the manner of the real outlaws, except that C. W. Moss in this part represents Henry Methvin rather than Daniel Jones. Methvin had joined the gang and, during breaks in its activities, had gone to visit his father in Arcadia, Louisiana. Law officers were tipped off about these visits, and they made a deal with Methvin's father. For assistance in laying a trap for Bonnie and Clyde, the senior Methvin received a promise that his son would not be prosecuted in Texas. Methvin then told his son to slip away from the outlaws as soon as he could. The movie shows C. W. Moss managing to evade his partner during a shopping trip to Shreveport, Louisiana, and it shows the senior Methvin pretending to change a tire on the road to get Bonnie and Clyde to slow down and come within firing range of the law officers who are hiding in the brush. The authorities warn Bonnie and Clyde to surrender, but the pair reach for their guns. A fusillade of bullets then causes instant death. All these details very closely follow the actual events in the last days of Bonnie Parker and Clyde Barrow.

In addition, the movie features a variety of background evidence that signals the filmmakers' attention to verisimilitude. Through props and film clips and other small details, *Bonnie and Clyde* gives audiences a feeling for life in the early 1930s. It incorporates, for example, the singing of Rudy Vallee, a rendition of the popular 1930 tune "We're in the Money," a film clip from the Hollywood movie *Gold Diggers of 1933,* presidential campaign posters for Franklin D. Roosevelt, Burma Shave signs, a segment from Eddie Cantor's radio program, and Ford V-8s (just like the fast cars the real Bonnie and Clyde used to outrun the law). These authentic-looking details help to ground the story specifically in the era when the Barrow gang carried out its exploits.

Thus, the movie remains relatively close to the historical record in many essential details. In cases where the filmmakers strayed from the evidence and applied fictional elements to the story, their editorializing tended to add glamorous qualities to Bonnie's and Clyde's characters or place their actions in more favorable light than did the authors of published histories.

When critics pointed to this evidence of fictionalizing to argue that the movie fails to represent the historical record accurately, they were showing more than just a concern about Hollywood's role as an interpreter of the past. They were interested in the movie's impact on American viewers in the 1960s, concerned that *Bonnie and Clyde'*s depictions of violent crime might somehow arouse people in the audience to commit aggressive acts of their own. Some worried about the cerebral effects, thinking that the movie could inspire others to commit violent crimes because it treats the protagonists as heroes. Others thought about the positive visceral effects, hypothesizing that the graphic scenes of bloodshed could excite the emotions of some people in the audience who were dangerous by nature and highly impressionable.

The gore in *Bonnie and Clyde,* which shocked many viewers in 1967, would become commonplace in many action movies of the succeeding decades. Splattering blood, flying body parts, slow-motion death, and related technical achievements would be featured in numerous crime, Western, war, and science fiction films. Americans became so familiar with graphic violence in the movies that the matter no longer seemed very controversial by the 1970s and 1980s. Similarly, Hollywood began to probe the lives of gangsters with more attention to the human qualities of individual criminals than was common in earlier movies (*The Godfather*, released in 1972, is a good example of the genre). From the perspective of the 1970s and 1980s *Bonnie and Clyde*'s sympathetic look at a pair of dangerous outlaws did not seem extraordinary.

In the context of the 1960s, however, the treatment did excite considerable public interest. During that era social psychologists such as Albert Bandura and Leonard Berkowitz were producing influential scholarship showing that violent depictions on film or television could raise levels of human aggressive behavior in experimental situations. When the National Commission on the Causes and Prevention of Violence issued its report in 1969, it summarized the findings of Bandura, Berkowitz, and others and devoted two volumes to the controversy about violence in the media. The debate had become intense, and *Bonnie and Clyde* served as a popular point of reference for many who argued about the movies' potentially negative impact on human behavior.[57]

Bonnie and Clyde's mythic treatment of its subjects and graphic depiction of bloodshed might have been excused by critics in another age as acceptable artistic flourishes, but in 1967 the issue of criminal violence seemed so pressing that the movie became a popular target for a number of worried and frustrated Americans. These critics directed their anger at the film because they saw it as both an example and a symbol of Hollywood's exploitation of violence. They claimed that the filmmakers were trying to turn the public's fascination with gore into huge profits. The critics' lively comments erupted at an important moment in the tumultuous 1960s—just a few years after graphic violence had become more prominent in the movies and real violence had become much more threatening in American life. Under these circumstances, the debates about *Bonnie and Clyde* revealed the emotions of the American people at an important time in their history, a period when the modern epidemic of criminal violence was first bursting on the scene.

6

Patton

"DELIBERATELY PLANNED AS A RORSCHACH TEST"

In a scene from *Patton,* the general (George C. Scott)
prepares to land on a beach in Sicily. Courtesy of
the Museum of Modern Art/Film Stills Archive.

*T*he American people were growing increasingly frustrated over the controversial war in Vietnam when Twentieth Century–Fox's movie *Patton* reached neighborhood theaters in early 1970. American combat troops had been heavily engaged in the fighting in Southeast Asia for five years, thousands of additional recruits were being transported to the region, and a peaceful settlement still seemed far away. In the United States tempers often exploded over the war. People identified as "hawks" and "doves" argued vociferously and sometimes came to blows. The ranks of the antiwar groups had been growing rapidly in previous years, particularly since the shock of the Tet Offensive in early 1968. Peace advocates held impressive demonstrations in cities around the country involving hundreds of thousands of participants, and more protests were expected in 1970. Many Americans sympathized with the demonstrators' complaints, but they did not themselves feel comfortable about marching or carrying placards. Troubled by the growing casualty lists and frustrated by the misplaced optimism of political and military leaders, they hoped for an early American exit from Vietnam. Hawks were also active in early 1970. They promoted patriotism, spoke enthusiastically about the power of the "Silent Majority," and dismissed critics of the war as naive liberals and hippies. Hawks were generally pleased that President Richard M. Nixon and leading members of his administration shared their disgust for the antiwar protests.[1]

Against this tense background the opening scene in *Patton* initially seemed to be a defense of the hawk's position. It looked like an argument for holding the line in Vietnam. The movie begins with a huge tableau of the American flag forming the setting for a stage. A jumble of voices in the background suggests that the scene is a crowded auditorium. Then a general's cry of "At-ten-shun!" is heard, and the soldiers' conversations quickly stop. A military band plays "The Star Spangled Banner," and General Patton comes to a smart salute. In a series of cuts the film shows close-ups of Patton's uniform and decorations—the cluster of stars, the decorations on his breast, and his pearl-handled revolvers. Patton then tells the assembled men that "the stuff we heard about America not wanting to fight, wanting to stay out of the war, was a lot of horsedung. Americans traditionally love to fight. All real Americans love the sting of battle." He goes on to point out that "Americans have never lost and will never lose a war, for the very thought of losing is hateful to Americans." Patton warns the soldiers that he does not want to receive any messages saying that "'we are holding our position.'" "We're not holding anything," he shouts. "We are advancing constantly and are not interested in holding anything except onto the enemy."

This stunning monologue, one of the most electrifying dramatic beginnings in Hollywood moviemaking, speaks powerfully for toughness in foreign policy, but it also brilliantly hints of significant questions about George S. Patton's posture toward war, questions that emerge through the rest of the movie. Patton's bravado, as the general is characterized by actor George C. Scott, sounds a bit unsettling in the opening scene. The viewer is encouraged to admire Patton's directness and machismo but is also left wondering whether the general appears too enthusiastic about warfare. Later scenes add to this sense of confusion, giving the viewer reason both to respect Patton and to criticize him. The general seems to be a man of courage, brilliance, and foresight but also a man of arrogance, bloodthirstiness, and intolerance.

A reviewer for the *New Yorker* described the contradictory nature of the story poignantly, saying Hollywood's Patton "appears to be deliberately planned as a Rorschach test." Patton could seem like a true hero to people who believe in military values, said the writer. To them, he would be "the red-blooded American who loves to fight and whose crude talk is straight talk." For people who despised militarism, however, the movie would show "the worst kind of red-blooded American mystical maniac who *believes* in fighting." In their eyes Patton would seem to be "symbolic proof of the madness of the whole military complex." In an emotionally powerful way the movie manages to portray the general both as a great man and as a crazy man.[2]

Twentieth Century–Fox's production did provide ample material to excite people with very different outlooks on the Vietnam War. It offered perspectives on Patton that could please or displease, allowing each viewer to walk away feeling that the movie confirmed a personal viewpoint. It was both pro-Patton and anti-Patton and prowar and antiwar (with obvious implications for the Vietnam controversy). This two-sided portrait constitutes an impressive achievement in view of the tumultuous times in which the movie appeared. With so much lively controversy surrounding the Vietnam experience, a drama about a blood-and-guts general who loved the excitement of battle easily could have alienated a sizable portion of its audience. That it did not had much to do with the way the filmmakers planned their production and the way they reacted to the changing conditions in American society during the period of the film's development.

The producer of *Patton* who nursed the movie to maturity was Frank McCarthy, a Hollywood executive with much personal experience working close to military leaders in World War II. McCarthy had been secretary to General George C. Marshall in the war years, and later he served as a brigadier general in the U.S. Army Reserves and as deputy chief of information at the army's Washington, D.C., office. McCarthy had met Patton during World War II, and in later years, when he became a staff producer with Twentieth Century–Fox, he decided that a movie about the controversial military figure could have tremendous box office potential. Patton was arguably the war's most successful field commander, a flamboyant and self-centered man, and a maverick. McCarthy recognized the general's brilliance in matters of war, but he also understood that Patton had "several Achilles Heels." Patton was a complex man, and to McCarthy this added up to "fine drama." In 1951 he proposed a movie about Patton to Twentieth Century–Fox's head of production, Darryl Zanuck, and won immediate approval. McCarthy then encountered many frustrating setbacks, and he was unable to complete his production for another nineteen years.[3]

One of the first objectives in planning the movie project was obtaining cooperation from the U.S. Army. This support seemed crucial, since portrayal of Patton's World War II battle scenes would require the use of much army equipment (tanks, trucks, cannon, and the like). Through the Department of Defense, Hollywood had received such valuable cooperation for the making of many war movies, and McCarthy did not expect great difficulty as he planned his new production. He was painfully surprised to discover, however, that the road to U.S. Army cooperation was bumpy.

Both the army and Patton's family placed obstacles in front of the movie project. At first some of the army brass feared that a motion picture about Patton would be heavily critical of the general. They thought that the film might give excessive attention to Patton's image as a man who slapped soldiers, acted in a rebellious manner toward the military establishment, and sought war with the Soviets. Representatives from the army and the Department of Defense wanted to be convinced that the script would please them. They also insisted that McCarthy win approval from the general's widow. Such a blessing could not be obtained, for Mrs. Beatrice Patton was not happy about the prospect of a movie dealing with the World War II career of her late husband. She felt that the media had been unfair to the general during the war years. Through a lawyer, she complained about an invasion of privacy and insisted that a Hollywood motion picture was likely to portray her husband inaccurately.[4]

When Mrs. Patton died in 1960 McCarthy thought he had an opportunity to move the project forward. He pressured the army to cooperate, saying that the story of Patton's military career was clearly in the public domain, and the army was improperly holding back support as a favor to members of the general's family. After some hesitation army leaders became more cooperative, but they still recommended that McCarthy seek a blessing from the surviving members of Patton's family. McCarthy tried and failed. Two of the three Patton children protested. Both were connected to the army (George S. Patton II, a lieutenant, and a daughter who was married to a career officer). George S. Patton II was particularly resistant. Sounding very much like the late general, he announced he would "shoot any S.O.B. who makes a movie about my father." His lawyer repeated the previously stated doubts about any movie's potential to deal with the general's life accurately, and he threatened legal action if the project went forward. This warning disturbed the assistant secretary of defense for public affairs, Arthur Sylvester, who expressed concern about the legal issues. Thus, McCarthy still lacked a full-fledged expression of support from the army.[5]

Then, in 1964, the project received a much-needed boost. Ladislas Farago's excellent 800-page biography *Patton: Ordeal and Triumph* appeared. The biography provided an excellent source of information about Patton, one that could free Hollywood from the various difficulties about ownership of the story. Darryl Zanuck and his son Richard quickly purchased the rights to the book. The senior Zanuck had been pleased with the box office receipts from *The Longest Day*. The 1962 production realistically depicts the D-Day experience in World War II, and Zanuck hoped that a cinema version of Patton's career could also draw a substantial audience. Zanuck worked a new deal with McCarthy (who had moved to Universal Studios) and announced that Mc-Carthy would produce the film through Twentieth Century–Fox.[6]

The U.S. Army had now turned cooperative, but its assistance seemed to come too late. Very little World War II equipment remained in the U.S. armories. The Defense Department no longer could offer McCarthy the battle hardware he needed to make his movie, and McCarthy had to look elsewhere for help. Fortunately, he discovered that the Spanish army was using much U.S. World War II–vintage military equipment, and the Spanish also had a fair amount of German hardware from Franco's days of friendship with Adolph Hitler. Furthermore, the variegated geography of Spain provided excellent settings for filming Patton's campaigns from North Africa and the Mediterranean to France and Germany (sections of Spain look very much like these locations). Finally, filming in Spain was relatively inexpensive.[7]

Twentieth Century–Fox attempted to settle any remaining questions about influence over the portrayal. Fox bought the rights to two additional Patton biographies and agreed to submit scripts for the examination of the U.S. military. Fox also asked the government to pass the script on to Patton's children. This offer was a gesture of cooperation; Fox did not request the family's approval of the script drafts.[8]

To begin planning the movie about Patton, McCarthy realized that he needed to build up his knowledge base about the general and the historical background of the war years. He consulted numerous books dealing with Patton, as well as books about General Omar Bradley, Dwight David Eisenhower, Field Marshal Sir Bernard Law Montgomery, Winston Churchill, and others. Particularly useful was General Omar Bradley's personal account, *A Soldier's Story* (Bradley's memoir gave McCarthy valuable ideas for the screenplay during the early planning, and the book continued to serve, along with Farago's volume, as a key source of information). McCarthy also turned to Eisenhower for help, and the former war hero and U.S. president provided useful assistance. Eisenhower wrote a "personal and confidential" letter that offered a "personal evaluation of my old friend." He spoke candidly of Patton's strengths and also of his faults. Eisenhower revealed that he had intervened on several occasions to protect Patton from efforts to remove him from command during the war, and he suggested that General Omar Bradley was a more balanced, effective, and competent commander than Patton. The former president appreciated Patton's genius for pursuit, however, saying that he defended Patton during the war when he received criticism "for some publicized and foolish episode."[9]

As in the case of many Hollywood films, several hands helped to shape the screenplay. Calder Willingham began the work by developing a treatment from McCarthy's notes and collected books. Francis Ford Copolla, recently out of film school, then turned the treatment into a script. For a brief time, however, while William Wyler was assigned as director, Copolla's script fell into disfavor. In 1967 McCarthy assigned Jim Webb to the script. Eventually Franklin Schaffner took the director's job, and at that time Edmund North received the call to rewrite Copolla's script.[10]

Several leading actors were invited to play Patton. George C. Scott was an early favorite of Zanuck's, and McCarthy agreed with Zanuck's recommendation, but Scott complained about a lack of subtlety in Jim Webb's characterization of Patton and refused to play the part. McCarthy then tried to enlist Burt Lancaster, Robert Mitchum, Lee Marvin, Rod Steiger, and John Wayne, without success. Eventually Scott agreed to work with Edmund North's revision of the original Copolla script. Scott proved to be a difficult partner for the filmmakers, however, especially for director Franklin Schaffner. Scott frequently took issue with the language in the script and complained about the difficulty of portraying Patton with adequate sophistication.[11]

Thanks to Scott's interest in creating a multidimensional character, as well as to McCarthy's commitment to presenting a representative portrayal of Patton's complex personality, the figure who appears on the screen demonstrates complex qualities. The multifaceted nature of the screen portrayal also owes much to the political pressures of the times. During the lengthy period that the *Patton* script was in development—1965 to 1969—the political environment in the United States changed dramatically, and the writers, the producer, and the director of *Patton* could not help but be influenced by the events. What had begun as a supposedly large-grossing movie about a popular historical figure turned out also to be a project with relevance to contemporary American politics. As such, *Patton* had potential for stirring a great deal of political controversy.

At first attention focused on the likelihood of bringing in huge profits by making an exciting movie about a genuine American hero. The idea of presenting a largely positive perspective of Patton was particularly evident in the detailed treatment for a screenplay that Calder Willingham prepared for Darryl Zanuck and Frank McCarthy in 1965. Willingham discussed Patton's character with McCarthy and then read the many books and notes McCarthy made available to him and inter-

viewed people who knew Patton (individuals referred to him by Mc-
Carthy). On completing his initial work, Willingham was enthusiastic
about the film's prospects for exciting audiences. "Given a first-class
production, I don't see how this picture can help but be an absolutely
staggering smash," he wrote. Patton's heroism would serve as the principal bait to hook the viewers. "Patton is a misunderstood and unap-
preciated hero of his country," said Willingham. A movie about his war
exploits would be a tremendously "human" story. It would become an
"exciting, thrilling action picture combined with an immensely moving portrait." Patton, said Willingham, "is an immensely appealing man
as well as heroic, and that's gold Frank, pure sheer gold." The movie
"could gross God knows how much money," said Willingham, and be
"a fantastically successful picture at the box office," as well as "an historic picture of enduring importance." Willingham confessed that he
was "touched again and again with inspiration" as he tried to design
the treatment, and he speculated that an actor like Burt Lancaster could
not fail to win an Academy Award in the role of Patton.[12]

Almost five years passed before the film outlined in the McCarthy-
Willingham discussions of July 1965 became a finished product. During that period American attitudes about the Vietnam War went
through dramatic transformations, and the filmmakers could not remain insulated from these developments. The story they were trying
to tell about a war hero from the past began to carry significant meaning for the controversies of the present. As the filmmakers discussed
the messages of their film and considered how to publicize them with
the press, they had to explain their portrait of Patton in the context of
modern-day questions about the American people's relationship to war
and the role of the military in American society.

In the 1965–69 period public opinion toward U.S. involvement in
the Vietnam War moved from general support for intervention to much
division about America's purpose in Southeast Asia. By 1969–70 many
Americans had became strongly disillusioned about U.S. involvement
in the fighting in Vietnam. They were disturbed about the rising U.S.
casualties and uncertain about how long it would take to convince the
North Vietnamese to surrender. Many began to think that the United
States could not win the war, and a number questioned the morality
of their country's destructive intervention in what seemed to be a civil war in a distant land. Discontent over the experience in Vietnam
prompted new questioning about U.S. military actions. Many criticized
the history of U.S. foreign policy, speaking of militarism and imperial-

ism, and a number expressed strong antiwar sentiments. Against this background a gung ho Hollywood portrait of a wartime military hero such as the one suggested by Calder Willingham could meet much audience resistance. Surely many viewers would not look kindly on a movie that celebrated the career of a battle-hungry cold warrior. Furthermore, many of these viewers would not be receptive to a film that romanticized war generally. Movie audiences of the Vietnam era were not like the audiences that watched *The Sands of Iwo Jima* enthusiastically in 1949 and cheered the memory of "the good war." In 1970 Americans had a distinctly "bad" war on their minds.

The producers of *Patton* were aware of the potential problems in making a movie about war at a time when antiwar sentiment was growing stronger. They did not want to present their story simply as a tale of guts and glory. Describing their plans for the movie to reporters in 1968 and 1969, producer Frank McCarthy and the man he selected as director, Franklin Schaffner, were quick to point out that the movie would not take a romantic view of armed conflict. "This is not a war film," said McCarthy.[13] He claimed that anyone watching the scenes his crew shot in Almeria, Spain, would see a graphic picture of the horrors of battle and appreciate the film's antiwar qualities.[14] Schaffner tried to anticipate controversy. He said that he did not expect to encounter any "pacifist" protests against the movie, "since our film will be distinctly antiwar." The picture, he emphasized, "will not sentimentalize or glorify Patton, nor will it be the usual kind of war movie."[15] McCarthy and Schaffner stressed that *Patton* was not going to idolize the general known as "Old Blood and Guts." McCarthy told reporters that his movie would present a close-up portrayal of Patton with "all his faults as well as his virtues," and Schaffner focused on a number of the general's less-endearing qualities when talking about the subject of his film.[16] Schaffner emphasized that Patton "was misguided and a man after a headline." He said that the general "hated peace and wanted to start trouble with the Russians." Schaffner reminded reporters that Patton "began to fall apart" after the war, but he also said that "we were lucky to have him during the two years that we needed him."[17]

To provide a means of viewing Patton with sympathy while recognizing his faults, the filmmakers stressed the idea that Patton represented an anachronism. They placed numerous references in the movie to Patton's chivalrous mentality and suggested that he was, in many ways, a sixteenth-century man trying to live in the twentieth century. They had German officers in the movie describe Patton as a "pure warrior" and made Patton appear to support this impression by saying, "God, how I hate the twentieth century." The screenplay shows Patton disliking automated warfare, yearning for the days of hand-to-hand combat, and wishing that he and Erwin Rommel could square off against each other in tanks (in a sort of jousting match) to decide the outcome of the war. The last scene places a windmill in the background, suggesting elements of *Don Quixote*.[18]

Patton moves cautiously across the minefield of public emotions about war and military leadership by presenting a carefully constructed dual image of the controversial general. *Patton* reveals the general's warts as well as his halos. It manages to depict his courage and genius while also showing that Patton's leadership could produce mangled bodies and broken men. The movie demonstrates Patton's extraordinary knowledge of military history, but it also shows that the general failed to integrate some of the fundamental moral lessons humanity could draw from the experience of war.

Much of *Patton*'s perspective is positive. The movie portrays George S. Patton as probably the most resourceful and effective general in the entire Allied command. German military leaders constantly voice praise for him, acting as if he could become the key factor in their defeat. They fear his movements and hold back troops from critical areas of battle to stand prepared for an attack from Patton's army. Audiences see why the Germans fear him so greatly; Patton possesses vast knowledge of the history of warfare and is able to understand the psychology behind his enemy's strategy. It seems almost impossible to stop him.

The movie shows Patton setting high standards for his men—even regarding the rules about proper military dress and decorum. At first the officers and men in his army think that his demands are excessive in view of the rough conditions they face in the North African desert. They soon realize, however, that Patton's standards help to mold a highly efficient military unit that is able to overcome earlier setbacks and drive out the Germans.[19]

The movie also shows Patton as a cultured and humane person. He is fluent in French, a connoisseur of fine wine and food, and a talented poet. His toughness can be tempered with warmth, as in the case of his encounter with a soldier in a hospital who was badly wounded in battle. On seeing the heavily bandaged youngster, Patton appears to shed a tear. He bends down, whispers some words of appreciation in the ear of the mangled warrior, and kisses his forehead.

The picture also portrays less-appealing aspects of Patton's character. For example, it leaves the viewer curious about the general's flamboyant style. Although Patton often seems to be colorful and dashing, he also appears to be arrogant, intolerant, and insensitive. He is driven by the idea of racing against British field marshal Montgomery so that he can win honors for defeating the Germans—even if it costs unnecessary loss of life for many American soldiers. Patton expresses so much enthusiasm for the war that the viewer becomes puzzled in interpreting the movie's message. When Patton says, "I love it. God help me, I do love it so," it is not clear whether the filmmakers want audiences to marvel at this winning display of aggressiveness, believe that Patton reflected a subtle sense of guilt when he asked God to help him, or think that Patton was insane. The movie leaves viewers wondering: did Patton make this statement because he believed that war is man's noblest undertaking, or does the comment demonstrate his lack of appreciation for the tragedy war can bring to soldiers and their families? The movie's portrayal of Patton makes the viewer ask whether America needs more generals like Patton in wartime (men who hunger for the opportunity to lead in battle) or more men like George Washington and Dwight D. Eisenhower (generals who were eager to finish an unwanted burden and retire from military life). The movie effectively forces these choices on the viewers, and it refuses to answer the questions definitively.

Patton displays several aspects of the general's character that raise questions about his state of mind. The film shows, for example, that Patton believed in reincarnation and talked as if he had been a warrior in ancient battles such as the Roman victory over the Carthaginians. In another segment the film shows Patton worrying in 1944 that the fighting may end before he has a chance to fulfill his glorious destiny. The scene takes place at a time when Patton has been denied a command. The general reports with frustration that some Germans tried to assassinate Hitler a few days before. "First thing you know, it'll all be over," says Patton, as he contemplates the possibility of a settlement without further contributions from him. Toward the end of the movie viewers see Patton making controversial statements that seem to be grossly simplistic observations about complex matters. Patton shows a willingness to allow former Nazis to take up key positions in postwar Europe and expresses eagerness to use Nazi and American troops to go after the "mongoloid Russians." War should not stop so quickly, he laments, because the United States will have to fight the Bolsheviks sooner or later.

These extraordinary comments leave viewers wondering what to make of Patton. Did his unorthodox beliefs about reincarnation reflect the thinking of a mystic? Did his preoccupation with destiny reveal an extreme egotist who would easily sacrifice lives to realize personal glory? Did his readiness to cooperate with some Nazis suggest insensitivity about the enormity of their crimes? Was his attitude toward the Russians an example of the worst kind of cold war fanaticism? In these matters, too, the movie does not deliver easy answers. It offers disturbing evidence but also makes Patton appealing in the broad context of its character study. The picture allows some viewers to dismiss the questions as largely irrelevant. Patton's extraordinary statements may seem to be only colorful comments from a "character" who enjoyed exaggerating his thoughts for maximum effect. At one point the movie hints that Patton consciously shaped his lively language, suggesting that even his best friends were not certain when he was serious and when he was acting. Against this complicated presentation of contradictory evidence, the movie lets viewers build their own assessment of the general.

Patton's treatment of the U.S. soldier's experience in war is similarly mixed. Although the movie does not convey the gung ho attitude of the earlier John Wayne stories about fighting in World War II, it does show how victorious armies can experience moments of glory. *Patton* displays U.S. soldiers being cheered by grateful Sicilians after liberation from Nazi control, and it reveals the tremendous pride U.S. soldiers took in contributing to the Allies' victories. Yet the film also demonstrates the ugly face of war, showing, for example, a body with legs blown off and the charred, smoking remains of an American soldier.

While working cautiously with the controversies about Patton and their implications for the times, the filmmakers also tried to present an objective picture. They hoped to create a reasonably authentic and well-documented portrait of the controversial general. The scriptwriters worked carefully with the evidence to identify people and places properly and to understand the chronology of military developments in North Africa, Sicily, and the European campaign. They drew much of the language Patton used in the movie directly from the historical record. For example, the speech George C. Scott delivers in the film to a women's group in England is almost a verbatim copy of the presentation Patton gave during the war, and the crew filmed the scene in the town where Patton made his comments.[20]

In some instances the filmmakers twisted the facts to support their story, but they did not take extraordinary liberties or dramatically misrepresent the historical record. For example, Patton spoke with a high-pitched voice, but actor George C. Scott played the role with his familiar gravely voice (the producers thought that Scott would sound unnatural if he attempted to imitate Patton completely).[21] The filmmakers also made some figures from history interchangeable so that they could limit the number of principal characters. For instance, they attributed the language of British field marshal Alan Francis Brooke to another British field marshal, Bernard Law Montgomery (Montgomery already had a key role in the story, and Brooke could be overlooked). Thus it is Montgomery, not Brooke, who says in the movie, "Don't wince, Patton. I shan't kiss you." Patton replies, "That's a pity, sir, because I shaved very closely this morning in preparation for getting smacked by you."[22] A more serious twisting of the evidence came in the manner in which the movie gives almost all the credit to Patton for driving Rommel out of North Africa. Historians of World War II have acknowledged more debt to the British than the film allows, and they have recognized the value of General Dwight D. Eisenhower's planning.[23]

The movie contains a number of themes that threatened to irritate British audiences. Not only does it underplay the important British contributions to Allied victories in North Africa, the Mediterranean, France, and Germany, but it also pokes fun at British soldiers and their leaders. The film makes their army appear to be less virile than Patton's army. It shows British soldiers wearing Scottish kilts performing a march in front of husky Americans who are somewhat bemused by the sight. Then the bagpipe music of the British army is drowned out by the hearty sounds of an American military band that strikes up "The Stars and Stripes Forever."

From the standpoint of international relations, the film particularly risked controversy treating the British military hero Field Marshal Montgomery with less than reverential respect. *Patton* portrays Montgomery as a haughty, spoiled, almost effeminate leader. It shows Montgomery waddling like a duck, wearing shorts, acting like a perfect snob, and speaking in what one movie reviewer described as an "anyone for tennis?" voice. The producers were trying to accentuate the differences between Patton and the field marshal and to dramatize a keen sense of competition between them. To create interest they juxtaposed the image of a muscular, crusty, swearing general with the image of an aristocratic, well-groomed, condescending one. Their portrayal had some basis in fact: Montgomery was a supreme egotist, and he was also, as he appears in the film, somewhat small and frail. The overall thrust of the portrayal is to exaggerate contrasts out of proportion, however, and it leaves viewers wondering whether this effete snob really could be the great British war hero. McCarthy knew he was flirting with trouble when he was designing the script. In 1967 he confessed, "We don't see much of the British in this movie, and their great hero, Montgomery, doesn't come off very well." McCarthy said that he hoped the filmmakers would "take every opportunity to build [the British] up and justify them from the audience's point of view even when American leaders are highly critical of them." He also told the writers to "bear in mind that Great Britain and the Commonwealth constitute by far our largest audience outside the United States."[24] Despite these recommendations to work carefully with the sensitive topic, the final version of *Patton* raised eyebrows in the United Kingdom. A number of British viewers expressed dismay at the shoddy treatment of their soldiers and their national hero.[25]

Less controversial, but equally challenging for the filmmakers in terms of crafting an exciting interpretation of history, was their handling of Patton's slapping of an American soldier. The filmmakers realized that the incident could serve as a critical turning point in the story, and in many ways the success of their character study would hinge on the way they handled this important moment in Patton's career. McCarthy and his associates decided that they needed to probe the psychology of Patton's behavior to make the incident understandable.

There were actually two slapping episodes, but the filmmakers simplified the story by focusing only on the case of Charles H. Kuhl. The incident occurred after Kuhl, an American soldier, had been admitted to an aid station in Patton's army. Kuhl received a diagnosis of "exhaustion." Evidently he was suffering psychological trauma from his experiences at the front, and his medical tag read, "Psychoneurosis anxiety state, moderately severe." Patton visited Kuhl while walking through the tent holding wounded soldiers. Seeing that Kuhl lacked obvious physical injuries, he asked what was the matter. "I guess I can't take it," Kuhl replied. Patton exploded in anger. He slapped Kuhl with his gloves, kicked him in the pants, called him a coward, and demanded that an officer send the "gutless coward" back to the front. A group of corpsmen then took Kuhl to a ward for examination and found he had a 102-degree temperature and chronic diarrhea. Also, a blood test showed that he was suffering from malaria. When the news of the incident reached the press back in America, many demanded that General Dwight D. Eisenhower put the reins on Patton. Shortly afterward Patton lost command of the Third Army.[26]

McCarthy reviewed evidence from a variety of books as he considered ways to explain Patton's behavior. He found that some authors, such as General Omar N. Bradley, appeared to defend Patton, explaining that Patton was simply trying "to purge the soldier of 'cowardice' by shaming him." McCarthy, however, thought that audiences would have difficulty understanding Patton's actions if they did not see the buildup of the general's emotions. McCarthy and the writers solved the problem by showing Patton driving along a road on which badly battered soldiers are marching. The scene in the hospital tent follows, beginning with Patton's visit to the beds of seriously wounded men. Against this background, Patton's outburst does not necessarily look like the act of a violent madman; it could appear to be a heartfelt expression of anguish from a general who deeply appreciated the courage of his fallen soldiers and was moved emotionally on seeing their desperate condition. Still, there is a vicious, almost uncontrolled look in George C. Scott's eyes when he lambastes Kuhl. The movie leaves a double message, explaining Patton's act and placing it under question.[27]

In a number of respects the filmmakers made considerable effort to render small details of history accurately and realistically. In planning the battle scenes, which were huge, complexly staged events, McCarthy and Schaffner accompanied General Omar N. Bradley on a tour of the sites of Patton's World War II campaigns. Then they traveled through Spain to find locales that nicely matched the appearance of the sites in North Africa, Sicily, and France. The sandy region of southeastern Spain has the appearance of the African desert, for instance, and snow-covered forests outside Segovia represent the Ardennes during the Battle of the Bulge. The Spanish army happily cooperated with the filmmakers by providing 3,000 soldiers to play the roles of both American and German soldiers. Spain also contributed hundreds of authentic World War II vehicles and the personnel to run them (including more than 200 tanks with crews).[28]

In attempting to depict the violence of World War II activities in a dramatic fashion, the filmmakers sometimes flirted with trouble. *Patton* features numerous spectacular explosions in which military vehicles blow into the air and moving tanks burst into flame. The American special effects artists and stuntmen on the set boasted that they had accomplished the tricks without experiencing even a small powder burn, but their Spanish counterparts were less effective in monitoring for safety. One Spanish stuntman suffered serious injury during an explosion and was in danger of losing his leg.[29] Injury on the set to humans, however, did not attract nearly as much press attention as the issue of injury to animals did. International controversy broke out when societies for the protection of animals in the United States and Britain criticized the filmmakers for using real mules for a scene in which Patton shoots two of the animals that are blocking traffic on a bridge. In the film Patton points his gun at the animals and fires. Soldiers then are seen tossing the carcasses into a river. An extra in the film told reporters that the crew killed the animals with strychnine and had also clubbed a donkey to death and blown up a horse by tying dynamite to its belly. Although the report brought the movie some unwanted publicity, it did not hurt its box office success. A few years later, however, the controversy surfaced again when *Patton* was to make its first appearance on television in the United States. In deference to humane society interests, the television version of the movie did not show the soldiers dumping the dead mules off the bridge.[30]

As for *Patton*'s handling of the most controversial issue—the general's zest for battle—most of the reviewers commented favorably, noting that the movie managed to handle the prickly topic fairly during a time of great sensitivity about the nation's painful experience in Vietnam. A headline in the *Wall Street Journal* read, "Viewing Patton: Pick Your Angle"; *Variety*'s headline reported, "Left, Right Hail War Picture," and the *Los Angeles Herald-Examiner* said "'Patton': Reaction Divided."[31] Richard Cuskelly of the *Herald-Examiner* noted that the movie makes General Patton seem like a monster to some and a genius to others. Even though the movie was a political film released during the period of the Vietnam War, noted Cuskelly, it could be greatly appreciated by both the Left and the Right. Liberals might watch the movie and say, "See, that's the sort of freak America produces . . . and idolizes during wartime," whereas conservatives could leave the theater commenting, "what we need are more leaders and Americans like Patton."[32]

The principal actor in *Patton* was pleased to see that movie reviewers appreciated the film's complex message. George C. Scott said that he had not wanted to play Patton as a "standard cliche," an "obvious gung-ho bully," or a "hero to please the Pentagon." Evidently Scott was reluctant to portray Patton in a completely favorable light because of his growing disenchantment with the Vietnam conflict. Scott admitted to reporters that he had been a hawk earlier but had become pretty much a dove, and he called the war in Vietnam "an obscenity." He said that he found many things to hate about Patton, yet he admitted respecting some of his qualities as a human being. Scott said that his main goal was to show the many facets of the man. He was generally pleased with the outcome, although he regretted having to please so many masters—the producers, the Pentagon, General Bradley and his book, and the Zanucks, to name a few.[33]

The producer and director were similarly pleased. Frank McCarthy said that he was glad he had not given in to pressures to take one stand or another. He wanted balance. Director Franklin Schaffner also said that he was happy about the balance. He said that he had aimed to make a biographical picture about a war figure that would not romanticize or falsify history in the style of the old movies starring Errol Flynn, John Wayne, or Clark Gable. Schaffner claimed that he had "wanted to see if biography could be done objectively"[34]

Not everyone could tolerate the movie's lack of a final judgment on its subject. Some reviewers thought that the filmmakers owed audiences an interpretation. For instance, Tom Ramage, writing in *Boston after Dark,* noted that the producers attempted a "balancing of the books" throughout the movie, juxtaposing favorable and unfavorable examples and taking caution not to go too far in one direction without quickly presenting equal evidence leaning in the other direction. This created a shortcoming. Ramage said that he was not asking for extreme deification or debunking, but the movie "should have made a judgment about the man behind the uniform."[35]

Some who called for a point of view made reference to the Vietnam conflict and asked whether there were lessons in Patton's story for contemporary times. One of the angriest criticisms of the movie's caution came from Peter Schjeldahl in the *New York Times*. Schjeldahl said that the film went "wrong" in "its fidgety refusal to deal with any of the issues it raised along the way." He said the movie plays "with the fires of political controversy" but always scrambles "to evade the pointed moral questions upon which it is always verging." Schjeldahl thought that *Patton* elicited thought about "some ambiguities in our national character and on the agony of our current history" but that the producers took the easy way out of controversy. He said that they avoided questions about how one person could be responsible for the deaths of hundreds of thousands of young men by painting Patton as a historical aberration, a Don Quixote. Schjeldahl felt "a justifiable urge to start throwing things at the screen" when he saw such great questions answered simply with the idea that the man was an anachronism. The producers should have addressed the relevance of the issues they raised, he insisted. "The differences between Patton publicly crowing about the million or two German casualties he had inflicted and a faceless aide [today] reciting in a modest tone the latest body count from Vietnam seems largely . . . one of style," Schjeldahl wrote. The spirit of old "Blood and Guts" was still evident in war-torn America. "Old generals don't die; they just make way for new generals."[36]

Interestingly, *Patton's* relationship to the Vietnam controversy took on new importance when one of the movie's most enthusiastic fans tried to draw contemporary lessons from the story portrayed on the screen. The individual was Richard M. Nixon, president of the United States. In the spring of 1970 Nixon was trying to decide whether he should sanction an invasion of Cambodia. The president had supported secret bombings of the country adjacent to Vietnam in an attempt to stop North Vietnam from supplying the communists in South Vietnam, but the infiltration had continued. The heroic image of General Patton seen in the movie helped to give the president courage to make a controversial decision about Cambodia. Nixon watched the movie with his family on 4 April 1970 and then watched it again on 23 April. A few days after his second viewing of the movie, Nixon gave the order to send U.S. and South Vietnamese troops into Cambodia. In tough language the president told a television audience, "we will not be humiliated, we will not be defeated." With Patton-like pride he declared that when the chips are down "the world's most powerful nation" should not "act like a pitiful helpless giant." He said that he would rather be a one-term president than have two terms at the "cost of seeing America become a second-rate power and to see this Nation accept the first defeat in its proud 190-year history."[37]

The college students' reaction to Nixon's decision was extraordinary. Many interpreted the invasion to mean that the United States was expanding its role in Southeast Asia rather than contracting it. On many campuses students met in emergency meetings, planned rallies, marched in demonstrations, and demanded that classes be canceled. In some locations the demonstrators attacked university property and local businesses (nonstudents who visited the campuses joined and sometimes led these activities). Strikes broke out on nearly 450 campuses. At Kent State, a public university in Ohio, national guardsmen assigned to the campus fired into the crowds of young people and killed four students.[38]

Despite the upheaval and tragedy, Nixon continued to manifest his enthusiasm for *Patton*. Discussion of the movie came up a short time later when the president brought forty-five business and financial leaders to a meeting at the White House to shore up confidence in his economic and war policies and, by implication, his leadership. Nixon asked the visitors whether any of them had seen *Patton*. After watching several hands go up in the crowd, he reminded the visitors of the way that the movie showed the general rescuing men trapped in the Battle of the Bulge. Nixon recalled that various generals thought Patton's plan could not work, yet Patton succeeded in completing "perhaps the greatest movement of forces in the whole history of warfare in a short time." The president described with particular pleasure the scene in the movie in which Patton calls in a clergyman the day before an invasion. Patton demands that the chaplain deliver a prayer for good weather on the day of battle. Nixon considered this story to be relevant to his own situation, telling the audience that "we have every chaplain in Vietnam praying for early rain." He received a burst of applause after concluding, "You have to have the will and determination to go out and do what is right for America." A short time later Nixon flew to his estate at San Clemente and brought along a 16-mm copy of *Patton*. He took the film to edify his staff. Presidential assistant Bob Haldeman urged members of the White House team to examine the movie so that they could better understand Nixon's behavior during a critical time in his leadership. One of these individuals, Secretary of State William Rogers, later saw Twentieth Century–Fox chairman Darryl Zanuck and reported that the president was a walking ad for the movie. *Patton* "comes up in every conversation," reported Rogers, who noted that aides frequently discussed the movie in the back corridors of the White House.[39]

Nixon's infatuation with *Patton* attracted interest from Hugh Sidey, a noted journalist who had been irritating Nixon at the time because of his critical articles. Sidey thought that the president's fondness for the World War II general was very revealing. He pointed out that Patton experienced much criticism and endured rejection, yet he remained steadfast in pursuing goals that seemed impossible (Nixon liked to see himself in the same pattern). Patton had the courage to take the bold stroke. Furthermore, Patton was a complex man, and so was Nixon. For a president who had just made a highly controversial decision about invading Cambodia, Patton's model served a useful purpose. It encouraged Nixon to hold the line despite the public uproar. Sidey questioned the wisdom of this approach, however, suggesting that the president might be drawing the wrong lessons from Patton's story. He referred to anthropologist Margaret Mead's reading of Nixon's interest in the general. World War II was different from the Vietnam War, Mead argued, and Nixon could be mistaken if he handled the challenges of 1970 in the manner that Patton dealt with the challenges of the 1940s.[40]

Despite his great admiration for the general's style, Nixon was unable to show nerves of steel when facing a national uproar over his decision to invade Cambodia. He made forceful declarations in a television speech announcing that America would "not be defeated," but he began to back off from a complete defense of his actions within a few days. Had General Patton been alive, he probably would have been disappointed by the president's shaky handling of the crisis.

Publicly Nixon pulled away from the truculent position he had established when he first announced the incursions into Cambodia, but privately he imitated the toughness of Patton. Nixon now demanded a much more aggressive posture in dealing with antiwar groups. He called in his staff and asked them to be tough with congressional critics. At the same time that he was promoting his interest in the movie *Patton*, he called in leaders from the CIA, the FBI, and the Defense Intelligence Agency. Nixon wanted these agencies to take bolder action in their intelligence and investigatory activities, and he told his staff that he was disappointed in the agencies' lack of aggressiveness. Nixon observed that the FBI and CIA had failed to quell the uproar during the period of antiwar demonstrations. He conveyed an interest in more unorthodox measures to deal with the problems. This discussion of tough treatment of student radicals and others who supposedly endangered the nation's security encouraged a member of the administration, Tom Huston, to make a proposal to the president calling for spying on private individuals, interception of the mails, and burglarizing homes. Nixon approved this extraordinary recommendation, but FBI director J. Edgar Hoover and Attorney General John Mitchell objected to it and convinced Nixon to put the plan aside.[41]

According to the president's top assistant, Bob Haldeman, May 1970 "marked a turning point for Nixon." He now gave more enthusiastic encouragement to secret activities, including a program of domestic surveillance. This mentality took Nixon and his men directly on the path to the Watergate scandals, and evidently the forceful model seen in *Patton* inspired the president to come out fighting.[42]

The lessons of *Patton* did not seem as obvious to the American public as they did to President Nixon. The population remained divided in assessing the leadership of the World War II general and in speculating on the film's meaning for the United States in 1970. Although some approved of Patton's toughness and sense of conviction, others were troubled by his enthusiasm for war. Some marveled at Patton's prescience in recognizing the need to destroy Soviet power as early as 1945; others felt that the movie served as a useful reminder of how cold warriors can draw the nation unnecessarily into armed conflict if they are allowed to influence American foreign policy. In these and other respects, the mixed public reception showed that the filmmakers had realized a unique achievement. Their movie had, indeed, served very much like a Rorschach test. It allowed people with diverse points of view to read their own messages into the multidimensional story about a complex figure from history. *Patton* helped Americans to articulate their heightened feelings with respect to the struggle in Vietnam and war in general.

PART 4

ACCENTING HEROISM

Celebrating the "Great Man" in the Documentary Style

7

All the President's Men

"THE STORY THAT PEOPLE KNOW AND REMEMBER"

Carl Bernstein (Dustin Hoffman) and Bob
Woodward (Robert Redford) investigate the
Watergate mystery in *All the President's Men*.
Courtesy of the Museum of Modern
Art/Film Stills Archive.

Warner Brothers' 1976 release *All the President's Men* gave audiences a powerful reminder of the ugly Watergate scandal that had destroyed the Republican administration of Richard Nixon just a few years before. The movie shows how *Washington Post* journalists Bob Woodward (played by Robert Redford) and Carl Bernstein (played by Dustin Hoffman) discovered and exposed corruption in the White House. It covers the early period of Woodward and Bernstein's investigations, showing the tremendous difficulties the young journalists faced in obtaining information, their determination to pursue the case despite many frustrating setbacks, and the excitement they experienced in discovering that the trail of scandal reached all the way to the highest office in the land. *All the President's Men* succeeds in making the complex web of intrigue understandable through a study in personalities. It reveals how two men with very different backgrounds and styles developed a cooperative relationship and managed to crack one of the most important political cases of the twentieth century.

Although the focus on personalities gives life to a story that otherwise might have been a confusing and perhaps boring examination of Washington shenanigans, the movie's concentration on Woodward and Bernstein's activities leaves the impression that the two journalists almost single-handedly brought down President Nixon's administration. Other major figures who contributed to the discovery of corruption receive almost no attention in the motion picture. Like many examples of cinematic history from Hollywood, *All the President's Men* tends to glamorize the achievements of a few individuals and overlook the roles of other people and other causes behind historical developments.

Despite this shortcoming, *All the President's Men* delivers a remarkably sophisticated glimpse of an important historical episode. It shows the tedious work of investigative journalists, presenting an inspiring story about the value of perseverance in the face of difficult obstacles. Furthermore, it demonstrates a commitment to authenticity throughout. With careful attention to detail, the filmmakers intelligently re-created the physical and mental environment in which the two newspaper reporters worked in the federal capital. Finally, the makers of *All the President's Men* succeeded in delivering an emotionally strong message. They made a powerful moral statement about the Watergate crimes. Few Hollywood films have offered such a boldly opinionated picture of an important episode from American political history. Indeed, the achievement was even more impressive in view of the timeliness of the subject. At the time of its release, the movie did not deal with a controversy from America's distant past, one for which the emotional partisanship had long passed. Rather, it presented judgments on a very recent political crisis, and the object of its criticism—the Nixon administration—still attracted many sympathizers in 1976.

The individual most responsible for bringing *All the President's Men* to the screen was Robert Redford, an accomplished movie actor who liked to work with stories about determined individuals who challenge "the system." Redford became fascinated with the activities of Woodward and Bernstein and sought the journalists' approval to make a movie about their exploits. After winning their support, he guided the film project through much of its development and helped to give the final production its committed and hard-hitting style.

Redford had been eager to produce a movie that reflected on Richard Nixon's leadership. Ever since his youth Redford had disliked Nixon. When he was thirteen years old Redford had received an athletic award from then-senator Richard Nixon. Years later Redford recalled that he "never believed a word [Nixon] said" at the event. On shaking Nixon's hand, he felt "absolutely nothing . . . it was just empty." As an adult Redford wondered why journalists did not sense President Nixon's insincerity and comment on it honestly in their publications. After revelations came out about Nixon's involvement in the Watergate scandals, Redford confessed that he wanted to believe that the president was responsible.[1]

Before news of the Watergate case broke in the press, Redford had not demonstrated much interest in politics. In fact, for many years he had not even shown much commitment to a career. In the years before he moved into acting, Redford had drifted into a number of different endeavors. He won an athletic scholarship to the University of Colorado but took little interest in his studies and received poor grades. Eventually he dropped out of college and engaged in a variety of jobs, operating a jackhammer, shoveling oil slick, and clearing pipelines.

Then he went to Europe for thirteen months to try his hand at sketching. Redford worked as an artist in Paris's Montmartre section. Later he moved to Florence to enroll in an art school. Frail from a poor diet and running out of money, he returned to the United States. Redford then married Lola Van Wegenen and enrolled in the Pratt Institute in New York. There he studied scenic design but soon took up acting on the advice of a friend. A lead role in Neil Simon's hit play *Barefoot in the Park* put him on the road to fame and fortune.[2]

Redford's success allowed him to be selective in his choice of scripts, and by the early 1970s, he was showing an interest in stories with political messages. Redford appeared in *Three Days of the Condor*, which deals with deceit and assassination in a CIA-type operation, and *The Candidate*, a story about a naive son of a former governor who is promoted for high office by a group of politicos. *All the President's Men*, however, was the film to which he gave the most personal enthusiasm in this period of his career.

The genesis of *All the President's Men* came during the presidential election campaign of 1972. At the time Redford became intrigued with the work of the two reporters for the *Washington Post*. He noticed that Woodward and Bernstein, obscure journalists with the newspaper, were publishing extraordinary revelations identifying the trail of wrongdoing in the Watergate break-in. Journalists for other prominent papers, such as those at the *New York Times*, as well as reporters associated with network television, on the other hand, offered relatively little new information. Why were they not as aggressive in pursuing the truth, he wondered? One day, when Redford was on a train in Florida to promote his movie *The Candidate*, he posed the question to some news reporters. The reporters gave him a cynical response, indicating that Watergate was business as usual in the nation's capital. The public probably would never learn the truth about the scandal, they speculated. Redford was appalled by the tone of the remarks, and as he read more articles by Woodward and Bernstein, he thought about turning their story into a movie.

As Redford learned about the character and background of the two reporters, the concept looked more and more appealing. Woodward and Bernstein reflected quite different personalities and styles, he discovered, yet they worked together effectively. Woodward was a graduate of Yale and a commissioned officer in the navy. He joined the *Post* from a position of privilege and was expected to rise quickly. Bernstein had been struggling to get ahead at the *Post* since he began as a copyboy at the age of sixteen. With less impressive credentials than Woodward, he won his assignment to the Watergate story by building a reputation as a scrappy competitor who relentlessly chased a story. Woodward was a WASP, Bernstein a Jew; Woodward was cool and controlled, Bernstein nervous and excitable. A movie about how these two men learned to work together in their sleuthing operation seemed very promising, Redford thought.[3] A study of contrasting personalities could provide an emotional hook to grab the audiences' interest.

Shortly after the November 1972 elections, Redford tried to contact Woodward and Bernstein to sound out his proposal for making a film about their reporting experiences. At the time the journalists were too busy with their investigations to give Redford much consideration. Bernstein did not return the actor's call, and Woodward explained to Redford that he could not break away from his work to arrange a meeting. In April 1973 Redford tried again. He told Woodward that he would be in Washington, D.C., for a screening of *The Candidate* and invited him to visit for a chat. Woodward came by but could not stay long. At the time Watergate events were breaking fast, for Nixon's top aides, Robert Haldeman and John Erlichman, had just resigned, and the president's counsel, John Dean, had been fired. Woodward did hear enough, though, to understand that Redford was still quite eager to make the movie.

During this time, the spring of 1973, Woodward and Bernstein had a book contract with Simon and Schuster. The journalists wondered how they were going to continue covering the scandal for the *Post* and complete the manuscript. When Bernstein heard that their lives could be further complicated because of a movie project, he replied, "First, let's get the damn book done." Redford persisted, and in time the parties worked out an agreement. Woodward and Bernstein received $450,000 for the movie rights to their publication. During their discussions Redford offered tips about the approaches the authors might take in their writing. He pointed out that readers were likely to be more interested in a book about *how* they discovered the information on Watergate than in a book that just reported *what* they discovered. Bernstein considered this recommendation to be misdirected. He thought that readers would react negatively to a volume that focused on the activities of two reporters; he worried that the format would make the two of them look egocentric. In time, though, *All the President's Men* did take the shape Redford recommended, and two years after publication Woodward acknowledged that "Redford was a factor in getting us to write the kind of book we wrote."[4]

After Redford achieved an understanding with Woodward and Bernstein, he sought cooperation from leaders at the *Washington Post*. Presenting an authentic picture of the operations of a major newspaper required assistance from these insiders, he thought. If his movie was to present a realistic depiction of the people at the *Post* and the working environment there, it would be important to gain access to the offices. Woodward wanted to talk with key figures in the operation and to observe the day-to-day activities. Katharine Graham, publisher of the *Post*, was wary, however. She preferred to keep a low profile for her newspaper and worried that the *Post* would appear to be congratulating itself for successful detective work if it cooperated extensively with the moviemakers. She also realized that the newspaper could not influence the movie's treatment of its activities in the investigation of the Watergate scandal. Giving the moviemakers free rein could result in some embarrassing portrayals. "Our interests are not the movie's interests," Graham explained. "I am concerned about having no control of what is in the movie." Graham did not even want Redford to use the *Post*'s name in the movie. That request was completely unacceptable for the producer/actor, for he intended to stage *All the President's Men* as a carefully designed reenactment of actual events.[5]

Graham's initial discomfort disturbed Redford and his associates. They thought that the resistance represented a form of censorship, something about which newspaper people are usually eager to complain. Redford thought that it would be ludicrous for individuals at the *Post* to tell him essentially that he could not make the movie. "What a bunch of garbage that would be," he observed later. "It would have been censorship, and movies are a medium just like newspapers, magazines, or books."[6] Redford left the clear impression that the movie was going to be made with or without the *Post*'s cooperation, and that it would be wiser to give the project a supportive blessing. Evidently Graham appreciated this reality. She did not say yes to several of Redford's requests, but she did not say no either, and the cooperation moved forward.

Ben Bradlee, the *Post*'s respected executive editor, represented another potential obstacle. Bradlee's cooperation was important, since he would be a prominent figure in the story (actor Jason Robards played his part). Bradlee thought that "journalists belong in the audience, not on the stage," and he worried that the reporters would have little recourse if the movie portrayed them inaccurately or unfairly. "Just remember pal," he told Redford, "that you go off and ride a horse or jump in the sack with some good-looking woman in your next film—but I am forever an asshole." Bradlee reminded Redford that the *Washington Post*'s leaders "will forever be known as we are portrayed in this movie." Despite these reservations, Bradlee cooperated, and he came to appreciate the finished product considerably.[7]

There were more challenges ahead, for Redford and his associates encountered difficulties trying to design an exciting script about the lives of investigative reporters. The Woodward and Bernstein saga contained no sex and violence, and the action in the story involved telephone calls, interviews, and note-taking. Also, Woodward and Bernstein's large book contained far too many incidents and events to include them all in a screenplay; deciding what to include and what to cut was not easy. Additionally, the public appeared to be sick of the Watergate story, which received media exposure day after day. Furthermore, no matter how carefully the writer worked to create excitement and suspense in the drama, audiences would know how the case turned out. How could the screenwriter make such a story riveting drama?

To face these challenges Redford sought help from an accomplished Hollywood writer who had prepared the screenplay for an earlier Redford movie, *Butch Cassidy and the Sundance Kid*. William Goldman brought impressive talent to the task, but his first effort to shape the complex record into an interesting movie script encountered difficulties. The Woodward and Bernstein book was packed with names and facts, and no obvious story line came to mind as Goldman went through his reading of it. The writer worked on a number of schemes for a screenplay and supplemented his understanding of the events with additional reading. Eventually he decided to throw away about one-half of the book and concentrate on the journalist team's early experiences in the Watergate investigation.[8]

At first it seemed that Woodward's would be the more difficult character to work with, but Bernstein became Goldman's bigger source of troubles. Goldman thought that Bernstein would be easier to create on paper because of idiosyncrasies in his personality. Woodward seemed to be particularly hard to develop as a main character in a movie because, as he admitted himself, "I'm especially boring. The way I live and work is undramatic."[9] In time, however, Goldman learned a great deal about Woodward's activities and viewpoints, because the young journalist became extremely cooperative. Woodward spent numerous hours with Goldman reviewing evidence and discussing particulars in the story. An early meeting with Bernstein, however, introduced a sour note in the relationships. Goldman made a remark about the incompetence of the White House conspirators, observing that they did a clumsy job with break-ins and cover-ups. "It's like a comic opera," he joked. Bernstein took offense. Goldman's remark seemed to diminish the difficulty of Bernstein's journalistic achievements and suggest that his discoveries were easy in the face of resistance by hapless adversaries. Discussions between the two became tender.[10]

Later a new element of tension emerged. Redford was partly to blame for the new difficulties, although his motives were decent. In an effort to encourage the cooperation of Woodward and Bernstein in his movie project, Redford had invited the journalists to contribute ideas regarding the script. Redford's openness apparently gave Bernstein incentive to take an aggressive role in mapping out a strategy for the screenplay. Rather than comment quickly on Goldman's initial draft, Bernstein held back his remarks and spent time ironing out some ideas of his own. Eventually Bernstein gave Redford a draft of a script plan that he had prepared with his friend Nora Ephron. This version presented Bernstein as an aggressive reporter and a Don Juan with women, while it characterized Bob Woodward as a colorless Elmer Fudd. Goldman was visibly shaken by the implied criticism of his work and Redford's suggestion that he should give Bernstein's script a serious reading. Redford resolved the crisis by turning down the proposed revision, telling Bernstein that "Errol Flynn is dead." The experience disrupted the production schedule, however. Goldman had difficulty getting back on track, especially when *Time* magazine reported that Bernstein had criticized his draft. Emotions became strained, and Redford recognized that he had made a bad judgment in placing Goldman in a delicate situation. His well-intentioned efforts to ensure that the screenplay would benefit from the input of the historical figures being portrayed on the screen brought mixed results. It worked in the case of the Woodward-Goldman relationship and backfired in the case of Bernstein-Goldman dynamics.[11]

The ultimate success of *All the President's Men* depended on more than just the screenwriter, of course. It rested on the shoulders of a number of production personnel, including the talented chief cinematographer, Gordon Willis. Above all, Redford received valuable assistance from the director of the film, Alan J. Pakula. Pakula had made a number of films, including *Klute*, which Redford liked very much. Most important, Redford was impressed by his direction of *The Parallax View*, a movie that effectively communicates a sense of conspiracy and fear. Redford waited until relatively late in the project to appoint Pakula. He had initiated overtures with other directors but was not successful in securing their services, and then he had to wait until Pakula was available. The delay also concerned Redford's desire to maintain control over the film for as long as he could. He wanted to get a strong version of the script in place before a director came on board. Redford understood that once the director took charge, that person would have the primary authority for establishing the film's direction.[12]

In trying to make the movie effective as drama, Pakula realized he faced a special challenge that other Hollywood directors did not usually confront. He wanted *All the President's Men* to re-create the journalists' experiences authentically, and that would require a realistic portrayal of their tedious work. Somehow he had to develop a sense of excitement out of a story of day-to-day research. Pakula needed to make routine activities—telephone calls, personal interviews, and examination of documents—appear interesting and important. He needed to show that the materials Woodward and Bernstein used—typewriters, pencils, pads, and library cards—served as important weapons that could bring down some of the most powerful men in the country. Pakula also wanted the story to show that journalism typically involves not the fast-paced dramatics seen in the 1931 Hollywood movie *The Front Page* but rather day in and day out plodding in pursuit of a lead. Investigative reporting is not physical, Pakula observed; it is intellectual. The production team needed to imagine ways to make this cerebral experience understandable to movie audiences.[13]

The principal solution was to design a documentary-like story that would establish a strong sense of realism. Pakula wanted the film to have "immediacy." *All the President's Men* would bombard viewers with so many authentic-looking details that viewers would feel as if they were present at the scene of history when watching the picture. The actors would look very much like the historical figures; sets would be designed to resemble the places where events actually occurred, and, through a television set placed in the offices of the *Washington Post*, viewers could see news broadcasts showing some of the real players in history (such as Richard Nixon, Richard Kleindienst, Ron Ziegler, and Spiro Agnew). Furthermore, in maintaining the documentary style, the film would not give audiences some of the advantages of perception typically featured in the movies. For example, in scenes showing Woodward and Bernstein asking questions over the telephone, viewers would not see the individual at the other end of the line. By limiting the audience's information solely to the voice heard over the phone (exactly what the reporter experienced), viewers would sense better the difficulty of trying to interpret a respondent's comments without seeing the individual's facial expressions. This format would also make audiences sensitive to the journalists' difficulty in extracting information from a conversation before the person at the other end chose to hang up. Pakula wanted audiences to see only what the reporters saw so that they would better appreciate the tensions reporters experienced.[14]

Bob Woodward thought that Pakula succeeded in capturing "the fundamental essence of journalism." Recalling the director's work on the film years later, Woodward praised Pakula for appreciating that, in journalism, "information is king." Journalists must pursue facts in difficult ways, seeking out individuals who will give them leads, Woodward explained. Interviews add up to no more than pieces of a puzzle. Some witnesses are noncooperative, others are cooperative, and some are cooperative but in ways that the journalist only partly understands. Lacking a complete picture of what happened, the journalist feels vulnerable. "You're out there," wondering why other journalists are not writing about the story that begins to take shape in your mind, explained Woodward. Pakula effectively communicated the sense of "wonderment" and "doubt" that an investigative reporter experiences—"the emotional and psychological dimensions" of journalism. During the time of production, Woodward thought that a story about the monotonous pursuit of names "can't possibly interest anyone." Yet Pakula managed to make his motion picture compelling by portraying the journalists' experiences "exactly as we lived," he said.[15]

Pakula and his colleagues also employed a number of artistic devices to communicate their message about the importance of journalism in sustaining American democracy. They found an opportunity to do this, for example, by focusing closely on a page in a typewriter in the opening moments of the movie. A tremendous pounding follows, and viewers become aware that a microphone close to the typewriter is amplifying the noise as the machine's keys print out the date of the Watergate break-in. The typewriter appears to send out cannon shots, suggesting the power of the press in exposing assaults on freedom. Later in the story audiences see Woodward and Bernstein flipping cards in the Library of Congress, searching for a sort of needle in a haystack that may provide a clue to the location of the Watergate trail. The camera then travels upward to the heights of the cavernous room. This scene cost $90,000 to photograph, but it was worth the price, for it intelligently communicates a feeling for the tremendous challenges the reporters faced in searching for leads in a bewildering maze of documents. The filmmakers also used lighting to convey a message about the workings of democracy. They shot scenes representing the *Washington Post*'s offices in bright, clean light and shot scenes around Washington, D.C., in darkness and shadows. The former suggests openness and honesty, whereas the latter suggests a secretive, menacing environment.

Following the plan to design the movie with documentary-like authenticity, Pakula and the production crew gave considerable attention to small historical details in the set design. Indeed, they made a greater effort to ensure the historical correctness of the props than was really necessary, for movie viewers were unlikely to take notice of these many details. Still, the care given to historical re-creation helped Redford and Pakula to advertise their movie as a realistic representation of the actual historical conditions and events. Their promotional literature stressed that the movie reproduces the environment of Woodward and Bernstein's investigations with considerable integrity.

Much of the work toward authentic re-creation went into the set design for the *Washington Post*'s offices, the location for many of the movie's scenes. Members of the production team visited the newspaper's Washington, D.C., offices, obtained architects' blueprints for the building, consulted with the firm that handled the interior decorating, and took hundreds of slide pictures of the rooms. After finishing this research they designed and constructed a 35,000-square-foot representation of the *Post*'s newsroom in Burbank, California (at a cost of $450,000). When executive editor Ben Bradlee visited California, he felt as if he were in his own office.[16] The production designers also gathered an abundance of authentic materials from the *Post*'s newsrooms to accent their commitment to verisimilitude. Sitting on the 200 reporters' desks seen in the film were 1972 calendars (with dates changed to match the date for the scene being shot). Also on the desks were 1972 telephone directories and 1972 newspapers (again, dated according to the day in the drama). Set designers also arranged to have 270 cartons of paper from the *Post*'s offices shipped to Burbank. These letters, pamphlets, newspaper clippings, copy papers, carbons, and reporters' notes were then distributed around the Burbank set and placed in the trash cans under each desk. In scenes showing the break-in at Watergate the filmmaker used $100 dollar bills in sequential order, just as the real burglars did, and they used the same model walk-ie-talkies.[17] Again, movie audiences were not likely to know about the care given to these details (unless they read the movie reviews), and the specificity in these historical re-creations did not significantly affect the film's interpretation of the Watergate story. Nevertheless, the efforts to use authentic materials made good advertising copy when promoters praised the motion picture as a serious examination of recent American history.

The producers' commitment to authenticity also appeared in the choice of locations and in the choice of actors. The filmmakers shot the scenes of the Watergate break-in at the Watergate complex in Washington, D.C., and they filmed scenes showing the burglars' lookout across the street from the Watergate complex at the Howard Johnson's motel where the stakeout actually occurred. In choosing actors the casting directors sought individuals with a strong physical resemblance to the people in Woodward and Bernstein's story. Promotional literature emphasized the resemblances. Publicity photos juxtaposed portraits of Robert Redford with Bob Woodward, Dustin Hoffman with Carl Bernstein, and actor Stephen Collins with CREEP treasurer Hugh Sloan. The similarities in physical appearance were striking, particularly in the case of the actor playing Hugh Sloan. In one minor role the representation was perfect. Frank Willis, the night guard at the Watergate building who reported his discovery of a taped door latch to the police in June 1972, played himself.

The makers of *All the President's Men* also put key production and acting personnel through a rapid course of instruction regarding the life of a *Washington Post* journalist. Several actors and technicians visited the *Post*'s offices in Washington for weeks at a time, including director Alan Pakula, writer William Goldman, Robert Redford, and Dustin Hoffman. The visitors sat alongside reporters while they performed their daily work, accompanied them on research assignments, attended meetings of the newspaper's editors, and generally observed language and behavior around the newsroom. Redford gravitated toward the editors in these visits, while Hoffman spent a great deal of time sitting in with reporters and clerks. An assistant director also joined the team in Washington and took abundant notes (he observed, for example, that contrary to popular images, little smoking took place in the newsroom). Some of the actors with less important roles received a lecture in California from one of the *Post*'s West Coast editors. To strengthen the portrayal of the burglars, Pakula talked at length with one of them (Bernard Barker), as well as with one of the police officers who conducted the arrest. A researcher for the movie spoke with one of the burglars' lookouts, who had operated from across the street.[18]

These efforts to approximate the historical reality, while admirable, could not guarantee that *All the President's Men* would examine the Watergate story with sophistication. It was not enough that Redford and Pakula got the furniture right in the *Washington Post*'s offices or hired actors whose features closely resembled the appearance of the actual figures in Washington, D.C. Redford and Pakula could cram each scene with authentic-looking details yet misinform their audiences about the lessons of the past.

One of the greatest temptations the filmmakers needed to resist was the tendency for a movie about crusading newspaper reporters to give a glamorous portrayal of the principal characters. It would be easy to make Woodward and Bernstein seem like national heroes. The filmmakers could depict the two journalists as humble giant slayers who brought down some of the most powerful men in the country by using their typewriters as weapons. The movie does this to a degree, and in this regard it misrepresents the story of how the president and his aides fell from power. Numerous other individuals helped to break the secrets of Watergate—journalists, members of Congress, judges, and special prosecutors, for example. *All the President's Men*, as might be expected, assigns an inordinate amount of credit to Bob Woodward and Carl Bernstein. Indeed, when the movie had its debut in Washington, D.C., many of the Watergate investigators who had made important contributions to the discoveries were upset that the film gave no attention to their activities. Other people were "more consequential than us," Woodward recalled years later, but "in a way they didn't exist," since *All the President's Men* did not deal with them. A movie has special power, Woodward noted, because the history it portrays "becomes the story that people know and remember."[19]

What people would know and remember in years to follow was, indeed, shaped by this popular motion picture. The image of the heroic investigative reporter remained strong in the public mind, especially for those who were poorly informed about politics. Talk about the Watergate case frequently referred to the story of the two young men from the *Washington Post* who uncovered details of the scandal. Easily overlooked in these discussions were the contributions of important figures who were not portrayed in *All the President's Men*, individuals such as federal judge John Sirica, special prosecutors Archibald Cox and Leon Jaworski, Senate Select Committee on Campaign Practices chairperson Sam Ervin, and a host of other figures.

Although the movie gives substantial credit to Woodward and Bernstein for breaking the case, it does at least recognize some of the journalists' flaws. *All the President's Men* reveals occasional overeagerness on the part of Woodward and Bernstein, who are seen bending some of the rules of their profession to extract information from the potential sources. In the movie Woodward and Bernstein bluff, cajole, deceive, and threaten as they try to shake details about the Watergate story loose from people who evidently know some clues to the puzzle. The journalists even extract some valuable information from members of a grand jury (clearly a violation of the law). Also, they reveal human qualities. Bernstein appears to be perpetually nervous in the movie and frequently stutters; Woodward seems to be a plodder—hardworking but conventional in style and socially unexciting. Neither demonstrates romantic interests.[20]

Although it shows some of the reporters' questionable activities, the movie never addresses questions about their ethics frontally. Woodward and Bernstein did, after all, get access to the credit card records of Watergate trickster Donald Segretti. The journalists also obtained phone records through a friend that helped them to trace links between the burglary and the activities of the Committee to Re-Elect the President. Was it proper for Woodward and Bernstein to break into private information for a good cause? The movie considers the question only briefly. Dustin Hoffman, portraying Bernstein, says, "George, I really feel bad doing something like this. You know that." George replies, "Don't give me any more of your liberal shit, okay Carl?" This is as close as the film comes to acknowledging that the supposed heroes may have assumed too easily that good ends justify questionable means.

Key figures at the *Washington Post*'s office also reveal some shortcomings in the movie. The *Post*'s editors get credit for their courage in pursuing the Watergate scandal with more energy than other managers in American journalism showed, but they are also seen as a disputatious, egotistical group. The editors compete aggressively with each other for influence over the newspaper's reporting; infighting and jockeying for position are evident in their deliberations (Goldman wrote these scenes into the script after witnessing similar competition at meetings at the *Post*, and some of the newspaper's editors were not pleased with the revealing dialogues he incorporated in the screenplay).[21] Furthermore, *All the President's Men* shows some of the editors demonstrating considerable uneasiness when Woodward and Bernstein produce their revelations. The managers worry that if they publish the reports, someone will sue the newspaper for libel, or leaders in the Nixon administration will become angry with the *Post* and complicate the reporters' efforts to cover events in the nation's capital. The editors' attitudes reflect the realistic concerns of executives who want their organization to win Pulitzer Prizes for investigative reporting but also are fearful about the risks involved when publishing shocking news reports. The movie's portrayal has basis in fact. The president was quite angry about Woodward and Bernstein's articles. When tape recordings of conversations in the White House were released a few years later, they revealed that Richard Nixon wanted to pressure the Federal Communications Commission not to renew the *Post*'s six radio and television broadcast licenses.

In dramatizing the story of Watergate, the makers of *All the President's Men* could have limited their movie's scope to an examination of the break-in and the discovery of those responsible for it and its cover-up. But the moviemakers also aimed at a much larger target. They traced connections between the break-in and other lawbreaking activities carried out under the Nixon administration that constituted significant challenges to government under the Constitution. In fact, *All the President's Men* provided a valuable history lesson worth repeating to a public that suffered historical amnesia in the years following Watergate. Too many Americans forgot what was at stake in the scandal, and consequently, they considered the crisis to be far less serious than it really was. *All the President's Men* offered them a useful reminder.

In the years after Nixon's resignation a significant portion of the American public believed that the former president had not committed crimes any more serious than those perpetrated by various other scandal-blemished presidents. Many of these people remembered Nixon fondly for his foreign policy achievements (opening relations with Communist China and improving the United States' relationship with the Soviet Union, for example), and they regretted that Nixon's supposedly small miscalculations in the Watergate matter tarnished his reputation badly (this interpretation was particularly noticeable in the public's responses to news of Nixon's death in 1994). They pointed out that other leaders in the White House had made mistakes, but Nixon got caught. Many claimed that the liberal media—Nixon's longtime enemies—brought him down by relentlessly publicizing his errors.

This distorted assessment gained popularity in the years after President Gerald Ford pardoned Nixon, and indeed, the pardon had a great deal to do with the warped perspective. If Richard Nixon had faced criminal charges, the public would have received a lengthy reminder of the Executive Office's alleged complicity in a wide range of political scandals. Court proceedings and news coverage would have lasted months, perhaps years, and the public would have gained a more thorough understanding of the breadth of the crisis and the role of the White House in it. Instead the public got only a limited lesson on the case's importance. Through media coverage of the investigations, particularly television broadcast of the Senate subcommittee hearings on Watergate, viewers received an excellent introduction to the problem. But television did not bring closure on the matter. The televised hearings aimed to discover what had occurred, not to punish the guilty. A courtroom was the appropriate forum for that kind of settlement. Watergate conspirators eventually were sentenced to prison and served time for their crimes, but the sentencing usually occurred away from the glare of television lights and at a time when public interest in Watergate was beginning to fade. More important, President Richard Nixon never had to confront definitive judgments about his own role in the Watergate affairs. Consequently, many Americans assumed that his transgressions were not very great. A number even speculated that, had the president revealed everything he knew from the moment of the June 1972 break-in, he could have finished his second term in office. These assumptions contrast sharply with the realities. The House Judiciary Committee voted for impeachment of the president on three major counts. If Nixon had experienced the impeachment process in the Senate and later had faced criminal proceedings without a presidential pardon, his apparent connections to the Watergate activities would have received more meaningful exposure.

There are several moments in *All the President's Men* that refer to the breadth of the Watergate crimes. The issue is addressed most directly near the end, after Woodward and Bernstein have been chasing the complex trail of evidence for months. The two reporters are still confused about the goals of the conspirators, and they are uncertain about how high the trail of criminal responsibility stretches into the upper ranks of the national government. Woodward then meets his contact— a White House insider whom he calls "Deep Throat"—and describes some of the facts he has learned in tracking the road to the break-in at the Watergate complex. Deep Throat warns Woodward that he and his partner are getting so bogged down in details about that story that they are missing the bigger picture. The informant urges Woodward to think about the broader meaning of the evidence he has studied. The conspirators, says Deep Throat, bugged conversations, followed people, designed phony press leaks, and faked letters. They canceled Democratic party campaign rallies, investigated the private lives of leading Democrats, planted spies, and stole documents. Woodward should recognize that the crimes involve much more than just a break-in at party headquarters, Deep Throat concludes. A short time later Woodward meets the informant again, and Woodward expresses frustration about his difficulty in getting to the heart of the crime. Deep Throat then reminds Woodward again to cast his eyes in high places. "It involves the entire U.S. intelligence community," he says. "The FBI, CIA, Justice—it's incredible." Deep Throat explains that "the cover-up had little to do with it. It was mainly to protect the covert operations." In other words, the break-in at the Watergate complex, although reprehensible, represents only the surface of the iceberg. Below the water was the complex form of a much larger scandal.

In the course of telling the story of Woodward's and Bernstein's investigations, the filmmakers revealed aspects of this deeper problem. They conveyed an important message about the way in which Nixon's men threatened democracy, for example, through a dialogue involving Carl Bernstein and CREEP saboteur Donald Segretti. Segretti had tried to create deception and confusion to undermine the candidacy of the leading Democratic contender for the White House in 1972, Edmund Muskie. The CREEP organizers who sent him worried about Muskie's popular appeal; they thought that Muskie could compete effectively against Nixon in the coming elections. If they could stop Muskie in the early primaries, his candidacy would quickly lose momentum. In support of this effort, Segretti, a young lawyer with a reputation for playing dirty tricks during his college days in California, sabotaged the Muskie campaign. He obtained some "Citizens for Muskie" stationery and used it to send letters to two other Democratic candidates for the presidency (Hubert Humphrey and Henry M. Jackson), accusing them of sexual misconduct. Segretti disrupted a Muskie fundraising dinner, and he planted agents at Muskie rallies carrying pro-busing posters (a sensitive issue in the Florida primaries). The trickster also assigned agents to appear at Muskie rallies to ask the candidate embarrassing questions, and Segretti placed an ad harmful to Muskie in newspapers and on radio stations. This interference in the Democratic party primaries succeeded in disrupting Muskie's efforts, and within a short time the Maine senator no longer seemed a viable candidate. Eventually the divided Democrats nominated South Dakotan George McGovern as their candidate for president, and McGovern proved to be an easy target for Richard Nixon. The incumbent president won the 1972 election with a convincing 60.7 percent of the votes cast.

All the President's Men does not provide elaborate details about Donald Segretti's efforts to sabotage Muskie's presidential campaign, but it does reveal enough information to sharpen the viewer's appreciation of the importance of Segretti's activities. The movie shows that Segretti and his CREEP backers tried to tamper with the democratic process, and judging by the outcome, it appears that they were rather successful. The tricks made an impact on a national race for the White House. *All the President's Men* also shows that the perpetrators of these crimes sometimes failed to recognize the seriousness of their transgressions. As Segretti tells Bernstein in the movie, "I honestly don't see what we did that was so goddam awful."

In a variety of other small ways the movie hints of the multitude of different illegal activities that got Nixon and his team in trouble—paying off the burglars for remaining silent, breaking into personal offices in search of incriminating evidence against individuals, circulating deliberate lies about public figures, destroying evidence, conducting illegal surveillance, and intimidating critics of the administration. The producers were unusually successful in cramming so many references to historical events in a Hollywood entertainment film. They succeeded in drawing attention to a number of controversial issues. Rather than apply a soft touch to their interpretation of the Watergate crimes, the moviemakers managed to drive at the heart of the scandal. They showed that it involved much more than just political hanky-panky at the opposition party's headquarters; "Watergate" concerned violation of many of the fundamental tenets of democratic government.

The filmmakers' forthrightness must be viewed in the context of the times, of course. Their movie went into production in the year after Richard Nixon's embarrassing exit from office. Although a number of Americans in 1975 continued to believe that Nixon had not committed serious crimes, many others were highly disgusted. They felt that the former president and his associates had broken the public's trust. The year 1975 offered a propitious environment for making a hardhitting motion picture about corruption in Washington.

Actions in Congress gave evidence of the new reform mood in the nation during the period when *All the President's Men* was in development. In 1973–74 the legislative branch became more assertive in dealing with the White House. Congress passed the War Powers Act in 1973, asking that the president consult with the legislative branch when dispatching troops to foreign lands and requiring a withdrawal of such troops within ninety days unless Congress authorized their continued use. More relevant to the Watergate scandal, in 1974 Congress voted for the Campaign Financing Act, which attempted to reform some of the abuses in financing elections. Then, in 1975 and 1976, Congress passed the Freedom of Information Act and other legislation designed to give citizens access to government documents that previously had been kept from public view. Congress also investigated the extraordinary abuses of power by the CIA and the FBI. None of these efforts completely corrected the dangers that historian Arthur Schlesinger Jr. associated with the "Imperial Presidency," but they gave evidence of the reformers' growing strength in American politics at the time when *All the President's Men* went into production and made its appearance in American theaters.[22] In many respects the movie's highly critical view of corruption reflected current political fashions in the angry days during and after the Watergate revelations.

The appearance of *All the President's Men* in the spring of 1976 was bad news for President Gerald Ford, coming as it did in the midst of a battle for the presidency. Any reminders about the nation's embarrassments under recent Republican leadership had the potential of hurting Ford's campaign. The incumbent president was already in trouble with voters for pardoning Nixon. Now Jimmy Carter had emerged as the Democratic presidential front-runner in the primaries by projecting the image of an honest politician from outside the Washington loop. To defeat Carter, Ford needed to keep the public's thoughts about Watergate to a minimum. The arrival of *All the President's Men* made that task difficult.

Some leaders in the Democratic party thought that the movie could help their cause. At the time of the film's release, Basil Patterson, vice chair of the Democratic National Committee, observed that there had been a national effort "to exclude from our consciousness the painful, unpleasant, unacceptable memories of the Watergate debacle." Patterson claimed that *All the President's Men* "revives all the recollections and the emotions."[23] William vander Heuvel, New York cochair for Jimmy Carter's presidential bid, agreed. Heuvel speculated that "the movie will have a major impact on the 1976 campaign" and observed that *All the President's Men* "takes a subliminal issue and puts it back in the front ranks of people's minds."[24]

Carter surged ahead in the polls in the months following the movie's release, but he slipped later in the year and beat Ford in November by only a small margin. Whether the motion picture made a difference in the close race is impossible to determine. The movie's effect on the American voting public, if significant, probably came not in the form of a direct influence on votes but in a vaguer sense of sowing doubts about Republican leadership, raising suspicions about a president who would pardon Nixon, and arousing general anger over the wrongs of Watergate.

All the President's Men opened to generally good reviews. Commentators praised the film for its realism and its thesis. *All the President's Men* is a morality play, wrote Joy Gould Boyum in the *Wall Street Journal*. Its lessons about freedom of the press and political corruption are familiar themes from grade school civic classes, yet the picture is "so exciting, so effective in building tension, and so ultimately moving, that we tend to experience its familiar materials almost as revelation," wrote Boyum.[25] Jack Kroll, commenting in *Newsweek,* saw similar virtues. *All the President's Men* "gets under your skin," he reported, because "behind the scrabbling style of the reporters lies a world of moral meaning."[26] The movie is "spellbinding" and "riveting," wrote Vincent Canby of the *New York Times*. It manages to show the young reporters "becoming thoroughly absorbed in seemingly unimportant minutiae," details that ultimately reveal a conspiracy of gigantic proportions. "'All the President's Men' is remarkable for its understatement, for the cliches it avoids, for all the things it doesn't do, as for the things that it does," wrote Canby.[27]

The understated documentary style did not please all. Some reviewers considered the emphasis on realism to be tedious. *All the President's Men* gives too much attention to details, they said, and too little consideration to drama. Writing in the *Washington Post*, Gary Arnold complained that *All the President's Men* "verges on being meticulous to a fault." Arnold found the story flat, lacking "highs and lows" and "ups and downs." It needs a "spark of showmanship and inspiration."[28] Similarly, Stanley Kauffmann of the *New Republic* complained that the movie delivers an "ultimately static and uncomfortable result." He noted that much of the film shows Woodward and Bernstein working on the telephone (with the other party not seen but heard as a filtered voice). This hardly seems to be the stuff of riveting drama.[29] *All the President's Men* features no "big scenes" and "no sudden confrontations," complained Robert Hatch in *The Nation*. Instead, it concentrates on journalists combing through lists looking for leads, ringing doorbells, and drinking numerous cups of coffee. The real villains in the Watergate story are not even portrayed on the screen. Hatch observed that Attorney General John Mitchell is only a voice on the telephone in the movie, and President Richard M. Nixon appears only as a face on a television screen in the *Washington Post*'s office. Attention to realism, in short, diminished the movie's potential for delivering a compelling story.[30] To these critics, the edification gained by the documentary style did not offset the losses created because of a format that they considered to be poorly suited for Hollywood.

Not surprisingly, some of the individuals who had been involved in the Watergate scandal and were mentioned or portrayed in *All the President's Men* were not pleased with the movie. They objected to the film's depiction of certain White House figures, and they challenged aspects of the movie's interpretation of history. Herbert G. Klein, the former White House communications director, thought that *All the President's Men* concentrates on the negative aspects of White House activities and ignores the "good deeds" of the president's advisers. Klein also criticized the movie for delivering forms of "character assassination." *All the President's Men* unfairly associates decent people with the scandals, he claimed, individuals such as Clark McGregor and Ken Clawson. The movie fails to distinguish between major and minor crimes. A typed note featured near the end of the film announces "Maurice Stans guilty," Klein noted, yet Stans's guilt pertained only to five technical misdemeanor violations (such as tardy reporting of a contribution and two disbursements). Charles W. Colson, the president's former counsel in the White House, agreed that Ken Clawson had not been treated fairly. Colson took issue with the movie's suggestion that Woodward and Bernstein feared that their phones were tapped and their lives were threatened. The danger did not really exist, Colson insisted, and the two intrepid journalists probably never felt insecure about their safety. Filmmakers probably threw this idea into the movie to breathe life into the plot, Colson guessed. He also complained that the movie gives too much credit to Woodward and Bernstein for exposing the Watergate scandals. *All the President's Men* fails to recognize the contributions of Seymour Hersh of the *New York Times*, as well as figures such as Senator Sam Ervin and special prosecutor Archilbald Cox, Colson observed.[31]

The argument that *All the President's Men* accentuates the role of Woodward and Bernstein in bringing down the Nixon administration was the most commonly repeated criticism of the film. It appeared in both favorable and negative reviews of the movie. Commentators were quick to note that many individuals played important roles in the exposures of 1972 to 1974. The objection was not surprising, of course, for history from Hollywood frequently concentrates on the activities of a hero or two and assumes that the principal characters almost single-handedly changed American politics. Redford, Goldman, and Pakula were well aware that their movie could not achieve a balanced examination of the Watergate investigations that would provide attention to all the major players. It was difficult enough to communicate an understanding of the complex web of corruption and to mention some of the many individuals associated with the scandal. Accordingly, the moviemakers focused tightly on the work of the two journalists.[32] This focus on the actions of Woodward and Bernstein evidently gave luster to their profession. During the year after the movie's release, application to journalism schools increased significantly.[33]

Not many other objections arose about the movie's presentation of recent history. In view of the many depictions of historical events in *All the President's Men,* it is remarkable that the moviemakers took so few hits regarding interpretation. Most commentators seemed to accept the film's rendition of the Watergate story as essentially true and argued instead about whether they thought the documentary style was effective. By basing their movie closely on Woodward and Bernstein's book, Redford, Pakula, and Goldman managed to protect themselves rather effectively from criticism of their interpretation. Woodward and Bernstein's writing also provided a shield against lawsuits. Ordinarily, a movie about the recent political behavior of real-life individuals can be risky. The living persons portrayed in such a film may try to sue a studio or the producers if they do not like the way they are depicted on the screen. Since no one had challenged Woodward and Bernstein's book in court, it seemed unlikely that there would be an attack on the same material if it appeared in the movie. Besides, many of the Watergate conspirators had been convicted by the time the movie came out; they were in no position to mount a legal campaign against the film's characterizations.

When William Goldman accepted the assignment to write a screenplay for *All the President's Men,* he suspected that he would face a difficult job making a successful drama out of the Watergate story.

Hollywood executives preferred to stay clear of political movies, evidently because they sensed that the public did not like them very much. "Message pictures" were often losers in the commercial entertainment business. When a social or moral message had to be incorporated in a motion picture, usually it would be soft-pedaled. Nonetheless, the story that Goldman, Redford, and Pakula constructed moves in opposition to these familiar standards. It strikes hard at the record of scandal, bluntly identifies the names of living culprits, and honestly demonstrates how widespread and serious was Watergate's assault on American democracy. The movie's toughness emanated from the peculiar times in which it was made, an era when Americans were outraged over the evidence of conspiracy and lies that had come out of Washington. Yet its sharpness can also be traced to the man who conceived the film. Robert Redford had communicated very few public statements about American politics before he created the 1976 movie. With *All the President's Men* he emerged as a political man and made an important contribution to the public's thinking about history.

All the President's Men does exaggerate the accomplishments of its two protagonists, Woodward and Bernstein. The movie ensured that, as Bob Woodward observed, their story would be the one about Watergate "that people know and remember."[34] The movie's tendency to glamorize the achievements of the reporters is common to the genre, however. Most Hollywood docudramas accent the heroic action of a few people and downplay the role of other individuals and the impact of broad, complex forces that can contribute to change. Despite this limitation, *All the President's Men* manages to deliver a bold and informed view of a significant crisis in American political life. As such, it represents one of Hollywood's better examples of cinematic history.

Norma Rae

"A FEMALE ROCKY"

Norma Rae (Sally Field) boldly urges
her fellow mill workers to join a union in
Norma Rae. Courtesy of the Museum of
Modern Art/Film Stills Archive.

When *Norma Rae* made its appearance in 1979, southern mill workers were in the midst of a long and frustrating fight with one of the nation's largest textile companies, J. P. Stevens. Laborers in the cotton-manufacturing industry had been trying to win union recognition for years, and they thought that they had achieved their goal in the struggle that culminated in the early 1970s (the movie depicts this campaign). In the following years, however, Stevens's executives developed a variety of excuses for inaction and managed to evade the organization of workers in their plants. In 1979, the year of *Norma Rae*'s release, many of the South's poor mill hands thought that they would continue to work for years in the biggest nonunion industry in the country. Then a surprise occurred. One year after the movie appeared in the theaters, a new president of J. P. Stevens announced that he would sign an agreement permitting union representation in his company's plants. Whether the movie made an impact on management's decision must be left to speculation, but it is clear that Hollywood's emotionally powerful look at the southern textile industry eloquently brought the mill hands' case to millions of Americans and helped to publicize the union's cause more broadly than the previous decade of labor's campaigning had done.

Norma Rae stimulated public awareness through a provocative exercise in cinematic realism. The movie exposes the ugly features of southern industrial life. It shows the mill hands' unpleasant working conditions, reveals the physical and mental hazards of their jobs, and demonstrates the difficulties they faced when they tried to improve their situation. *Norma Rae* communicates this picture in the form of a partisan, documentary-style drama. It confronts viewers with a realistic vision of an exploitive work system, prompting sympathy for the victim.

In a more subtle way the movie makes a case for feminism as well. Unlike many Hollywood films of previous years that focus on men's lives when telling stories about struggles of the weak against the powerful, *Norma Rae* examines the battles of a feisty female. It shows that a woman can be a leader in a clash between workers and their employers. The movie tracks the real-life experiences of a dynamic individual from Roanoke Rapids, North Carolina, who played a significant role in winning union representation from the J. P. Stevens company. The person's actual name was Crystal Lee (she will be referred to here by that name; she had a separate maiden name and three different surnames from different marriages). Crystal Lee grew up in a family of mill workers, labored in a variety of jobs, including work in the textile industry, and then, rather suddenly, discovered an interest in collective representation for the mill hands. She became a valued assistant to a union agent and eventually lost her job because of her activities in support of a union.[1] *Norma Rae* portrays her as she was in real life—not someone particularly cognizant of the ideology of women's liberation but an individual whose bold actions demonstrated the possibilities for women workers as active agents in the transformation of their own lives.

In focusing on the gutsy actions of this determined woman, *Norma Rae* leaves the impression that Crystal Lee was almost alone among the mill workers in forcing J. P. Stevens to its knees. The movie portrays Crystal as a heroic, action-oriented figure who galvanized previously compliant blue-collar workers into resistance. The real story is much more complex, of course. Various other people contributed to the union victories, and the struggle covered many years and locales (not just the brief period and the specific plant suggested in the movie). Still, Crystal Lee's contribution to the union campaign was significant, and her specific case is representative of the experiences of many mill workers during the difficult years of organizing activity.

Two female producers created *Norma Rae,* and their interest in feminism led them to consider Crystal Lee's story as material for Hollywood. Tamara Asseyeu and Alex Rose came on a report on Crystal Lee's activities in a 1973 article in the *New York Times Magazine* and quickly sensed its potential. When the author, Henry P. Leifermann, released a book-length study in 1975, *Crystal Lee: A Woman of Inheritance,* Asseyeu and Rose bought an option on it. Asseyeu was interested in making socially conscious films, and Rose wanted to develop "character-driven" movies about "American sub-cultures" and the "human condition." Crystal Lee's case offered all this and more; it provided an appealing story about a female David battling Goliath. In the new age of feminist consciousness the film's tale of a fighting heroine could excite the interest of female moviegoers.[2]

Asseyeu and Rose planned their film at a time when American society was becoming increasingly receptive to women's issues. In the decade before *Norma Rae*'s appearance (1969–78) the feminist movement in the United States recorded a number of significant gains. In the early 1970s the National Organization of Women saw dramatic increases in membership, and its lobbyists succeeded in pressing members of Congress for reforms. The Equal Rights Amendment passed the House of Representatives in 1971 and the Senate in 1972 (but it did not achieve ratification), and Congress included Title 9 in the 1972 Education Amendment, a measure that prohibits sex discrimination in educational institutions. In 1973 the Supreme Court ruled on *Roe v. Wade,* permitting abortions under certain conditions, and the American Telephone and Telegraph Company settled a discrimination suit that brought $38 million in back pay to 15,000 women and minority males who had suffered job discrimination. Various religious groups began to ordain women as ministers for the first time in the 1970s, while in politics figures such as Shirley Chisholm, Bella Abzug, Barbara Jordan, and Elizabeth Holtzman began to draw national attention. Rosalynn Carter, the president's wife, established a reputation as a "Steel Magnolia" in the White House. The women's movement also made an impact on journalism. Female editorial staff members working at *Time, Newsweek,* and other publications made charges about sex discrimination and won promises of improvement, and established women's periodicals such as *Vogue* and *The Ladies Home Journal* began to give more coverage to issues concerning economic and sexual liberation. Also, magazines such as *Ms.,* which directly celebrated the liberationist cause, appeared in the 1970s. In short, the era in which Tamara Asseyeu and Alex Rose tried to promote Crystal Lee's story was a period of growing awareness and improving opportunities for women.[3]

During the 1970s a number of screen actresses played strong female characters. Meryl Streep, Barbra Streisand, Bette Midler, Cicely Tyson, Diane Keaton, Jane Fonda, Vanessa Redgrave, Sissy Spacek, Shirley McLaine, and Anne Bancroft had displayed vibrant personalities in Hollywood productions. Two films of the late 1970s in particular indicated Hollywood's growing interest in women's issues. *Julia* (1977) shows Jane Fonda as a talented playwright who visits a friend who has become a humanitarian crusader in 1930s Germany (played by Vanessa Redgrave), and *The Turning Point* (1978) presents Anne Bancroft

and Shirley McClaine as former friends who are fighting over the choices between career and marriage that they made years before. Then
came Sally Field as Norma Rae in what Asseyeu and Rose claimed to
be the first major Hollywood movie produced by two women working without a male partner.

In crafting their story Asseyeu and Rose wanted to give audiences
insight into the causes of Norma Rae's independent-mindedness and
aggressiveness. They felt that they needed to attribute her emergence
as a union leader to specific factors. In developing a thesis about the
sources of Norma Rae's dynamic personality, they tried to draw a connection between her behavior in the workplace and her behavior in
her personal life. They suggested that Norma Rae's many romantic li-
aisons in her younger years represented the rebellious actions of a
southern woman who, until the union fight came along, considered
flirtatious behavior to be a manner of exhibiting distaste for conventions and a hunger for independence. Small southern communities
provided few outlets for a spirited and energetic woman, they suggested; sexual escapades offered one avenue of expression.

Research by Jacquelyn Dowd Hall published seven years after the
release of *Norma Rae* appears to support this perspective. Hall examined the case of a Tennessee nylon plant in 1929 and found a pattern
in the characters of the "disorderly women" who played prominent
roles in a 1929 strike. Some of the leaders were "new women" of the
1920s, young people who led unconventional private lives and often
were called "lewd women" by the people who sought to discredit their
union activities. The strike activists—women like Crystal Lee in a later age—were often young and single. Some had children out of wed-
lock. These outspoken women were sexually expressive, and they
addressed the authorities in a provocative manner when presenting
their case for union. Opponents feared their sexual power and considered their style of protest to be distasteful. Thus, the "erotic subtext"
associated with the strikers' behavior suggests some of the sources of
the mill worker's courage and rebelliousness.[4]

This view of rambunctious southern women finding ways in which
to channel their energy became a central message in the promotion
of *Norma Rae*. When seeking underwriters for the production and in
promoting the movie with the public, *Norma Rae*'s creators described
their movie as a woman's story rather than a laborer's story. They
stressed the film's contribution to feminist thinking rather than to
unionist thinking. Nonetheless, the movie does project a very strong

pro-union bias, and its attention to the concerns of working people is even more prominent in the story than its attention to feminist issues. The pro-union agenda was not prominent in the promotional efforts, however, because both the movie industry and American society seemed to be more receptive in the 1970s to feminist sentiment than to unionist sentiment.

The movie's sympathy for blue-collar workers owes much to the man who became the director, as well as to the producers. Asseyeu and Rose chose Martin Ritt, a liberal-minded filmmaker with a long record of making movies about underdogs. Ritt had grown up in New York City. His father, an immigrant, was an engineer who displayed wide-ranging intellectual interests, and his mother was an outspoken native of Brooklyn. As a youngster Martin Ritt showed only occasional interest in his studies but a passion for baseball that remained strong throughout his life. He went to college on a football scholarship and later took up acting in New York City. Because of his large, muscular appearance, Ritt frequently played the role of a tough guy in his theatrical performances. He participated actively in New York City's agit-prop theater and began directing. Eventually he turned to Hollywood movies and television productions. Ritt's financial position improved substantially, but he remained a lively critic of society with a leftist perspective. He rarely expressed satisfaction with a presidential candidate, and in election years he usually told his friends that he intended to write in the name of Hugo Black. Ritt's record of social consciousness got him into trouble during the Red Scare: he was blacklisted. After some difficult years Ritt made a comeback. By the time he began directing *Norma Rae* he had established an impressive reputation for making movies that address important social questions.[5] These included *The Molly Maguires* (1970), about a secret union of anthracite coal miners in Pennsylvania in the 1870s; *The Great White Hope* (1970), which deals with the racial prejudice confronted by America's first black heavyweight boxing champion; *Sounder* (1972), which portrays the efforts of members of a black Louisiana family to keep their lives in order in times of depression and prejudice; *Conrack* (1974), about a teacher who tried to educate poor blacks in the South Carolina sea islands; and *The Front* (1976), which deals with abuses against left-wing scriptwriters during the Red Scare.

The production notes for one of Ritt's films (*The Front*) observe that the director wanted his movies to anger people. Ritt said, "I care very deeply about which is the right way for people to go."[6] Such comments

in promotional materials often reflect the imagination of the marketing agents rather than the real feelings of the artist. In Ritt's case, however, the words were representative. Ritt already had an enviable Hollywood record of producing movies that examine the problems of the
poor, the neglected, and the inarticulate and that draw attention to
questions about individual rights and human dignity.

Ritt agreed to work on the story of Crystal Lee with the understanding that he could choose his own writers. Asseyeu and Rose agreed to
the arrangement, and Ritt turned to Irving Ravetch and Harriet Frank
Jr., a husband-and-wife team that had worked with him on a number
of previous movies. The writers based their script largely on Leifermann's book; they did not add much additional research when they
designed the screenplay.[7]

Asseyeu and Rose now had key production personnel in place, but
they needed someone to play Crystal Lee. When a good draft of the
script was ready, they tried to enlist a noted actress for the main role
so that they could market their product with underwriters more successfully. In each case they were turned down. Faye Dunaway, Diane
Keaton, Jill Clayburgh, Meryl Streep, Jane Fonda, and others declined
their invitations. Julie Christie's name also entered the discussions, but
the producers could not see the British actress in the role of a southern mill worker. Eventually they found Sally Field, an actress not
known for playing sophisticated roles. She had appeared in television
series (*Gidget* and *The Flying Nun*) and as a low-class, sexy friend of Burt
Reynolds in a farcical comedy about truck driving (*Smokey and the Ban-
dit*). Some people in the production organization harbored doubts about
her ability to handle such a serious dramatic role. Field destroyed the
criticisms with a performance that won her an Academy Award for best
actress.[8]

Still, the producers had to find a studio and financing for their
movie, a difficult task in view of the film's transparently pro-union
agenda. Ritt realized that he would face a challenge trying to convince
a major studio to take on the project. Hollywood had never established
much of a record for examining the issue of union organization. Occasionally a film such as *Black Fury* drew public attention (the 1935
movie is about a coal miner who became a union leader and fought
against company thugs). In fact, many of Hollywood's examinations
of organized labor show union corruption (as in the 1954 picture *On
the Waterfront*). Two films about blue-collar workers appeared in American theaters a year before the release of *Norma Rae,* but they do not

provide a strong pro-union perspective. *Blue Collar* (1978) shows workers turning to criminal activity after suffering boredom on the assembly line (while the union leaders are co-opted by the local power apparatus), and *F.I.S.T.* (1978) tells the story of a union leader somewhat like Jimmy Hoffa who is corrupted by the labor movement's connections with mobsters. For the most part, however, Hollywood stayed clear of dramas about unions. The political conservatism of Hollywood's business leaders and the producers' inclination to avoid controversial subjects made pro-union pictures rare products. Furthermore, Hollywood executives worried about labor relations within their own industry. They were sensitive to the organized pressure put on them by guilds involving technicians, writers, actors, directors, and others.

The changing economic and political environment further compounded the difficulties for *Norma Rae*'s developers. Public sentiment had been turning more hostile toward unionism. In the late 1970s many Americans worried about the corruption of large labor organizations (they especially recalled the racketeering charges against Teamster leader Jimmy Hoffa). Americans also complained that high wages and complicated work rules won by the unions were making American industry less competitive than before. Within a few years Americans would elect Ronald Reagan to the presidency and usher in a new conservative era, bringing union clout in Washington, D.C., to its lowest ebb since the Great Depression. Across the ocean sentiment was also hostile. In the late 1970s Margaret Thatcher rose to power in Great Britain, building much of her support on public unhappiness about the power of organized labor and the Labour party.

Asseyeu and Rose understood the complexity of marketing a pro-union movie in the economic and political environment of the 1970s. Indeed, they failed to get support for their project from Columbia Pictures, Warner Brothers, and United Artists partly because of the picture's subject matter. Consequently, they obscured some of the film's partisan features by emphasizing that their movie would be above all about the maturation of a woman. They pressed this theme in selling the concept to Twentieth Century–Fox. Banking on the recent success of *Rocky* (1976), they spoke of their film as a story about "a female Rocky," that is, another movie about a determined underdog, except in this case the film could prove particularly appealing to women. Asseyeu, Rose, and Ritt accentuated this idea further when promoting the movie with the press. They described *Norma Rae* as an exciting examination of a spirited female mill worker who demonstrated little personal direction until a union organizer came to town and inspired her to fight for her rights. They pointed out that sexual escapades constituted just about the only kind of rebellion a headstrong woman like Norma Rae could imagine while living in a small southern town. Then the labor movement came into her life and helped to raise her consciousness to a higher level.[9]

Martin Ritt, speaking in behalf of the production, argued that his movie looks more realistically at some of the challenges women in America were facing in the 1970s than do other Hollywood films of the time that deal with women's issues. Too many of these pictures focus on middle-class women who are disturbed, neurotic, and "slightly erotic," he said. *Norma Rae,* instead, looks at a working-class female who had genuine reasons to rebel. It shows Norma Rae beginning her awakening awkwardly as she gropes for an understanding of her role in a southern mill community that expected women to be docile. It is a picture about a woman's growing self-assertion. Ritt acknowledged that the film carries this larger meaning regarding women's consciousness, but he insisted that it was not meant to be a "political" film or "a union or a labor film."[10]

It took more than a feminist message to convince leaders at Twentieth Century–Fox to gamble on Asseyeu's and Rose's picture. Executives at Fox also viewed the subject as risky, particularly because they could not make a confident judgment about likely revenues. A film like *Norma Rae,* lacking big-name stars and dealing with a serious social issue, could easily prove disappointing at the box office. In a different period Asseyeu and Rose probably would not have received a favorable nod at Fox either, but they were fortunate to approach the studio at a time when its executives were excited about the extraordinary profits they had earned from the first of the *Star Wars* films. Under these conditions the executives were willing to gamble on a long-shot message film such as *Norma Rae.*[11]

Locating a working textile mill to serve as an authentic set presented yet another challenge for the filmmakers. They sent scouts through the southeastern states, where the greatest concentration of mills could be found, but encountered resistance. Mill owners were not eager to open their factories for the filming of a pro-union movie, and they did not want their regular operations interrupted by the activities of filmmakers. Asseyeu and Rose especially hoped to identify a location in North Carolina, where Crystal Lee had lived, but they received a cold response. Eventually the production crew located an old factory in

Opelika, Alabama, that, because of poor earnings, appeared likely to close. Its owners, who lived in Chicago, were happy to receive the $150,000 fee from the production company for use of their facilities, and they were pleased to learn that manufacturing at the plant could continue during the period of the shooting. The fee helped to keep their plant open for another year. Authenticity was relatively easy to achieve in the dark, noisy environment of the Opelika factory. Lint dust blew around the rooms, and the floors shook from the vibrations of the machinery. The production crew members had to operate with earplugs and masks over their noses and mouths.[12]

As production planning for the movie moved forward, Asseyeu, Rose, and Ritt encountered a new obstacle: Crystal Lee began demanding greater influence over the film. She would not sign a paper giving the producers artistic control of the story. As in the case of most Hollywood films dealing with living persons, the producers wanted signed releases from the principal people being depicted in the drama. The documents were to give the filmmakers complete authority to tell the story in any way that they wished. Producers typically seek such guarantees to avoid unexpected interference with their artistic decisions. Editorial interference can greatly complicate efforts to design a cogent story, and it can be quite expensive if forced on the production during the period of work on the set. The releases also help to prevent legal challenges. Suits, although difficult for the plaintiff to win, often prove to be a nuisance to the producers and involve costly fees. Because of these difficulties filmmakers often do not have a choice about whether to operate with the releases, for the studios will not give a production financial support without them (indeed, the studios need the releases to obtain insurance). In the case of *Norma Rae* the producers got documentation from some key figures, but Crystal Lee insisted on editorial influence over the script before she would sign.[13]

Crystal Lee felt emboldened in part because she was being courted by another filmmaker who wanted to tell her story on the screen. Barbara Kopple, creator of the much-praised documentary *Harlan County, U.S.A.*, thought that the example of Crystal Lee's courage in standing up to J. P. Stevens would make an exciting film. She promised Crystal Lee the right to approve the script if she would agree to a relationship in which Kopple would direct a picture about her. Crystal Lee found this proposal appealing and considered working exclusively with Kopple. Asseyeu and Rose had bought the rights to Leifermann's book, however, and because Crystal Lee had sold her rights to Leifermann, the two Hollywood producers had legal authority to tell her story. Since Asseyeu and Rose held the necessary rights to move forward and had financing, whereas Kopple's project remained in an earlier stage of development, the Hollywood producers could overcome Kopple's competition. Still, Asseyeu, Rose, and Ritt preferred to have Crystal Lee's enthusiastic cooperation, and they made aggressive efforts to obtain it.[14]

The producers and the director tried to win Crystal Lee's support by examining the script with her and her lawyers and agreeing to make adjustments in a number of places in the story. With regard to a few scenes, however, the parties could not come to an agreement. Crystal Lee was unhappy, for example, with the script's treatment of the main character's promiscuous youth. The draft includes a dramatic scene in which Norma Rae tells her children about her past sexual adventures when she realizes she has become a public figure in the fight for unionization and senses that her past is likely to be scrutinized by her enemies. Worried that her children will soon hear nasty rumors about her private life circulated by anti-union people, she informs her children of affairs with three men and identifies the fathers of two of her children. Ritt thought that this scene would be critically important for understanding Norma Rae's character. The film could not effectively excite audience interest, he argued, if it did not show its female subject maturing beyond her undirected, flirtatious beginnings. Furthermore, the story was public information, having appeared both in Henry Leifermann's *New York Times Magazine* article and in his book. Ritt thought that he could not budge on such an important element for character development, and Crystal Lee remained displeased about the plan to incorporate the material. Other points of disagreement emerged, too. Crystal Lee took issue with references in the script to Norma Rae's indulgence with alcohol, and she criticized the writers for focusing on her personal life, maintaining that the movie needed to give broader attention to the labor union movement and the many other people who contributed to its struggle.[15]

Negotiations continued up to the period when the producers were planning to begin work on the set. Ritt appealed to idealism in the final stages, maintaining that Crystal Lee ought to allow the screenwriters greater freedom of expression, for ultimately their efforts were likely to help her cause. *Norma Rae* would probably be the only pro-union picture ever made by a major studio, he said, and therefore it deserved her cooperation. Ritt also traveled to North Carolina with a $25,000 check in hand as a financial inducement. Crystal Lee continued to hold

out for editorial control, however, and soon discovered that the movie project was proceeding without her. The screenwriters made some
last adjustments in the script, giving the story a generic quality in various places rather than the appearance of a specific story about Crystal Lee. Because of legal difficulties, Ritt later promoted the movie as
"a fictionalized composite of several such women who became mili-
tantly involved in trying to unionize southern textile mills." *Norma Rae*
would have been called *Crystal Lee;* the mill worker's resistance forced
the adoption of a fictional name. By holding out beyond a point of a
workable compromise, Crystal Lee lost her best opportunity to gain
national fame from her personal story.[16]

Despite her reservations, Crystal Lee readily identified with the movie
when Twentieth Century–Fox released it, because *Norma Rae*'s appearance helped the campaign to unionize J. P. Stevens's plants. In 1979
Crystal Lee was a full-time employee of the Amalgamated Clothing and
Textile Workers Union (ACTWU), and she was traveling around the
country to promote the union's boycott of goods manufactured by
Stevens. Through public appearances and speeches she tried to convince
audiences not to purchase Stevens's cotton products until the company
agreed to end its years of resistance to union organization. In the course
of making these presentations, her celebrity as the "real Norma Rae"
helped to place her in numerous television appearances on talk shows.
She used these opportunities to slip in appeals for the boycott. Then, after
a taxing cross-country tour, she arrived in Hollywood. There she was
honored in a gala benefit for the boycott sponsored by the Screen Actor's Guild and the AFL-CIO, and for the first time she met Sally Field,
the actress who portrayed her in the movie.[17]

Norma Rae received a warm reception from the public and the critics, and it helped Martin Ritt to win the kind of artistic acclaim that
he had failed to achieve in many of his earlier efforts at movie making. The movie won five Academy Awards, grossed $12 million by the
mid-1980s, and continued to draw profits from video sales and occasional reruns on television in succeeding years. Crystal Lee received
nothing for the movie at first, because she had refused to sign the
agreement with the filmmakers. Her lawyers continued to negotiate,
and eventually she received a settlement check of $52,000.[18]

A year after the movie's release good news came for Crystal Lee and
others who had worked for unionization in the mills. In 1980 Whitney Stevens of the J. P. Stevens textile company signed a historic agreement with the ACTWU that gave workers in many of his company's

plants union representation. The action represented an extraordinary turnaround for the company, for J. P. Stevens was well known for its extreme resistance to labor organization. Before Whitney Stevens became the CEO in 1980, the company had resisted coming to terms with union leaders in its Roanoke Rapids, North Carolina, mills even though the workers had achieved an important election victory for union representation six years earlier. Instead of accepting the results of the employees' vote, J. P. Stevens's leaders had tried to avoid dealing with the union through a variety of delaying tactics.[19]

Many factors explain J. P. Stevens's turnaround. The appearance of new leadership in the company was a factor, as was the firm's desire to get beyond conflicts over unionization so that it could concentrate on the vital matter of modernization. Stevens's leaders also probably recognized that they were likely to sell the company within a few years, and it would be difficult marketing a business with a troubled history of labor-management relations (indeed, West Point Peperell purchased J. P. Stevens in the 1980s). Public pressure no doubt also played a role in convincing Stevens's management to negotiate with the union after years of inflexibility. This pressure came not only from the ACTWU's highly publicized campaign urging consumers to boycott J. P. Stevens's products but also from the sympathy aroused by *Norma Rae*. The appearance of the movie in 1979 aggravated Stevens's situation, because the news media responded by featuring numerous human interest stories about Crystal Lee's fight against the company. It is difficult to determine precisely what role the film played in influencing the decision of Stevens's executives to reach a settlement in 1980, but the timing of Stevens's announcement is suggestive. *Norma Rae* helped to bring a close to the firm's longstanding policy of intransigence.

Norma Rae makes its case against companies like Stevens and in behalf of the long-exploited mill workers by presenting history from the "bottom-up," giving a highly detailed account of the difficult lives of the South's poor and inadequately educated industrial hands. It shows the mill workers' shabby clothing, their worn looks, and their poor health. It depicts their naïveté about the benefits of protecting themselves through unions and their timidity in confronting management with their needs. The movie displays their depressing work environment with its noisy, crowded, dirty, and dangerous conditions. In these respects and in many other ways *Norma Rae* appears to be a Hollywood-style documentary. It looks like drama based closely on the facts of life in the mill communities. *Norma Rae*'s power in evoking sympathy for the factory workers, mostly women, stems from its realistic presentation. The movie appears to tell the truth about suffering and asks for the viewer's empathy.

Norma Rae does not tell the complete truth, of course. The filmmakers made some adjustments in the story for dramatic purposes, and they had to revise their characterization of the central figure in the picture because Crystal Lee would not cooperate sufficiently. More important, *Norma Rae* overemphasizes the role of specific individuals in the union campaign. It focuses on the actions of two highly motivated people, overlooking the work of others who made important contributions to labor's cause. Despite these shortcomings, *Norma Rae* constitutes one of Hollywood's better examples of cinematic realism. It bombards viewers with an abundance of detailed evidence about Crystal Lee's experiences and the life of cotton mill workers that reflects, to a considerable degree, actual conditions in North Carolina's factories. Overall the filmmakers interpreted the historical record with integrity.

For example, the movie throws light on changes in the legal environment during the 1960s and 1970s that opened opportunities for laborers like Crystal Lee to criticize management's practices. *Norma Rae* hints of important developments that began to affect the balance of power between management and labor and opened the way for eventual union victories such as the one at Roanoke Rapids, North Carolina. In the years preceding Crystal Lee's actions the National Labor Relations Board and the courts intervened in labor's favor in a number of instances. The pressure against J. P. Stevens came in reaction to a long string of violations committed over several years. The courts established rules of fair play in the plants, thereby giving union organizers better means of communication with employees. This involvement helped to bring a number of mill hands over to the union side.

As *Norma Rae* shows, the new rules allowed an organizer like Eli Zivkovich, who led the Roanoke Rapids drive, to work far more effectively than had organizers of previous years. In the movie the character representing Zivkovich (named Reuben Warshovsky in the film) draws Norma Rae to a meeting through a notice that J. P. Stevens was required to post on its bulletin boards. The film also shows Warshovsky entering the mill and walking around the work rooms to make sure that the company kept its obligation to post the union's notices. Eli Zivkovich actually did visit the plant where Crystal Lee worked to check the bulletin boards, and just as the film demonstrates, management showed tremendous consternation when forced to abide by the rules.

The scene in *Norma Rae* showing Warshovsky warning supervisors about the danger of trying to restrict his visit is authentic, too; Eli Zivkovich told the managers that they could be held in contempt of court and sent to jail if they denied his right to check the plant. Similarly, the scene in which Norma Rae wears a large union button to work after she joins the movement effectively conveys the impact of outside intervention. The workers' right to wear such buttons in the work setting and to speak to their fellow workers about joining a union was protected under the new rules. The film also shows Norma Rae's supervisors violating these regulations by pressuring her to remove her union button (Crystal Lee had the same experience).[20]

Although the movie shows a number of ways in which the National Labor Relations Board's and the courts' intervention helped Eli Zivkovich to recruit for the ACTWU, it does not reveal one of the most important developments that attracted Crystal Lee and other mill hands to their first union meeting. In 1973 the U.S. Court of Appeals for the Second Circuit in New York ordered J. P. Stevens to place in the workers' hands a strongly stated apology for its past labor violations. The document had to be mailed to every worker's home at company expense and be posted on every bulletin board in the Stevens mills. Furthermore, it was to be read to groups of workers in the plant during company time. The extraordinary apology had to include a pledge that workers would not be punished for union membership, and it specifically listed the kind of intimidation that no longer could be practiced (such as discharge from service, downgrading of work level, and restriction of movement). Crystal Lee received a copy of this apology in the mail, and it became the initial stimulus that led her to thinking about joining the union. The document displayed J. P. Stevens's vulnerability and helped to give her and other mill hands the courage to take actions their predecessors would have been too fearful to consider.[21]

To a degree, however, the movie exaggerates the impact of this outside intervention. Warshovsky throws around so many warnings about bringing civil contempt charges against anyone who interferes with him that the movie leaves the impression that the National Labor Relations Board had achieved extraordinary power over J. P. Stevens's relations with its employees by 1973–74. The impression appears especially when Warshovsky tells Norma Rae that she cannot be fired for her union activities. Later he assures her, "There's not a goddamn thing they can do to touch you." It would have been more correct to suggest that management was finding it increasingly difficult to bring pressure on pro-union workers, but not impossible. Indeed, Crystal Lee was fired for her protests, and she claims that she later was blacklisted from employment in other textile plants in North Carolina because of her audacity.

In its overall presentation of Crystal Lee's experiences, however, the movie offers a portrayal that stays reasonably close to the facts. The "real Norma Rae's" mother was a weaver, and her father was a mill mechanic (as the movie portrays them). Like her parents, Crystal Lee took jobs in the textile plants, but she did not like the mill environment. She was troubled by the ugly working conditions: the noise of machines, the high temperatures and humidity in the plants, the abundance of cotton-lint dust floating in the air, and of course, the low wages. Like many other mill workers, she tried to find different means of employment. Alternatives were scarce in the mill towns, however. Crystal Lee worked for a while as a waitress and then as a hostess but eventually returned to the mills. She was employed in a J. P. Stevens plant in Roanoke Rapids when her life suddenly took a dramatic turn.

The developments that changed her situation in 1973 began with the appearance of the apologetic letter in her mail from J. P. Stevens, followed by the appearance of a notice about a union meeting on the plant bulletin board. Crystal Lee had not been a union enthusiast before. She remembered her father's warning that association with a union was a ticket to unemployment, and she recalled school lessons of her youth indicating that unions created troublesome strikes and taxed their members with dues.[22] The announcements aroused her curiosity, however, and she thought about the benefits her second husband enjoyed as a union member in a paper plant. Crystal Lee decided to attend the ACTWU's meeting. When she arrived at the event, she discovered that only four or five whites were present, along with about seventy blacks (the site of the meeting was an African-American church). Crystal Lee joined the meeting without hesitation. Years later, thinking about the need for cooperation between white and black workers, she expressed thanks that she had been "color blind" when she entered the African-American church.[23]

The African Americans were eager to attend the meeting because their ministers supported the union cause. Black preachers allowed union organizers to speak in their churches on Sunday mornings, and they referred to the need for unions in their sermons. Blacks in Roanoke Rapids were also interested in the union because they had grown angry over the preferential treatment whites received in advancing up the ranks of leadership in the plant. They observed that the relatives and neighbors of company managers often were promoted more quickly than were black workers who had more seniority. These factors led them to give the union a warmer initial reception than the whites did.[24]

At the meeting Crystal Lee heard an inspiring speech by fifty-five-year-old Eli Zivkovich, an agent for the ACTWU. Zivkovich addressed problems that were on the employees' minds and pointed to his union organization as the key to improved conditions. The day after the meeting Crystal Lee appeared in the mill proudly wearing a union button. Management's posture toward her changed abruptly. Instead of treating her like a favored worker, the supervisors made her the target of constant monitoring and pressure.[25]

Months later, after Crystal Lee became the principal ally in Zivkovich's efforts to organize the plant, she saw a provocative notice from management posted on the plant bulletin board. The message aimed to split white and black employees and weaken the cause of labor organization by suggesting that blacks would control the union if it won representation in the plant (white workers outnumbered blacks in the plant by about three to one). A few days later another anti-union message appeared—this one concerning wages—and Crystal Lee began to copy the notice so that she could give the details to Zivkovich. Three supervisors gathered around her and insisted that she stop her activity and return to work. Crystal Lee continued copying, and when the managers told her that she was fired, she insisted on staying until the chief of police himself took her away. While waiting for the chief to arrive, Crystal Lee mounted a table in her workroom and held up a sheet of cardboard with the word *UNION* marked on it in large letters. She turned around slowly, demonstrating her bold message to the assorted hemmers, terry cutters, and packers in the room. Stunned by her actions, the workers stopped their work and turned off their machines. The room became silent. Then the police chief took her away to book her on disorderly conduct charges. Crystal Lee did not leave calmly. She kicked, twisted, and screamed, and she had to be stuffed into the squad car.[26]

The movie relates Crystal Lee's story with considerable precision. It makes a few artistic adjustments (combining the posted notices about blacks and wages into one, for instance), and it tightly compresses the time in which events occurred. Overall, however, it presents the picture accurately. *Norma Rae* also establishes a number of small details about Crystal Lee's life with considerable authenticity. For example, Crystal Lee's father was overprotective, as is the figure in the movie. Many of the experiences in Norma Rae's turbulent year—her boredom with her job, the excitement she discovered in the union campaign, her resistance to company intimidation, and the revelations she made to her children about her past romances—parallel the experiences of Crystal Lee.

Also, the movie provides a sensitive picture of life inside many of the mills. Working conditions for the southern mill hands were frequently very difficult, and *Norma Rae* effectively demonstrates several of the most important problems. The movie presents the difficulties with particular force in the opening minutes, when audiences hear the roar of the textile machines and sense that the looms' tremendous vibration makes verbal communication in the plant almost impossible. Employees shout and gesticulate to make themselves understood, and Norma Rae's mother suffers from hearing loss. Cotton-lint dust floats across the air in the workrooms and gathers on the machinery. The workers appear to be exhausted from the heat inside the buildings. Pipes hanging from the ceiling shoot mist into the room to keep the humidity at the desired levels for the best weaving (mills typically maintained temperatures of eighty degrees and humidity levels at 65 percent). All these elements in the film are authentic; noise, lint, and vapor added to the discomfort of southern mill workers, who often worked in dreary, enclosed, windowless work environments much like the one seen in the movie. Indeed, many textile workers developed "brown lung disease" (byssinosis) and eventually died from respiratory problems. Company physicians often dismissed the workers' complaints about their breathing and coughing by concluding that the individuals were suffering from merely "a little touch of asthma."[27]

Norma Rae makes its case for organized labor by detailing the life of textile workers in the American South both in the workplace and in their social environment. The film reveals not only harsh working conditions in the plants but also the mill workers' limited education. In a variety of subtle ways *Norma Rae* offers a sampling of the history and culture of the southern "lintheads," showing the plainness of their lives while they resided in the isolated environment of the mill towns. *Norma Rae* strikes an emotional note for unions by suggesting that southern mill hands lived like nineteenth-century workers in late twentieth-century America.

As *Norma Rae* demonstrates, a mill worker's child grew up much like

a second-class citizen in southern textile towns. In school and in play
the mill children were socially and geographically segregated from the
children of more affluent families. Mill workers lived in separate neighborhoods (often on the "other" side of the railroad tracks), attended
their own churches, sent their children to their own schools, and
bought goods separately at a company commissary.[28] The movie conveys this social division authentically. When the union leader in the
movie says to assembled workers at an organization meeting, "You are
known as trash to some," he uses the exact words that Crystal Lee
employed to describe the way that the town's middle- and upper-class
citizens viewed the mill hands. In this social environment a romance
between an uptown boy and a mill girl could lead to trouble. The young
man could face social ostracism. Upper-crust males sometimes exploited
girls from the mill community for brief sexual relationships, but they
usually did not marry them. Crystal Lee experienced this problem
when a young man from across town who later went to law school
would not publicly acknowledge his earlier romantic relationship with
her or the child he fathered with her.[29] The movie reveals this situation in a scene at a baseball game in which a well-dressed figure named
Ellis accidentally encounters Norma Rae. It becomes evident that Ellis
is the father of Norma Rae's son Craig, but Ellis will not visit the youngster or take responsibility for what resulted from an escapade in the
backseat of his Cadillac six years before.

Of course, the filmmakers did take some liberties in fashioning the
story. They overemphasized the heroine's role in forcing change, accentuated personality differences, and conveniently placed the central
character in places where Crystal Lee was not situated.

Above all the movie concentrates heavily on the activity of a few
key individuals. It leaves the impression that the union victory in the
mills was almost solely due to the labors of Norma Rae (Crystal Lee)
and Reuben Warshovsky (Eli Zivkovich). In fact, it resulted from the
efforts of several union organizers (not one) who went to Roanoke
Rapids and the courage of numerous mill hands who risked their jobs
by handing out union literature, recruiting new members, and openly acknowledging their association with the union. Individuals such as
James Boone, Bennett Taylor, Robert Mallory, Alice Tanner, Dorothy
Lynch, Maurine Hedgepeth, and Carolyn Brown—figures not known
beyond the city of Roanoke Rapids and unrecognized in the movie—
played important roles in the union effort.[30] Indeed, some of the mill
hands believed that Crystal Lee hogged publicity and staged the dem-

onstration on the workroom table to draw attention to her own activities. Crystal Lee's personality and style clearly irritated some of her coworkers.[31] The movie acknowledges this tension, however, showing the employees' resistance to Norma Rae's behavior when she works as an organizer in Warshovsky's office. With regard to the role of multiple figures in winning union recognition, Crystal Lee herself is quick to point out that she was just one of several important people in the struggle. She also observes that African Americans made particularly important contributions to the cause, and one of these unrecognized heroes (Joseph Williams) lost his job before she did because of pro-union activity.[32]

The movie's concentration on two principal characters is not surprising, of course. Like most Hollywood films about historical events, *Norma Rae* tells a big story through the lives of a few exciting personalities. The technique effectively engages the audience's interest, but it also distorts the manner in which the union made progress in Roanoke Rapids.

The filmmakers also altered some important details about the two principal characters to create an intriguing dramatic structure. To accentuate the differences between Norma Rae and Reuben Warshovsky, they made Warshovsky a strongly ethnic Jewish New Yorker. This contrast gives the story an interesting romantic twist, suggesting the growth of mutual admiration between two people from very different cultures. The individual whom Warshovsky represents (Eli Zivkovich) was actually a former coal miner who had been a United Mine Workers' Union agent. Crystal Lee insists that their relationship was more like a father-daughter association than a romantic attraction, which the movie suggests. She emphatically notes, too, that she and Zivkovich never went swimming naked together (the movie shows Norma Rae and Warshovsky swimming in this fashion but never shows them developing a sexual relationship). In another bending of the facts, the filmmakers showed Norma Rae working in the terrible conditions of the weaving rooms when she began her confrontation with management. Actually, Crystal Lee's job in the J. P. Stevens plant in the early 1970s involved folding towels and preparing gift boxes. She worked in much cleaner and safer conditions at the time than the many other mill hands who labored in the noisier and dirtier stages of the manufacturing process.[33]

Despite these fabrications and misrepresentations, *Norma Rae* does an impressive job of portraying the personal experiences of a specific woman in Roanoke Rapids, North Carolina, and of communicating a general sense of southern mill workers' lives. Clyde Bush, who became a principal spokesperson for the textile union in Roanoke Rapids in the years after the representation election, said in 1991 that the movie "basically gives a real good view of life inside a textile plant."[34] Crystal Lee agreed. She called *Norma Rae* "as true to life as a movie can be" when she reflected on its accomplishments in 1991.[35]

Norma Rae was marketed to the American public as a story about a female "Rocky" and as a film that exudes feminist spirit while not overtly preaching feminism. It was an important contribution to Hollywood storytelling about strong-headed and courageous women, but it also constituted an unusual attempt by the movie industry to give a sophisticated examination of union issues from the worker's point of view. A fortuitous involvement of sympathetic people helped to produce this perspective, particularly the leadership of two socially conscious female producers and the direction of a champion of the underdog, Martin Ritt. Hollywood went on to make many more movies in the 1980s and 1990s sympathetic to the problems of secretaries, restaurant workers, factory hands, and other employees, but those films generally focus on the personal struggles of individuals rather than the efforts of workers to organize collectively. *Norma Rae*, in this regard, stands in high relief as a Hollywood film that sent a powerful pro-union message through the force of cinematic realism.

Shortly after Gore Vidal's *Lincoln: A Novel* appeared as a docudrama on NBC Television, Gabor Boritt, a Civil War specialist, took issue with the program's treatment of Lincoln's presidency. Commenting at a conference of scholars interested in film and history, Boritt complained that the drama takes too many liberties. Vidal and the filmmakers had been too eager to make their presentation entertaining, he complained, and consequently, they wove excessive fiction into their history. Boritt's criticism was not appreciated by some of the delegates. The most vociferous opposition came from Peter Stead, a historian and film scholar. Stead complained that Boritt failed to understand the purpose of televised entertainment such as Vidal's *Lincoln*. The television drama had not been designed to replicate past events, Stead argued. Instead, Vidal and NBC had created an imaginative perspective that constituted art as well as history. Holding a novelist or a dramatist to strict standards of scholarly presentation serves no useful purpose, Stead insisted; in fact, such pressures can stifle artistic creativity.

Unfortunately, delegates at the conference chose sides. In conversations following the exchange they endorsed Boritt's call for scholarly integrity or praised Stead for recognizing that historical dramas frequently must interpret the past in ways that are different from the techniques of written history. The selection of one or the other pole in this debate was lamentable, because the concerns of *both* Boritt and Stead were relevant to a discussion of Hollywood's treatment of history.

As the case studies in this book demonstrate, questions about responsible portrayals of historical events are appropriate when assessing popular movies that can affect the way millions view the past. To claim that "anything goes" in the name of artistic license is to invite fictional excesses that can grossly distort the public's understanding. Cinema is a powerful tool for communicating feeling and opinion about the past; if historians believe that the tool has been employed irresponsibility, they should articulate their concerns forcefully, as Boritt did.

Still, historians cannot treat dramatic entertainment simply as non-fiction brought to life with actors. They should recognize the need to incorporate speculation and myth and to take poetic leaps when presenting history on the screen. Cinema offers abundant chances for constructing imaginative visions of the past, and it is not surprising that artists often manipulate images liberally in pursuing these opportunities. In this respect Peter Stead gave proper recognition to the art form when he counseled receptivity to the experimentation in Gore Vidal's novel and NBC's television program.

There is no hard-and-fast rule for judging the handling of history on the silver screen. The filmmaker's activity in interpreting the past is complex. Cinematic historians make diverse choices in shaping scripts, selecting scenes and characters, dubbing sound, and editing images. Each historical movie reflects a rich variety of artistic decisions that can be scrutinized. On close examination the observer may find reason to offer mixed judgments. Some of the filmmakers' decisions will appear to deserve praise; others will seem to warrant criticism. In the popular press, however, measured judgments are rendered only occasionally. More typically, commentators make emotion-laden assessments. In the style of television's popular reviewers of Hollywood fare, they encourage audiences to respond with blanket indictments or enthusiastic praise. Judgments frequently appear in the form of thumbs up or thumbs down.

The case studies included here suggest the value of a more complex consideration of Hollywood's handling of history. *Mississippi Burning*, for example, overlooks the contributions of blacks to their own freedom movement and exaggerates the FBI's role in achieving civil rights gains, but it effectively re-creates the frightening milieu of the racist South. *JFK* presents speculation as fact and manipulates evidence, yet it imaginatively exposes audiences to a plethora of intriguing questions about the Warren Commission's report and draws attention to important debates about Kennedy's policies in Vietnam that have been the subject of serious scholarship. Although *Sergeant York* romanticizes the life of the World War I hero, it sent an important message to audiences in 1941 about the value of fighting for freedom. *Missing* suggests blame for the personal tragedy of Charles Horman on the basis of skimpy evidence, but in a broader sense, it communicates significant warnings about the danger of U.S. connections in foreign countries with right-wing leaders during the cold war years. *Bonnie and Clyde* offers a romantic view of a pair of brutal killers, yet it brilliantly re-creates the environment of poverty and crime in middle America during the depression years. *Patton* carefully avoids making a final judgment about its enigmatic subject, but the overall effect of this ambivalence is to stir audiences to think about war and peace. Both *All the President's Men* and *Norma Rae* make their leading characters appear to be more influential than they really were, yet the films relate stories of Davids fighting Goliaths with considerable authenticity.

A dramatically positive or negative assessment of Hollywood's handling of history often develops out of a limited consideration of a movie's relationship to the past, one that relies solely on examination of the finished product. Judgments that rely specifically on analysis of the motion picture—its story and its imagery—often rest on superficial evidence. It is far more useful to step behind the film. By viewing the history of a movie's development, we can better understand how producers, writers, and directors struggled with questions about historical interpretation during the formative stages of their creative work. It is also useful to step around the motion picture. Seeing the film in the context of the times and observing the way in which filmmakers and critics debate questions about interpretation take the analysis beyond simplistic black-and-white assessments. By going behind and around the motion picture, we connect the discussion to larger issues and give greater dimension to our efforts to consider what happens to history when Hollywood filmmakers get their hands on it.

Preface

1. See, for example, John E. O'Connor and Martin Jackson, eds., *American History/American Film;* Terry Christensen, *Reel Politics;* John H. Lenihan, *Showdown.*

For useful discussions about the way in which Hollywood films may or may not reflect conditions in society, see Peter C. Rollins, *Hollywood as Historian,* 1; Robert B. Ray, *A Certain Tendency of the Hollywood Cinema,* 11; Pierre Sorlin, "Historical Films as Tools for Historians," in John E. O'Connor, ed., *Image as Artifact,* 51; Michael Ryan and Douglas Kellner, *Camera Politica,* xi; Stephen Prince, *Visions of Empire,* 2–3; Michael Parenti, *Make-Believe Media,* 1–17; Philip Davies and Brian Neve, *Cinema, Politics and Society in America,* 1; Robert A. Rosenstone, "Genres, History, and Hollywood," 367–69; Lawrence L. Murray, "The Feature Film as Historical Document," 10–11; Lary May, *Screening out the Past,* 237; William Hughes, "The Evaluation of Film as Evidence," in Paul Smith, ed., *The Historian and Film,* 64; and Bruce Crowther, *Hollywood Faction.*

2. They draw inspiration from Siegfried Kracauer, *From Caligari to Hitler.*

3. Garth Jowett, *Film, the Democratic Art: A Social History of American Film;* Robert Sklar, *Movie-Made America;* Clayton R. Koppes and Gregory D. Black, *Hollywood Goes to War.*

4. See, for example, Robert C. Allen and Douglas Gomery, *Film History;* Tim Bywater and Thomas Sobchack, *An Introduction to Film Criticism;* J. Dudley Andrew, *The Major Film Theories;* Philip Rosen, ed., *Narrative, Apparatus, Ideology;* Bill Nichols, ed., *Movies and Methods;* Noel Carroll, *Mystifying Movies;* David Bordwell, *Making Meaning;* Robert Sklar and Charles Musser, eds., *Resisting Images;* David Bordwell, Janet Staiger, and Kristen Thompson, *The Classical Hollywood Cinema;* John E. O'Connor, ed., *The Image as Artifact;* Janet Staiger, *Interpreting Films;* and Ian Jarvie, *Philosophy of the Film.*

Introduction

1. Michael Parenti, *Make-Believe Media,* 58.

2. Daniel Leab, "The Moving Image as Intrerpreter of History—Telling the Dancer from the Dance," in John E. O'Connor, ed., *Image as Artifact,* 83.

3. Pierre Sorlin, *The Film in History,* 21.

4. Russell B. Nye, "History and Literature: Branches of the Same Tree," in Robert H. Bremmer, ed., *Essays on History and Literature,* 145.

5. Ibid., 148–49.

6. Ibid., 146.

7. Theodore Roosevelt quoted in ibid., 132.

8. Simon Schama, "Clio Has a Problem," 32–34.

9. Simon Schama, *Dead Certainties: Unwarranted Speculations* (New York, 1991), 320.

10. Daniel J. Walkowitz, "Visual History," 60.

11. Daniel J. Walkowitz quoted in Barbara Abrash and Janet Sternberg, eds., *Historians and Filmmakers,* 13.

12. Robert A. Rosenstone, "History in Images/History in Words," 1184.

13. Ibid., 1184.

14. Ibid., 1181.

15. Robert A. Rosenstone, "*JFK:* Historical Fact/Historical Film," *American Historical Review* 97, no. 2 (Apr. 1992): 509.

16. Rosenstone, "History in Images/History in Words," 1180. Rosenstone drew some of these ideas from Hayden White, who has written in a related way in *Tropics of Discourse,* 121–30. White has also written about history and film in "Historiography and Historiophoty."

17. Marcus Raskin, "'JFK' and the Culture of Violence," *American Historical Review* 97, no. 2 (Apr. 1992): 487.

18. James M. McPherson, "The *Glory* Story," *New Republic,* 8–15 January 1990, 26–27.

19. Warren Susman, *Culture as History,* 11.

20. Ibid., 9.

21. Richard Slotkin, *Gunfighter Nation,* 3–45.

22. For examples of reviewers' responses to *Quiz Show* and the questions raised about the movie's interpretation of history, see Max Frankel, "This Is Your Life," *The New York Times Magazine,* 9 October 1994, 32; Robert Goldsborough, "Quiz Show Draws Wrath of Exec's Relative," *Advertising Age,* 24 October 1994, 54; John Leo, "Faking It in 'Quiz Show,'" *U.S. News and World Report,* 17 October 1994, 24; Richard Zoglin, "Why 'Quiz Show' Is a Scandal," *Time,* 10 October 1994, 91; Richard Bernstein, "For $64,000, What Is 'Fiction'?" *New York Times,* 4 September 1994, H1; John Simon, "Questionable Questions," *National Review* 46, no. 19 (10 Oct. 1994): 76–78; Jeffrey Hart, "'Van Doren' and 'Redford,'" *National Review*

46, no. 21 (7 Nov. 1994): 78. For Robert Redford's views on the message of the movie, see Anthony DeCurtis, "Robert Redford: The Rolling Stone Interview," *Rolling Stone*, 6 October 1994, 74–77, 98.

Chapter 1 *Mississippi Burning*

1. See the *New York Times*, 30 March 1989, C22, for the story on the Academy Awards. For a good overview on the history of the campaigns for civil rights, see Harvard Sitkoff, *The Struggle for Back Equality* (New York, 1981). For discussions of the Philadelphia, Mississippi, murder cases, see Seth Cagin and Philip Day, *We Are Not Afraid: The Story of Goodman, Schwerner, and Chaney and the Civil Rights Campaign in Mississippi* (New York, 1988); William Bradford Huie, *Three Lives for Mississippi* (New York, 1964; rprt., 1968). For information on the FBI's activities in the cases, see Don Whitehead, *Attack on Terror: The FBI against the Ku Klux Klan in Mississippi* (New York, 1970); Neil J. Welch and David W. Marston, *Inside Hoover's FBI: The Top Field Chief Reports* (Garden City, N.Y., 1984).

2. Whitehead, *Attack on Terror*, 142.

3. Ibid., 125; Cagin and Day, *We Are Not Afraid*, 393–95.

4. Robert Brent Toplin's interview with Chris Gerolmo, 18 November 1991.

5. Ibid.

6. Robert Brent Toplin's interview with Alan Parker (via fax), 19 August 1993.

7. Interview with Chris Gerolmo.

8. Ibid.; Robert Brent Toplin's interview with Fred Zollo, 19 November 1991.

9. Interview with Chris Gerolmo.

10. Interview with Alan Parker; *Mississippi Burning* production notes, 11–26, in the *Mississippi Burning* file at the Academy of Motion Picture Arts and Sciences (AMPAS) archives, Los Angeles.

11. Cagin and Day, *We Are Not Afraid*, 367–85.

12. David Halberstam, "Mississippi Burning," *Premier*, February 1989, 97.

13. Cagin and Day, *We Are Not Afraid*, 344.

14. *Mississippi Burning* production notes, 15–16.

15. Gavin Smith, "Mississippi Gambler: Alan Parker Rides Again," clipping in the *Mississippi Burning* file at the AMPAS archives; Stuart Klawars, "Films," *The Nation*, 2 January 1989, 26.

16. *Time*, 9 January 1989, 58.

17. Coretta Scott King, "Hollywood's Latest Perversion: The Civil Rights Era as a White Experience," clipping in the *Mississippi Burning* file at the

AMPAS archives. Carolyn Goodman Eisner, the mother of slain civil rights worker Andrew Goodman, agreed with the view that *Mississippi Burning* gives inadequate attention to the contributions of African Americans (Robert Brent Toplin's interview with Carolyn Goodman Eisner, 1 August 1993).

18. Robert Brent Toplin's interview with Julian Bond, 15 December 1994.

19. Interview with Chris Gerolmo; interview with Fred Zollo.

20. Huie, *Three Lives for Mississippi,* 114–17.

21. *Mississippi Burning* production notes, 27.

22. Interview with Alan Parker.

23. Klawars, "Films." See also Harvard Sitkoff, "Mississippi Burning," *Journal of American History* 76, no. 3 (Dec. 1989): 1019–20.

24. Cagin and Day, *We Are Not Afraid,* 393, 395. Two books that served as important sources of information in designing the story (Whitehead's *Attack on Terror* and Welch and Marston's *Inside Hoover's FBI*) do not feature evidence about FBI-led intimidation and violence similar to the kind depicted in the movie.

25. Interview with Chris Gerolmo.

26. Ibid.

27. Interview with Alan Parker.

28. Welch and Marston, *Inside Hoover's FBI,* 105, 108.

29. "Civil Rights Burned," *New York Times,* 30 December 1988, I:30.

30. Ron Austin, "Letter to the Editor," *Los Angeles Times,* 4 February 1989.

31. Sitkoff, "Mississippi Burning," 1019.

32. Patrick Buchanan, "Hollywood's Never-Never Mississippi," *Los Angeles Herald-Examiner,* 25 January 1989.

33. "Facts for Burning," *The Economist,* 7 January 1989, 79.

34. Richard Schickel, "The Fire in the South," *Time,* 5 December 1988, 90.

35. Halberstam, "Mississippi Burning," 97.

36. Alan Parker quoted in Smith, "Mississippi Gambler," 29.

37. Ibid., 30; interview with Alan Parker.

38. Alan Parker quoted in Wayne King, "Fact vs. Fiction in Mississippi," *New York Times,* 4 December 1988, II:15.

39. Ibid.

40. Interview with Chris Gerolmo.

41. Interview with Fred Zollo.

42. Ibid.

43. Ibid.

44. Interview with Carolyn Goodman Eisner.

Chapter 2 *JFK*

1. George Will, "'JFK' Makes a Hash of History," *Wilmington Morning Star* (N.C.), 26 December 1991, 11A.

2. Robert Brent Toplin's interview with Zachary Sklar, 1 August 1993.

3. Robert Dam Anson, "The Shooting of 'JFK,'" in *JFK: The Book of the Film* (New York, 1992), 218.

4. Ibid., 218–24.

5. Ibid., 224–28; Robert Brent Toplin's interview with John Newman, 6 August 1993.

6. Gary Crowdus, "Clarifying the Conspiracy: An Interview with Oliver Stone," *Cineaste* 14, no. 1 (1992): 27; Crowdus, "Getting the Facts Straight: An Interview with Zachary Sklar," *Cineaste* 14, no. 1 (1992): 28, 30; Crowdus, "Striving for Authenticity: An Interview with Jane Rusconi," *Cineaste* 14, no. 1 (1992): 33, 35.

7. Interview with Zachary Sklar.

8. Interview with John Newman.

9. For criticisms of this view, see, for example, Alexander Cockburn, "Cockburn Replies," in *JFK: The Book of the Film*, 478–83.

10. See, for example, Cockburn, "Cockburn Replies," 478–83; *The Nation*, 6–13 January 1992, 7; Ronald Steel, "Mr. Smith Goes to the Twilight Zone," *New Republic*, 3 February 1992, 30–32.

11. *Newsweek*, 23 December 1991, 49 (quotation); Lisa Grunwald, "Why We Still Care," *Life*, December 1991.

12. *Time*, 23 December 1991, 70; Anson, "The Shooting of 'JFK,'" 97; Tom Bethell, "Reality Check for Another Movie Myth," *Los Angeles Times*, 1 December 1991, M5; "Oliver Stone's Patsy," *New York Times*, 30 December 1991, A34; Frances Frank Marcus, "Kennedy Film Puts Originator of a Conspiracy Theory in the Limelight," *New York Times*, 20 December 1991; Anthony Lewis, "'J.F.K.,'" *New York Times*, 9 January 1992, A23; Tom Wicker, "Does 'J.F.K.' Conspire against Reason?" *New York Times*, 15 December 1991.

13. *Newsweek*, 23 December 1991, 99 (quotation); Robert Brent Toplin's interview with Oliver Stone, 24 August 1993.

14. For debates about Attenborough's depiction, see, for example, "False Gandhi," *New Republic*, 21 March 1983, 9–11; Richard Grenier, "The Truth about Gandhi," *The Bulletin* (Australia), 28 June 1983, clipping in the *Gandhi* file at the Academy of Motion Pictures Arts and Sciences (AMPAS) archives, Los Angeles; John Briley, "'Gandhi' Is True: The Screenwriter Defends the Film," *Los Angeles Herald-Examiner*, 20 March 1983.

15. James O'Bryne, "The Garrison Probe: The Story Hollywood Won't Tell," in *JFK: The Book of the Film*, 234–40.

16. Arthur M. Schlesinger Jr., "'JFK': Truth and Fiction," *Wall Street Journal,* 10 January 1992.

17. James N. Giglio, "Oliver Stone's 'JFK' in Historical Perspective," *Perspectives,* April 1992, 19.

18. Steel, "Mr. Smith Goes to the Twilight Zone," 30.

19. Robert Dallek, "Kennedy Was No Dove" (letter to the editor), *New York Times,* 3 January 1992, A10.

20. Noam Chomsky, *Rethinking Camelot: JFK, the Vietnam War, and U.S. Political Culture* (Boston, 1993).

21. Kenneth O'Donnell and David Powers, who were advisers to Kennedy and close to him, support the conclusion that the president was "determined to pull out of the Vietnam War"; see their *"Johnny, We Hardly Knew Ye": Memories of John Fitzgerald Kennedy* (New York, 1973), 16–19 (quotation on 17). See also Theodore C. Sorensen, *The Kennedy Legacy* (New York, 1969), 208. George Herring, author of one of the most popular histories of U.S. military actions in Vietnam, points out that we do not know what Kennedy would have done in Vietnam, but judging by his actions in office, one must conclude that he expanded American involvement in the country to a dangerous level; see his book *America's Longest War: The United States and Vietnam, 1950–1975* (New York, 1986), 106–7.

22. Many of the arguments outlined here are discussed in Jim Marrs, *Crossfire: The Plot That Killed Kennedy* (New York, 1989), 90–312.

23. Richard B. Stolley maintains that *Life* did not try to conceal the Zapruder film from public view; see Stolley, "The Zapruder Film: Shots Seen round the World," in *JFK: The Book of the Film,* 410–13.

24. Tom Squitieri, "JFK Autopsy Disputed," *USA Today,* 3 April 1992, A2.

25. Lawrence K. Altman, "Doctors Confirm Kennedy Autopsy Report," *New York Times,* 20 May 1992, I:13.

26. Jacob Cohen, "Yes, Oswald Alone Killed Kennedy," *Commentary,* June 1992, 32–33, 36–37.

27. Ibid., 37.

28. William Manchester, "No Evidence for a Conspiracy to Kill Kennedy," in *JFK: The Book of the Film,* 452.

29. The strongest detailed argument pointing to Oswald as the lone killer is Gerald Posner, *Case Closed: Lee Harvey Oswald and the Assassination of JFK* (New York, 1993).

30. Manchester, "No Evidence," 452.

31. Daniel Patrick Moynihan, "The Paranoid Style," in *JFK: The Book of the Film,* 328–31.

32. Oliver Stone quoted in Tom Jacobs, "Deadly Hawks," *Los Angeles Daily News,* 20 December 1991.

33. Crowdus, "Clarifying the Conspiracy," 26.

34. Oliver Stone, "Stone Shoots Back," in *JFK: The Book of the Movie*, 230.

35. Oliver Stone, "The Flicker of an Eye Means Nothing in Print," *Los Angeles Times*, 26 March 1992, B7.

36. Ibid.; Ellen Goodman, "Oliver Stone's Hijacking of History," *New York Times*, 4 January 1992, A21.

37. Oliver Stone, "Oliver Stone Talks Back," in *JFK: The Book of the Film*, 353.

38. Oliver Stone quoted in Anson, "The Shooting of JFK," 221.

39. Oliver Stone, "The JFK Assassination—What about the Evidence?" *Washington Post*, 24 December 1991, A13.

40. Crowdus, "Clarifying the Conspiracy," 25.

41. Oliver Stone quoted in Will, "'JFK': Paranoid History."

42. George Lardner Jr., "On the Set: Dallas in Wonderland," *Washington Post*, 19 May 1991, D1.

43. *Washington Post*, 2 June 1991, D3.

44. Oliver Stone, "Who Is Rewriting History?" *New York Times*, 20 December 1991, A35.

45. Oliver Stone quoted in Tom Jacobs, "Deadly Hawks."

46. Stone, "Who Is Rewriting History?"

47. Oliver Stone quoted in Philip McCombs, "Oliver Stone, Returning the Fire," *Washington Post*, 21 December 1991, F6.

48. Interview with Oliver Stone.

49. David Belin, "Earl Warren's Assassins," *New York Times*, 7 March 1992, 25.

50. George Lardner Jr., "On the Set," D1; George Lardner Jr., ". . . Or Just a Sloppy Mess?" *Washington Post*, 2 June 1991, D3.

51. Tom Wicker quoted in "The 'JFK' Version," *Boston Globe*, 19 December 1991; *Chicago Sun-Times*, 29 December 1991, 39.

52. Stanley Kauffmann, "Yes, 'JFK' Again," *New Republic*, 6 April 1992, 27.

53. Edward Jay Epstein, "The Second Coming of Jim Garrison," *The Atlantic Monthly*, March 1993, 90.

54. G. Robert Blakey quoted in "The 'JFK' Version."

55. Gerald R. Ford and David W. Belin, "Kennedy Assassination: How about the Truth?" *Washington Post*, 17 December 1991, A21.

56. "'JFK' Comes under Fire," *New York Daily News*, 22 December 1991 (Mark Lane quotation); Lardner, "On the Set," D1 (Weisberg quotation).

57. John Connally quoted in William Pack, "Connally Slams 'JFK' Film," *Houston Post*, 24 December 1991.

58. Jack Valenti quoted in Bernard Weintraub, "Valenti Denounces Stone's 'J.F.K.' as a Smear," *New York Times*, 2 April 1992, B1.

59. "Twisted History," *Newsweek,* 23 December 1991, 47.

60. "Hollywood: History by Default," *New York Times,* 25 December 1991, 30; Anthony Lewis, "J.F.K."

61. Charles Krauthammer, "'JFK': A Lie, but Harmless," *Washington Post,* 10 January 1992, A19.

62. Arthur Schlesinger Jr., "'JFK': The Truth and Fiction."

63. Interview with Oliver Stone.

64. Interview with Zachary Sklar.

65. Crowdus, "Clarifying the Conspiracy," 25.

66. Stone, "Who Is Rewriting History?" A35.

67. In August 1993 the National Archives opened a large collection of previously closed papers for public view. Many documents still had not been released by that date, however. See Tim Weiner, "Papers on Kennedy Assassination Are Unsealed, and '63 Is Revisited," *New York Times,* 24 August 1993, 1, 8.

68. George Lardner Jr., "Ex-Warren Staffers Urge JFK Data Release," *Washington Post,* 31 January 1992, A7.

69. *Cineaste* 14, no. 1 (1992).

70. Marcus Raskin, "'JFK' and the Culture of Violence," *American Historical Review* 97, no. 2 (Apr. 1992): 487.

71. Ibid.

72. Robert A. Rosenstone, "*JFK:* Historical Fact/Historical Film," *American Historical Review* 97, no. 2 (Apr. 1992): 509.

73. Ibid., 509, 511.

Chapter 3 *Sergeant York*

1. For a review of the details of York's life that the movie portrays, see Sam K. Cowan, *Sergeant York and His People* (New York, 1992), 15–43, 270–72. Thomas Doherty put the film's contribution in perspective by noting that *Sergeant York* recasts World War I, helping to change its image from a useless slaughter to a crusade worthy of American participation; see Doherty, *Projections of War: Hollywood, American Culture and World War II* (New York, 1993), 100.

2. In his memoirs of work as a Hollywood screenwriter, Howard Koch recalled that he and the other three writers took "extravagant liberties" in portraying York's "backwoods rearing and his courtship of a neighbor girl"; see Koch, *As Time Goes By: Memoirs of a Writer* (New York, 1979), 73. These dramatic flourishes regarding York's personal life are not surprising for a feature film, however, and compared to the treatment of famous figures in later Hollywood movies, they are relatively mild examples of dramatic license.

3. David D. Lee, *Sergeant York: An American Hero* (Lexington, Ky., 1985), 100.

4. Rudy Behlmer, ed., *Inside Warner Brothers* (New York, 1985), 185. For details on Lasky's earlier work, see Thomas Schatz, *The Genius of the System: Hollywood Filmmaking in the Studio Era* (New York, 1988), 71–72, 81.

5. Lee, *Sergeant York,* 102.

6. The deal that Lasky and York negotiated included the following for York: $25,000 in advance, $25,000 on release of the motion picture, 4 percent of any gross over $3 million, 5 percent of gross over $4 million, 6 percent over $6 million, and 8 percent over $9 million. See Nick Roddick, *A New Deal in Entertainment: Warner Brothers in the 1930s* (London, 1983), 211.

7. Abem Finkel to Hal Wallis, 9 January 1941, "Sergeant York," box 1712 (Warner Brothers Collection, University of Southern California).

8. Lee, *Sergeant York,* 101–4.

9. Doherty, *Projections of War,* 92–98; Clayton R. Koppes and Gregory D. Black, *Hollywood Goes to War,* 20–37; Bernard F. Dick, *The Star-Spangled Screen: The American World War II Film* (Lexington, Ky., 1985), 67, 93.

10. Lasky was primarily interested in the production's monetary potential; he interfered very little in matters of planning the artistic presentation and the film's interpretation of history (Robert Brent Toplin's interview with Howard Koch, 6 August 1993).

11. Finkel to Wallis, 9 January 1941.

12. Ibid., 4–5.

13. Ibid., 6.

14. Ibid., 6–8.

15. Ibid., 2–3.

16. Albert F. Ganier to Jesse L. Lasky, 30 April 1940, "Sergeant York" (Warner Brothers Collection, University of Southern California); Jesse Lasky to Hal Wallis, 29 April 1940, inter-office memo, "Sergeant York" (Warner Brothers Collection, University of Southern California).

17. Bill Rice, "The Private Life of a Motion Picture," "Sergeant York" (Warner Brothers Collection, University of Southern California), 8.

18. Research department to Captain Carlysle, 23 April 1941, "Sergeant York" (Warner Brothers Collection, University of Southern California); Research department to Jesse Lasky, 26 April 1941, "Sergeant York" (Warner Brothers Collection, University of Southern California); Research department to Eric Stacey, 26 April 1941, "Sergeant York" (Warner Brothers Collection, University of Southern California).

19. *Sergeant York* production notes (Warner Brothers Collection, University of Southern California).

20. Julien Josephson and Harry Chandlee to Jesse Lasky, 8 May 1940, "Sergeant York" (Warner Brothers Collection, University of Southern California), 24, 27. Howard Koch, one of the writers, was of pacifist inclination at the time and had to wrestle with his own conscience in designing the movie's message about York's acceptance of the soldier's role (interview with Howard Koch).

21. Josephson and Chandlee to Lasky, 8 May 1940, 25.

22. Ibid., 27–28.

23. Lee, *Sergeant York*, 25–39.

24. Ibid., 112–13.

25. Harry Chandlee to Jesse Lasky, 15 October 1942, "Sergeant York" (Warner Brothers Collection, University of Southern California).

26. Cowan, *Sergeant York*, 11–152; Lee, *Sergeant York*, 6–18.

27. Lee, *Sergeant York*, 18–21.

28. Lee, *Sergeant York*, 20–47; Cowan, *Sergeant York and His People*, 15–43.

29. Lee, *Sergeant York*, x, 55, 65–67, 95, 99.

30. Alvin York quoted in ibid., 110.

31. "Speech by Sergeant Alvin York at Arlington on May 30, 1941," "Sergeant York" (Warner Brothers Collection, University of Southern California). On the reception for York and the movie in Washington, D.C., which included numerous political leaders and diplomats, see Jesse Lasky to Jack Warner, 1 August 1941 (telegram), "Sergeant York" (Warner Brothers Collection, University of Southern California).

32. Koppes and Black, *Hollywood Goes to War*, 38–39.

33. "23 Years after Argonne: Jesse Lasky Brings Life Story of Sergeant York to Screen," *Newsweek*, 14 July 1941, 61–62; "When Pacifists Fight," *Catholic World*, October 1941, 87.

34. "The Screen," *Commonweal*, 18 July 1941, 306.

35. Ibid.

36. "New Picture: Sergeant York," *Time*, 4 August 1941, 70.

37. Gerald P. Nye quoted in Lee, *Sergeant York*, 111.

38. Gerald P. Nye quoted in Koppes and Black, *Hollywood Goes to War*, 40.

39. Harry Warner quoted in ibid., 44.

40. *Propaganda in Motion Pictures*, hearings before a subcommittee of the Committee on Interstate Commerce, United States Senate, First Session on S. Res. 152, 9 to 26 September 1970 (Washington, D.C., 1942), 339–48. For additional comments from the Warners regarding questions about partisanship in their movies, see Behlmer, ed., *Inside Warner Brothers*, 188–90; and Dick, *The Star-Spangled Screen*, 68.

Chapter 4 *Missing*

1. Robert Brent Toplin's interview with Elizabeth Horman, 6 December 1991.

2. Robert Brent Toplin's interview with Nathaniel Davis, 9 December 1991; Nathaniel Davis, "Missing Evidence," *Washington Post*, 29 April 1987, A19.

3. Carla Hall, "The Scars after 'Missing,'" *Washington Post*, 18 January 1983, D1, D11 (Davis quotation on D11).

4. Robert Brent Toplin's interview with Thomas Hauser, 1 December 1991.

5. Robert Brent Toplin's interview with Eddie Lewis, 4 December 1991.

6. Flora Lewis, "New Film by Costa-Gavras Examines the Chilean Coup," *New York Times*, 7 February 1982; Jeffrey Wells, "Costa-Gavras on 'Missing,'" *The Film Journal*, 15 February, 1982. For Costa-Gavras's perspective on making "political" films, see Gary Gilson, "Interview with Costa Gavras," *Film and History* 13, no. 2 (1973): 11–20. Constantin Costa-Gavras quoted in Guy Flatley, "Movies Are Passions and My Great Passion Is Politics," *New York Times*, 11 January 1970, II:15.

7. Robert Brent Toplin's interview with Constantin Costa-Gavras, 20 September 1993.

8. Ibid.

9. "'Missing' Film Makers Sued for Libel," *Los Angeles Times*, 12 January 1983.

10. Constantin Costa-Gavras quoted in Marc Levitin, "'Missing': More Controversy for Costa-Gavras," *BAM*, 12 March 1982, clipping in the *Missing* file at the Academy of Motion Pictures Arts and Sciences (AMPAS) archives, Los Angeles.

11. Lewis, "New Film by Costa-Gavras."

12. Constantin Costa-Gravas quoted in "U.S. Takes Issue with Costa-Gavras Film on Chile," *New York Times*, 10 February 1982.

13. Lewis, "New Film by Costa-Gavras."

14. Vincent Canby, "Costa-Gavras' Striking Cinematic Achievement," *New York Times*, 14 February 1982.

15. Jeffrey Hart, "Our Media Fabricates These Stories, as in the New Film 'Missing,'" *Los Angeles Herald-Examiner*, 16 February 1982.

16. Peter Rainer, "Our Movies Are Prisoners of Their Politics," *Los Angeles Herald-Examiner*, 29 February 1982.

17. Patrick Buchanan, "If You Want to Know What Really Happened during the Coup in Chile, Do Not See Missing," *Los Angeles Herald-Examiner*, 27 February 1982.

18. Robert Brent Toplin's interview with Donald E. Stewart, 29 November 1991.

19. Thomas Hauser, *The Execution of Charles Horman: An American Sacrifice* (New York, 1978), 31–33.

20. Ibid., 25, 31–33, 40–43.

21. *Covert Action in Chile, 1963–1973,* staff report of the Select Committee to Study Government Operations with Respect to Intelligence Activities, United States Senate (Washington, D.C., 1975), 1, 3.

22. Ibid., 2, 37, 38 (quotation).

23. Robert J. Alexander, *The Tragedy in Chile* (Westport, Conn., 1978), 275–76; Alan Angell, "Chile since 1958," in Leslie Bethell, ed., *Latin America since 1930: Spanish South America,* 340–41, vol. 8 of *The Cambridge History of Latin America,* 11 vols. (Cambridge, 1991).

24. Angell, "Chile since 1958," 344, 347–48, 355; Alexander, *The Tragedy in Chile,* 297–300; *Time,* 24 September 1973, 45–46; Paul E. Sigmund, *The Overthrow of Allende and the Politics of Chile, 1964–1976* (Pittsburgh, 1977), 227–29, 234–35, 283–87.

25. Angell, "Chile since 1958," 357–59; Sigmund, *The Overthrow of Allende,* 228; Alexander, *The Tragedy of Chile,* 297–300, 322–23.

26. Seymour Hersh observes that Allende's leadership had been hurt severely by the internal economic and political problems in Chile, "but those problems were compounded by the clandestine C.I.A. interference, as the Senate Intelligence Committee discovered in 1975"; see Hersh, *The Price of Power: Kissinger in the Nixon White House* (New York, 1981), 638.

27. Henry Kissinger, *White House Years* (Boston, 1979), 683; see also 653–58.

28. Paul E. Sigmund, "Crisis Management: Chile and Marxism," in John D. Martz, ed., *The United States' Policy in Latin America: A Quarter Century of Crisis and Challenge, 1961–1986* (Lincoln, Nebr., 1988), 164–66; Sigmund, *The Overthrow of Allende,* 285; Alexander, *The Tragedy in Chile,* 218, 231.

29. Much of the writing about the coup has been polemical; writers have either criticized the right-wing military leaders who led the coup and blamed U.S. involvement for much of what happened or defended the coup as a necessary effort against dangerous left-wing radicals. For a sampling, see Edy Kaufman, *Crisis in Allende's Chile: New Perspectives* (New York, 1988); Samuel Chavkin, *The Murder of Chile: Eyewitness Accounts of the Coup, the Terror, and the Resistance Today* (New York, 1982); James R. Whelan, *Allende: Death of a Marxist Dream* (Westport, Conn., 1981); Suzanne Labin, *Chile: The Crime of Resistance* (Richmond, U.K., 1982); Francisco Orrego Vicuña, ed., *Chile: The Balanced View* (Santiago, 1975); *White Book of the Change of Government in Chile* (Santiago, n.d.).

30. *Missing* production notes, 9, in the *Missing* file at the AMPAS archives, Los Angeles; Houser, *The Execution of Charles Horman*, 5–8, 45–47, 51.

31. Hauser, *The Execution of Charles Horman*, 51–67.

32. Ibid., 195.

33. Ibid., 193; interview with Thomas Hauser.

34. Interview with Nathaniel Davis.

35. Interview with Thomas Hauser.

36. Interview with Nathaniel Davis.

37. Interview with Donald E. Stewart.

38. Ibid.

39. Dale Pollock, "Criticism May Not Be 'Missing,'" *Los Angeles Times*, 13 February 1982.

40. Interview with Nathaniel Davis.

41. Nathaniel Davis, "Missing Evidence."

42. Nathaniel Davis to Theodore S. Wilkinson, 15 April 1991 (in the possession of Nathaniel Davis).

43. Constantin Costa-Gavras quoted in "U.S. Takes Issue with Costa-Gavras Film."

44. The production notes released to the press at the time of the movie's appearance are quite explicit about the connections with Charles Horman's case. In considerable detail they describe Horman's experiences and the background of events during Allende's regime at the time of the military coup.

45. Nathaniel Davis quoted in "Former Diplomats File $150 Mil Libel Suit re 'Missing,'" *Hollywood Reporter*, 2 January 1983.

Chapter 5 *Bonnie and Clyde*

1. David Newman, one of the movie's original developers, said that he was greatly surprised by the movie's tremendous popular reception (Robert Brent Toplin's interview with David Newman, 18 December 1991).

2. David Newman and Robert Benton, "Lightning in a Bottle," in Sandra Wake and Nicola Hayden, eds., *The Bonnie and Clyde Book* (London, 1972), 16.

3. Charles E. Silberman, *Criminal Violence, Criminal Justice* (New York, 1978), 29–31.

4. Robert Brent Toplin, *Unchallenged Violence: An American Ordeal* (Westport, Conn., 1975), 27–28.

5. *Crime in the United States: Uniform Crime Reports, 1970* (Washington, D.C., 1971), 2–21.

6. Toplin, *Unchallenged Violence*, 16–31.

7. For a variety of perspectives on this debate, see Robert B. Dykstra, *The Cattle Towns* (New York, 1968), 123–33; Joe B. Frantz and Julian Ernest Choate Jr., *The American Cowboy: The Myth and the Reality* (Norman, Okla., 1955), 77, 84–92; W. Eugene Hollon, *Frontier Violence: Another Look* (New York, 1974), 106–23; Richard Maxwell Brown, *No Duty to Retreat: Violence and Values in American History and Society* (New York, 1991), 39–86.

8. See, for example, Robert Ardrey, *African Genesis* (New York, 1966); Robert Ardrey, *The Territorial Imperative* (New York, 1966); Desmond Morris, *The Naked Ape: A Zoologist's Study of the Human Animal* (New York, 1968); Konrad Lorenz, *On Aggression* (New York, 1966).

9. Garth Jowett, *Film*, 206.

10. Bosley Crowther, "Screen: 'Bonnie and Clyde' Arrives," *New York Times*, 14 August 1967; Bosley Crowther, "Run Bonnie and Clyde," *New York Times*, 3 September 1967, 2:1.

11. Sarris's article of 24 August 1967 is reproduced in Wake and Hayden, *The Bonnie and Clyde Book*, 222.

12. Pauline Kael, "Crime and Poetry," in Wake and Hayden, *The Bonnie and Clyde Book*, 201–6.

13. *New York Times*, 11 September 1967, 2:7.

14. *Time*, 8 December 1967, 66–74.

15. Joseph Morganstern, "The Thin Red Line," *Newsweek*, 8 August 1967.

16. Arthur Penn quoted in David Zinman, *Fifty Grand Movies of the 1960s and 1970s* (New York, 1986), 209.

17. Arthur Penn, "Bonnie and Clyde: Private Morality and Public Violence," in Wake and Hayden, *The Bonnie and Clyde Book*, 7–10 (quotation); John Gelmis, *The Film Director as Superstar* (London, 1971), 227.

18. Gelmis, *The Film Director as Superstar*, 227.

19. Vincent Canby, "Arthur Penn: Does His 'Bonnie and Clyde' Glorify Crime?" *New York Times*, 17 September 1967.

20. *Newark Advocate*, 26 June 1971.

21. Bob Thomas, "The Bonnie Days of Clyde," *Los Angeles Herald-Examiner*, 4 May 1968, B7.

22. *Newark Advocate*, 26 June 1971.

23. *Mass Media and Violence*, vol. 9A, Mass Media Hearings, a report to the National Commission on the Causes and Prevention of Violence (Washington, D.C., 1969), 202.

24. Crowther, "Screen." See also Crowther's article of 14 August 1967, which is reprinted in Wake and Hayden, *The Bonnie and Clyde Book*, 221.

25. "Director Arthur Penn Weighs Balance of 'Bonnie and Clyde' Yocks and Shocks," *Variety*, 30 March 1967.

26. Curtis Lee Hanson, "An Interview with Arthur Penn," *Cinema*, Summer 1967, 10–13.

27. Penn, "Bonnie and Clyde: Private Morality and Public Violence," 10.

28. Ibid., 7–9.

29. Canby, "Arthur Penn."

30. Robert Hatch, "Films," *The Nation*, 30 October 1967; "Bonnie and Clyde," a sampling of reviews in promotion materials for the film, microfiche, American Academy of Motion Pictures Arts and Sciences (AMPAS), Los Angeles.

31. *Time*, 8 December 1967, 73.

32. Richard Gilman, "Gangsters on the Road to Nowhere," *New Republic*, 4 November 1967.

33. Interview with David Newman. For a good overview of the movie's production and the public reception it received, see Lawrence L. Murray, "Bonnie and Clyde," in John E. O'Connor and Martin A. Jackson, *American History/American Film*, 237–56.

34. David Newman and Robert Benton, "Lightning in a Bottle," 19–22 (quotation on 22).

35. David Newman and Robert Benton, "The New Sentimentality," *Esquire*, July 1964, 31; interview with David Newman.

36. Interview with David Newman.

37. Newman and Benton, "Lightning in a Bottle," 19; interview with David Newman.

38. Newman and Benton, "Lightning in a Bottle," 16–19.

39. Gelmis, *The Film Director as Superstar*, 223.

40. Warren Beatty quoted in Suzanne Munshower, *Warren Beatty: His Life, His Loves, His Work* (New York, 1983), 61–62.

41. Newman and Benton, "Lightning in Bottle," 26.

42. Gelmis, *The Film Director as Superstar*, 224.

43. Newman and Benton, "Lightning in a Bottle," 18.

44. Arthur Penn quoted in Canby, "Arthur Penn," 2:21. See also Robert Joseph, "Bonnie and Clyde—Heroes of the Hopeless," *Los Angeles Times*, 6 November 1967; André Labarthe and Jean-Louis Comolli, "The Arthur Penn Interview," in Wake and Hayden, *The Bonnie and Clyde Book*, 168.

45. Robert Towne, "A Trip with Bonnie and Clyde," *The Bonnie and Clyde Book*, 185–86. Warren Beatty also stressed the thesis about the "unfairness of our society" during the Great Depression. See Munshower, *Warren Beatty*, 61–62.

46. John Toland, "Sad Ballad of the Real Bonnie and Clyde," *New York Times Magazine*, 18 February 1969.

47. Gelmis, *The Film Director as Superstar*, 225; Newman and Benton, "Lightning in a Bottle," 27–28; Canby, "Arthur Penn."

48. Robin Wood, *Arthur Penn* (New York, 1970), 84–90; Richard White-hall, "Read a Good Filmscript Lately," *Los Angeles Free Press*, 11 August 1967.

49. "The Arthur Penn Interview," *The Bonnie and Clyde Book*, 165–72.

50. H. Gordon Frost and John H. Jenkins, *I'm Frank Hamer: The Real Life of a Texas Police Officer* (Austin, 1968), 179, 187–95; Wood, *Arthur Penn*, 75; Joseph, "Bonnie and Clyde—Heroes of the Hopeless"; Phil Casey, "Show-ing up the Real Bonnie and Clyde," *Los Angeles Times*, undated clipping in the *Bonnie and Clyde* clipping collection at the AMPAS archive, Los Ange-les. A review in *Films in Review* claimed, for example, that "there is *evil* in the *tone* of the writing, acting, and direction of this film, the calculated effect of which is to incite in the young the delusion that armed robbery and murder are mere 'happenings.'" The quotation is in Lawrence J. Quirk, *The Films of Warren Beatty* (Secaucus, N.J., 1979), 142. For a critical histo-ry of the activities of Bonnie Parker and Clyde Barrow, see John Treherne, *The Strange History of Bonnie and Clyde* (New York, 1984). A more sympa-thetic discussion of their activities is Emma Krause Parker, *The True Story of Bonnie and Clyde* (New York, 1968).

51. Toland, "The Sad Ballad of Bonnie and Clyde," 27 (quotation), 29; Casey, "Showing up the Real Bonnie and Clyde"; Texas Jim Cooper, "The True Story of Bonnie and Clyde and Their Pursuer," *Texas Suburban News*, 2 November 1967.

52. Toland, "Sad Ballad of the Real Bonnie and Clyde," 29; Frost and Jenkins, *I'm Frank Hamer*, 179; Sidney Skolsky, "Tintype: Bonnie Parker," in the *Bonnie and Clyde* clippings folder at the AMPAS archives, Los Ange-les.

53. Crowther, "Run, Bonnie, Run."

54. Casey, "Showing up the Real Bonnie and Clyde"; Joseph, "Bonnie and Clyde—Heroes of the Hopeless."

55. Mike Royko, "Bonnie and Clyde? They Want No Part of It," *Los Angeles Times*, 3 March 1968.

56. Toland, "Sad Ballad of the Real Bonnie and Clyde"; Frost and Jen-kins, *I'm Frank Hamer*, 200–210; Treherne, *The Strange History of Bonnie and Clyde*, 252–55. See also John Toland's earlier writing on Hamer in his book *The Dillinger Days* (New York, 1963; rprt. 1969), 281–83.

57. See, for example, Albert Bandura, Dorothea Ross, and Sheila Ross, "Transmission of Aggression through Imitation of Aggressive Models," *Journal of Abnormal and Social Psychology* 63 (1961): 575–82; Bandura, Ross, and Ross, "Imitation of Film-Mediated Aggressive Models," *Journal of Ab-normal and Social Psychology* 66 (1963): 3–11; Bandura, "What TV Violence

Can Do to Your Child," in Otto N. Larsen, ed., *Violence and the Mass Media* (New York, 1968), 128; Leonard Berkowitz, *Roots of Aggression* (New York, 1969); *Mass Media and Violence,* vols. 9A and 9B. See also *Television and Growing Up: The Impact of Televised Violence,* report to the surgeon general, United States Public Health Service, from the Surgeon General's Scientific Advisory Committee on Television and Social Behavior (Washington, D.C., 1972).

Chapter 6 *Patton*

1. William Safire, *Before the Fall: An Inside View of the Pre-Watergate White House* (Garden City, N.Y., 1975), 171–80.

2. "The Man Who Loved War," *New Yorker,* 31 January 1970, 73.

3. Laurence Suid, *Guts and Glory: Great American War Movies* (Reading, Mass., 1978), 244.

4. Ibid., 245.

5. "Patton," *Los Angeles Herald-Examiner,* 5 February 1970; John L. Scott, "Movie's Aim: Tell Patton Saga the Way It Happened," *Los Angeles Times,* 12 January 1969.

6. Vincent Canby, "Patton: He Loved War," *New York Times,* 8 February 1970.

7. Henry J. Taylor, "Film on Patton Captures Life and Times in WWII," clipping in the *Patton* file at the Academy of Motion Picture Arts and Sciences (AMPAS) archives, Los Angeles.

8. Francis O. Beeman, "The Real Blood and Guts to Stand in Twentieth's 'Patton,'" 8 October 1968. In the *Patton* microfiche file at the AMPAS archives, Los Angeles.

9. Dwight Eisenhower quoted in Suid, *Guts and Glory,* 247–48.

10. Ibid., 249–51.

11. Ibid., 249, 252–55.

12. Calder Willingham to Frank McCarthy, 12 July 1965, inter-office memo (Twentieth Century-Fox collection, UCLA).

13. Frank McCarthy quoted in Taylor, "Film on Patton Captures Life and Times." See also Vernon Scott, "Britain May Declare War," *Citizen News,* 4 May 1970, clipping in the *Patton* file at the AMPAS archives, Los Angeles.

14. William Wolf, "World War II Revisited in Spain for Patton Saga," 5 May 1969, clipping in the *Patton* file at the AMPAS archives, Los Angeles.

15. Franklin Schaffner quoted in "Fox's Patton Will Avoid 'Berets' Type of Hip-Hip Hooray," *Variety,* 9 October 1968.

16. Taylor, "Film on Patton Captures Life and Times."

17. Franklin Schaffner quoted in Beeman, "The Real Blood and Guts to Stand in Twentieth's Patton."

18. Frank McCarthy to James Webb, 4 October 1967, inter-office memo, in the *Patton* file at the AMPAS archives, Los Angeles; "Synopsis of 'Patton,'" 5 December 1969, in the *Patton* microfiche file at the AMPAS archives; Rex Reed, "George Is on His Best Behavior Now," *New York Times*, 29 March 1970.

19. "Synopsis on 'Patton.'"

20. The writers based much of the script on Ladislas Farago's biography *Patton: Ordeal and Triumph* (New York, 1964).

21. Richard Cuskelly, "'Patton': Reaction Divided," *Los Angeles Herald-Examiner*, 1 July 1970.

22. McCarthy to Webb, 4 October 1967, 44.

23. Lloyd Steele, "Orchestra of Death," *Los Angeles Press*, 4 April 1970.

24. McCarthy to Webb, 4 October 1967, 33.

25. Scott, "Britain May Declare War"; "'Patton': A British Review," *Los Angeles Herald-Examiner*, 20 February 1970.

26. Farago, *Patton*, 325–27.

27. McCarthy to Webb, 4 October 1967, 41–43.

28. William Wolf, "World War II Revisited for Patton Saga," clipping in *Patton* file at the AMPAS archives, Los Angeles; Taylor, "Film on Patton Captures Life and Times."

29. Taylor, "Film on Patton Captures Life and Times."

30. Robert Brent Toplin, *Unchallenged Violence: An American Ordeal* (Westport, Conn., 1975), 213.

31. John J. O'Connor, "Viewing Patton: Pick Your Angle," *Wall Street Journal*, 3 May 1970; "Left, Right Hail War Picture," *Variety*, 11 February 1970, 3; Cuskelly, "'Patton': Reaction Divided."

32. Cuskelly, "'Patton': Reaction Divided."

33. Reed, "George Is on His Best Behavior Now."

34. Scott, "Britain May Declare War;" Cuskelly, "Patton: Reaction Divided."

35. Tom Ramage, "'Patton': Georgie in Review," *Boston after Dark*, 11 March 1970.

36. Peter Schjeldahl, "Is 'Patton' a Lie?" *New York Times*, 14 June 1970 (quotation); "Stanley Kaufman on Films," *New Republic*, 7 March 1970; Lloyd Steele, "Orchestra of Death," *Los Angeles Press*, 10 April 1970.

37. Richard Nixon quoted in Stephen E. Ambrose, *Nixon: The Triumph of a Politician, 1962–1972*, 322, 345, vol. 2 of *Nixon*, 3 vols. (New York, 1989).

38. Ibid., 345.

39. William Rogers quoted in Hugh Sidey, "The Presidency: Anybody See Patton?" clipping in the *Patton* file at the AMPAS archives, Los Angeles.

40. Ibid.

41. Ambrose, *Nixon,* 2:361–62. For an overview of Nixon's reaction to the antiwar protests and encouragement of domestic surveillance, see Theodore H. White, *Breach of Faith: The Fall of Richard Nixon* (New York, 1975), 128–36. Also instructive is H. R. Haldeman, *The Ends of Power* (New York, 1978), 104–7.

42. Haldeman, *The Ends of Power,* 107. Regarding the movie, Tom Wicker noted Henry Kissinger's remark that when Nixon felt pressed, his romantic streak surfaced and he saw himself "as a beleaguered military commander in the tradition of *Patton*"; see Wicker, *One of Us: Richard Nixon and the American Dream* (New York, 1991), 585.

Chapter 7 *All the President's Men*

1. David Downing, *Robert Redford* (New York, 1982), 165 (quotation); "Watergate: Now the Movie," *Newsweek,* 2 June 1975; Jack Hirshberg, "The Day the Sundance Kid Brought Washington to Its Knees, *Los Angeles Magazine,* April 1978.

2. David Castell, *The Films of Robert Redford* (London, 1974), 4, 8, 11, 26, 33; Downing, *Robert Redford,* 13–24, 78, 160–65.

3. Castell, *Films of Robert Redford,* 33–35; "Watergate on Film," *Time,* 29 March 1976, 56; Robert Brent Toplin's interview with Bob Woodward, 31 August 1993; J. Anthony Lukas, *Nightmare: The Underside of the Nixon Years* (New York, 1976), 272.

4. Bob Woodward and Carl Bernstein quoted in "Watergate on Film," 56. Commenting on the experience years later, Woodward said that although Redford did influence the narrative's shape, Redford was not completely responsible for the book's personal approach to the subject (interview with Bob Woodward).

5. Jack Hirshberg, *A Portrait of All the President's Men* (New York, 1976), 48.

6. Ibid., 48–49; Charles Champlin, "'President's Men': A Film That Was Made, Not Born," *Los Angeles Times,* 13 March 1977; Richard Cuskelly, "Woodstein and Watergate," clipping in the *All the President's Men* file at the Academy of Motion Picture Arts and Sciences (AMPAS) archives, Los Angeles.

7. Ben Bradlee quoted in Joy Gould Boyum, "Reliving the Watergate Days," *Wall Street Journal,* 5 April 1976; Robert Brent Toplin's interview with Ben Bradlee, 24 April 1992.

8. Robert Trent Toplin's interview with William Goldman, 6 August 1993; William Goldman, *Adventures in the Screen Trade: A Personal View of Hollywood and Screenwriting* (New York, 1983), 233–35.

9. Bob Woodward quoted in Hirshberg, *A Portrait of All the President's*

Men, 93; "All the President's Men: Production Feature," in the *All the President's Men* file at the AMPAS archives, Los Angeles; *New York,* 1 April 1976, 61; Larry Clein, "Progress Report: 'All the President's Men,'" *American Film,* October 1975.

10. Goldman, *Adventures in the Screen Trade,* 234–35.

11. Ibid., 238–40; interview with Bob Woodward; "Watergate: Now the Movie."

12. Boyum, "Reliving the Watergate Days"; "Redford/Hoffman: All the President's Men on Location in Washington, D.C.," microfiche in *All the President's Men* file at the AMPAS archives, Los Angeles.

13. "Watergate on Film," *Time,* 29 March 1976.

14. One commentator, Nat Hentoff, praised the film for its realism, saying, "In some places the gritty familiarity is so compelling that a watching reporter gets hit with the nagging feeling that he's missing a deadline while sitting there" (quoted in Michael Schudson, *Watergate in American Memory: How We Remember, Forget, and Reconstruct the Past* [New York, 1992], 113).

15. Interview with Bob Woodward.

16. These were Bradley's sentiments, but newspapers erred in attributing these words to him. Actually, his daughter made the statement (interview with Ben Bradlee). Redford/Hoffman, *All the President's Men,* microfiche in the *All the President's Men* file at the AMPAS archives, Los Angeles.

17. "Watergate on Film."

18. Hirshberg, "The Day the Sundance Kid Brought Washington to Its Knees"; Clein, "Progress Report"; "Hollywood Meets the Press: A Post-Script," *Los Angeles Times,* 4 May 1975.

19. Interview with Bob Woodward.

20. Redford had tried to incorporate a romantic interest for Woodward, but he, the writer, and the director agreed to drop the idea in later drafts (Goldman, *Adventures in the Screen Trade,* 243).

21. Ibid., 238.

22. Arthur M. Schlesinger Jr., *The Imperial Presidency* (New York, 1973).

23. Basil Patterson quoted in "'All the President's Men' and Gerald Ford: Trouble Ahead?" *New York,* 12 April 1976.

24. William vander Heuvel quoted in ibid.

25. Boyum, "Reliving the Watergate Days."

26. Jack Kroll, "Behind the Front Page," *Newsweek,* 5 April 1976.

27. *New York Times,* 8 April 1976; 11 April 1976.

28. Gary Arnold, "'President's Men': Absorbing, Meticulous . . . and Incomplete," *Washington Post,* 4 April 1976, K1.

29. Stanley Kauffmann, "Mysteries," *New Republic,* 24 April 1976, 16.

30. Robert Hatch, "Films," *The Nation,* 24 April 1976, 505.

31. "Some of the President's Men Talk back to the Movie," *New York Times,* 23 May 1976, 2:1.

32. It is interesting to note that Stanley I. Kutler gave relatively small attention to the work of Woodward and Bernstein in his large-scale study of the Watergate story; see Kutler, *The Wars of Watergate: The Last Crisis of Richard Nixon* (New York, 1990), 324, 458–59.

33. "Hollywood Meets the Press: A Political Script," *Los Angeles Times,* 4 May 1975; Molly Haskell, "Journalism Goes to the Movies," *Village Voice,* 12 September 1976; Wayne Warga, "'President's Men': Answering a Call to the Post," *Los Angeles Times,* 15 August 1975.

34. Interview with Bob Woodward.

Chapter 8 *Norma Rae*

1. The best overview of her story is Henry Leifermann, *Crystal Lee: A Woman of Inheritance* (New York, 1975). For descriptions of factory life in the mills and the mill workers' strike, see Mimi Conway, *Rise, Gonna Rise: A Portrait of Southern Textile Workers* (Garden City, N.Y., 1979).

2. Robert Brent Toplin's interview with Tamara Asseyeu, 20 January 1992; Robert Brent Toplin's interview with Alex Rose, 22 January 1992.

3. For overviews of these developments, see Winifred D. Wandersee, *On the Move: American Women in the Seventies* (Boston, 1988); Toni Carabillo, Judith Meuli, and Jane Bundy Cside, *Feminist Chronicles, 1953–1993* (Los Angeles, 1993).

4. Jacquelyn Dowd Hall, "Disorderly Women: Gender and Labor Militancy in the Appalachian South," *Journal of American History* 73, no. 2 (Sept. 1986): 356, 372–76, 379, 382.

5. Robert Brent Toplin's interview with Adele Ritt, 20 May 1991; Robert Brent Toplin's interview with Irving Ravetch and Harriet Frank Jr., 8 January 1992.

6. *The Front* production notes, in the *Norma Rae* collection at the Academy of Motion Pictures Arts and Sciences (AMPAS) archives, Los Angeles.

7. Interview with Irving Ravetch and Harriet Frank Jr.

8. Interview with Tamara Asseyeu; interview with Alex Rose.

9. Interview with Alex Rose; interview with Tamara Asseyeu.

10. Clarke Taylor, "The On-Camera, Off-Camera Drama of Crystal Lee Jordan," *Los Angeles Times,* 4 March 1979.

11. Interview with Alex Rose.

12. Ibid.; interview with Tamara Asseyeu.

13. Tamara Asseyeu to Robert Brent Toplin, 22 January 1992 (in the possession of the author).

14. Ibid.; Robert Brent Toplin's interview with Barbara Kopple, 27 January 1992.

15. Stephen Klein, "Original of 'Norma Rae' Dubious," *Variety,* 28 February 1979; "Fabric of 'Norma Rae' Story Questioned; Suit May Follow," *Variety,* 2 March 1979.

16. "Fabric of 'Norma Rae' Story Questioned" (quotation); "Original of 'Norma Rae' Dubious"; interview with Alex Rose; interview with with Tamara Asseyeu; Eunice Field, "Real Norma Rae 'Not Bitter' over Not Receiving Any Money," *Hollywood Reporter,* 14 March 1980.

17. Harry Bernstein, "Norma Rae—a 'Lint Head' Fighting Her Fight," *Los Angeles Times,* 15 March 1980; Beverly Stephen, "The Real 'Norma Rae' Fights On," *Los Angeles Times,* 6 July 1980, 7:10; Mary Beth Murrill, "Sally Field Meets Real Norma Rae," *Los Angeles Herald-Examiner,* undated clipping in the *Norma Rae* file at the AMPAS archives, Los Angeles.

18. "Real Life Norma Rae Snubbed by Field," *Variety,* 14 August 1985.

19. Chester Goodrich, "A Year after J. Stevens, Union Settled, Firm Is Pushing Program to Revive Profits," *Wall Street Journal,* 9 October 1981, 48.

20. Leifermann, *Crystal Lee,* 110–11, 120–25, 130.

21. Ibid., 110.

22. Robert Brent Toplin's interview with Crystal Lee Sutton, 13 October 1991.

23. Ibid.

24. Robert Brent Toplin's interview with Bennett Taylor, 9 February 1992.

25. Leifermann, *Crystal Lee,* 111–20.

26. Victoria Byerly, *Hard Times Cotton Mill Girls: Personal Histories of Womanhood and Poverty in the South* (Ithaca, N.Y., 1986), 206–12.

27. Wayne Flint, *Poor but Proud: Alabama's Poor Whites* (Tuscaloosa, Ala., 1989), 102–4; Jacquelyn Dowd Hall, James Leloudis, Robert Korstad, Mary Murphy, Lu Ann Jones, and Christopher Daly, *Like a Family: The Making of a Southern Cotton Mill World* (Chapel Hill, N.C., 1987), 358–63.

28. Flint, *Poor but Proud,* 94–103.

29. Leifermann, *Crystal Lee,* 82–83.

30. Interview with Bennett Taylor.

31. Robert Brent Toplin's interview with Maurine Hedgepeth, 18 January 1992.

32. Interview with Crystal Lee Sutton.

33. Ibid.

34. Robert Brent Toplin's interview with Clyde Bush, 16 October 1991.

35. Interview with Crystal Lee Sutton. Years before, Crystal Lee was more critical of the film; see Stephen Rebello, "The Real People: How Hollywood Told Their Stories—and Forever Changed Their Lives," clipping in the *Norma Rae* file at the AMPAS archives, Los Angeles.

SELECTED BIBLIOGRAPHY

Abrash, Barbara, and Janet Sternberg, eds. *Historians and Filmmakers: Toward Collaboration.* A roundtable held at the New York Institute for the Humanities, New York University, 30 October 1983. New York, 1983.

Abrash, Barbara, and Daniel J. Walkowitz. "Sub/versions of History: A Mediation on Film and Historical Narrative." *Historical Workshop Journal* (1994): 203–14.

Allen, Jean Thomas. "Film History: A Revisionist Perspective." *Journal of the American Film and Video Association* 35 (Fall 1983): 5–9.

Allen, Robert C., and Doublas Gomery. *Film History: Theory and Practice.* New York, 1985.

Alvaray, Luisela. "Filming the 'Discovery' of America: How and Whose History Is Being Told." *Film Historian* 5, no. 1 (1995): 35–44.

Andrew, J. Dudley. *The Major Film Theories.* London, 1976.

Arnheim, Rudolph. *Film as Art.* Berkeley, Calif., 1956.

Balio, Tino, ed. *The American Film Industry.* Madison, Wis., 1976.

Basinger, Jeanine. *A Woman's View: How Hollywood Spoke to Women, 1930–1960.* New York, 1993.

———. *The World War II Combat Film: Anatomy of a Genre.* New York, 1986.

Bazin, André. *What Is Cinema?* 2 vols. Berkeley, Calif., 1968, 1971.

Bergman, Andrew. *We're in the Money: Depression America and Its Films.* New York, 1971.

Biskind, Peter. *Seeing Is Believing.* New York, 1983.

Bordell, David. *Making Meaning: Inference and Rhetoric in the Interpretation of Cinema.* Cambridge, Mass., 1989.

Bordwell, David, Janet Staiger, and Kristen Thompson. *The Classical Hollywood Cinema: Film Style and Mode of Production to 1960.* New York, 1985.

Bordwell, David, and Kristin Thompson. *Film Art: An Introduction.* Reading, Mass., 1979.

Breitbart, Eric. "From the Panorama to the Docudrama: Notes on the Visualization of History." *Radical History Review* 25 (1981): 115–25.

Bremner, Robert H., ed. *Essays on History and Literature.* Columbus, Ohio, 1966.

Brownlow, Kevin. *Behind the Mask of Innocence: The Social Problem Films of the Silent Era.* New York, 1990.

Burns, E. Bradford. "Conceptualizing the Use of Film to Study History." *Film and History* 4 (Dec. 1974): 1–11.

Bywater, Tim, and Thomas Sobchack. *An Introduction to Film Criticism: Major Critical Approaches to Narrative Film.* New York, 1989.

Carr, E. H. *What Is History?* New York, 1961.

Carroll, Noel. *Mystifying Movies: Fads and Fallacies in Contemporary Film Theory.* New York, 1988.

Caughie, John, ed. *Theories of Authorship.* Boston, 1981.

Chandler, D. G. "War and the Past: The Historian and the Media." *History Today* 31 (Aug. 1981): 54.

Christensen, Terry. *Reel Politics: American Political Movies from "Birth of a Nation" to "Platoon."* New York, 1987.

Clark, Michael, ed. *Politics and Media: Film and Television for the Political Scientist and Historian.* Fairview Park, N.Y., 1979.

Cohn, William H. "History for the Masses: Television Portrays the Past." *Journal of Popular Culture* 10, no. 2 (Fall 1976): 280–88.

Conkin, Paul K., and Roland N. Stromberg. *Heritage and Challenge: The History and Theory of History.* Arlington Heights, Ill., 1989.

Corliss, Richard., ed. *The Hollywood Screenwriters.* New York, 1972.

Crowther, Bruce. *Hollywood Faction: Reality and Myth in the Movies.* London, 1984.

Current, Richard N. "Fiction as History: A Review Essay." *Journal of Southern History* 52, no. 1 (Feb. 1986): 77–90.

Curtis, James C. "To Be a Muse or to Be Amusing." In *Material Culture and the Study of American Life,* ed. Ian M. G. Quimby, 201–18. New York, 1978.

Custen, George F. *Bio/Pics: How Hollywood Constructed Public History.* New Brunswick, N.J., 1992.

Davies, Philip, and Brian Neve. *Cinema, Politics, and Society in America.* New York, 1981.

Davis, Natalie Zemon. "Any Resemblance to Persons Living or Dead: Film and the Challenge of Authenticity." *Yale Review* 76 (Sept. 1987): 461–77.

Eagleton, Terry. *Literary Theory: An Introduction.* Minneapolis, 1983.

Eitzen, Dirk. "Against the Ivory Tower: An Apologia for 'Popular' Historical Documentaries." *Film Historian* 5, no. 1 (1995): 25–34.

Ellis, Jack. C. *A History of Film.* 3d ed. Englewood Cliffs, N.J., 1990.

Ferro, Marc. *Cinema and History.* Detroit, 1988.

Fischer, David Hackett. *Historians' Fallacies: Toward a Logic of Historical Thought.* New York, 1970.

Foster, Harold M. *The New Literacy: The Language of Film and Television.* Urbana, Ill., 1979.

Fraser, George MacDonald. *The Hollywood History of the World: From One Million Years B.C. to Apocalypse Now.* New York, 1988.

Furhammar, Leif, and Folke Isaksson. *Politics and Film.* London, 1971.

Gabler, Neil. *An Empire of Their Own: How the Jews Invented Hollywood.* New York, 1988.

Gomery, Douglas. *Movie History: A Survey.* New York, 1991.

———. *Shared Pleasures: A History of Movie Presentations in the United States.* Madison, Wis., 1992.

Goodwyn, Lawrence. "Modern History and Modern Films: The Paradox of 'Political Education' in Filmmaking." *Film Library Quarterly* 12, nos. 2–3 (1979): 24–27.

Grenier, Richard. Introduction to "Historians and the Movies: The State of the Art." *Journal of Contemporary History* 19, no. 1 (Jan. 1984): 1–4.

Hampton, Benjamin. *History of the American Film Industry.* New York, 1931.

Herlihy, David. "Am I a Camera? Other Reflections on Films and History." *American Historical Review* 93, no. 5 (Dec. 1988): 1186–92.

Higham, Charles. *Hollywood at Sunset: The Decline and Fall of the Most Colorful Empire since Rome.* New York, 1972.

Hollander, Anne. *Moving Pictures.* Cambridge, Mass., 1991.

Huaco, George. *The Sociology of Film Art.* New York, 1965.

Hudson, Thomas. *Hollywood and History: Costume Design in Film.* New York, 1987.

Jackson, Martin A. "The Future of Film in History." *History Teacher* 3 (Mar. 1970): 10–12.

Jacobs, Lewis. *The Rise of the American Film.* New York, 1939.

Jarvie, Ian. *Movies as Social Criticism: Aspects of Their Social Psychology.* Metuchen, N.J., 1978.

———. *Philosophy of the Film: Epistemology, Ontology, Aesthetics.* New York, 1987.

———. *Sociology of the Movies.* New York, 1970.

Jowett, Garth. *Film, The Democratic Art: A Social History of American Film.* Boston, 1976.

Jowett, Garth, and James M. Linton. *Movies as Mass Communication.* Beverly Hills, Calif., 1986.

Kerr, Paul. *The Hollywood Film Industry: A Reader.* London, 1986.

Kindem, Gorham. *American Film Industry: A Case Studies Approach.* Carbondale, Ill., 1982.

———. *The American Movie Industry: The Business of Motion Pictures.* Carbondale, Ill., 1982.

Knight, Arthur. *The Liveliest Art.* New York, 1979.

Koppes, Clayton R., and Gregory D. Black. *Hollywood Goes to War: How Politics, Profits and Propaganda Shaped World War II Movies.* New York, 1987.

Kracauer, Siegfried. *From Caligari to Hitler: A Psychological Study of the German Film.* Princeton, N.J., 1948.

————. *Theory of Film.* New York, 1960.

Kuehl, Jerry. "Television History: The Next Step." *Sight and Sound* 51, no. 3 (Summer 1982): 188–89.

Lang, Robert, ed. *The Birth of a Nation.* New Brunswick, N.J., 1994.

Lazarus, Paul N. III. *The Movie Producer.* New York, 1985.

Lenihan, John H. *Showdown: Confronting Modern America in Western Film.* Urbana, Ill., 1980.

Levine, Lawrence W. *The Unpredictable Past: Explorations in American Cultural History.* Oxford, 1993.

Maltby, Richard. *Harmless Entertainment: Hollywood and the Ideology of Consensus.* Metuchen, N.J., 1983.

Marsden, Michael T., John G. Nachbar, and Sam L. Gross Jr. *Movies as Artifacts: Cultural Criticism of Popular Film.* Chicago, 1982.

Mast, Gerald, ed. *The Movies in Our Midst: Documents in the Cultural History of Film in America.* Chicago, 1982.

————. *A Short History of the Movies.* Indianapolis, 1981.

Mast, Gerald, and Marshall Cohen, eds. *Film Theory and Criticism.* New York, 1970.

May, Lary. *Screening out the Past: The Birth of Mass Culture and the Motion Picture Industry.* New York, 1980.

Mayer, Arthur. *The Movies.* New York, 1957.

McKerns, Joseph P. "Television Docudramas: The Images as History." *Journalism History* 7, no. 1 (Spring 1980): 24–27.

Mellencamp, Patricia, and Phillip Rosen. *Cinema Histories, Cinema Practices.* Frederick, Md., 1984.

Metz, Christian. *Film Language: A Semiotics of the Cinema.* New York, 1974.

————. *The Imaginary Signifier: Psychoanalysis and the Cinema.* Bloomington, Ind., 1982.

Miller, Mark Crispin, ed. *Seeing through Movies.* New York, 1990.

Mitchner, James A. "Historical Fiction." *American Heritage* 33 (Apr.–May 1982): 44–48.

Murray, Lawrence L. "The Feature Film as Historical Document." *Social Studies* (Jan.–Feb. 1977): 10–14.

Musburger, Robert B. "Setting the Stage for the Television Docudrama." *Journal of Popular Film and Television* 13, no. 2 (Summer 1985): 93–101.

Nichols, Bill. *Ideology and the Image: Social Representation in the Cinema and Other Media.* Bloomington, Ind., 1981.

————, ed. *Movies and Methods: An Anthology.* Berkeley, Calif., 1976.

O'Connor, John E. "History in Images/Images in History: Reflections on the Importance of Film and Television Study for an Understanding of the Past." *American Historical Review* 93, no. 5 (Dec. 1988): 1200–1209.

————. *The Image as Artifact: The Historical Analysis of Film and Television.* Malabar, Fla., 1990.

O'Connor, John E., and Martin A. Jackson. *American History/American Film: Interpreting the Hollywood Image.* New York, 1979.

————. *Teaching History with Film.* Washington, D.C., 1974.

Parenti, Michael. *Make-Believe Media: The Politics of Entertainment.* New York, 1992.

Pitts, Martin R. *Hollywood and American History: A Filmography of over 250 Motion Pictures Depicting U.S. History.* Jefferson, N.C., n.d.

Poland, Dana. *Power and Paranoia: History, Narrative and the American Cinema, 1940–1950.* New York, 1986.

Prince, Stephen. *Visions of Empire: Political Imagery in Contemporary American Film.* New York, 1992.

Pronay, Nicholas. "The 'Moving Picture' and Historical Research." *Journal of Contemporary History* 18 (July 1983): 365.

Quart, Leonard, and Albert Auster. *American Film and Society since 1945.* Westport, Conn., 1991.

Raack, Richard C. "Historiography and Cinematography: A Prolegomenon to Film Work for Historians." *Journal of Contemporary History* 18 (July 1983): 411–38.

Ramsaye, Terry. *A Million and One Nights.* New York, 1926.

Ray, Robert B. *A Certain Tendency of the Hollywood Cinema, 1930–1960.* Princeton, N.J., 1985.

Reimers, K. F., and H. Friedrich, eds. *Studies in History, Film and Society III: Contemporary History in Film and Television.* Munich, 1982.

Robert, Randy. *Hollywood's America: Reflections on the Silver Screen.* St. James, N.Y., 1993.

Roddick, Nick. *A New Deal in Entertainment: Warner Brothers in the 1930s.* London, 1983.

Roffman, Peter, and Jim Purdy. *The Hollywood Social Problem Film: Madness, Despair, and Politics from the Depression to the Fifties.* Bloomington, Ind., 1981.

Rogin, Michael Paul. *Ronald Reagan, the Movie, and Other Episodes of Political Demonology.* Berkeley, 1987.

Rollins, Peter C., ed. *Hollywood as Historian: American Film in Cultural Context.* Lexington, Ky., 1983.

Rosen, Philip, ed. *Narrative, Apparatus, Ideology: A Film Theory Reader.* New York, 1986.

Rosenstone, Robert A. "Genres, History, and Hollywood: A Review Article." *Comparative Studies in Society and History* 27, no. 2 (Apr. 1985): 368–70.

———. "The Historical Film as Real History." *Film Historian* 5, no. 1 (1995): 5–24.

———. "History in Images/History in Words: Reflections on the Possibility of Really Putting History into Film." *American Historical Review* 93, no. 5 (Dec. 1988): 1173–85.

———. *Revisioning History: Film and the Construction of a New Past.* Princeton, N.J., 1994.

Ryan, Michael, and Douglas Kellner. *Camera Politica: The Politics and Ideology of Contemporary Film.* Bloomington, Ind., 1990.

Salmi, Harru. "Film as Historical Narrative." *Film Historian* 5, no. 1 (1995): 45–54.

Sarris, Andrew. *The American Cinema.* New York, 1968.

———. *Politics and Cinema.* New York, 1978.

Schama, Simon. "Clio Has a Problem." *New York Times Magazine,* 8 September 1991, 32–34.

Schneider, Alfred R. "Keeping Television History Honest—and Entertaining." *Christian Science Monitor,* 30 June 1988, 39.

Short, K. R. M. *Feature Films as History.* Knoxville, Tenn., 1981.

Sklar, Robert. "Documentary: Artifice in the Service of Truth." *Reviews in American History* 3, no. 3 (Sept. 1975): 299–304.

———. *Movie-Made America: A Cultural History of American Movies.* New York, 1975.

Sklar, Robert, and Charles Musser, eds. *Resisting Images: Essays on Cinema and History.* Philadelphia, 1990.

Slotkin, Richard. *Gunfighter Nation: The Myth and the Frontier in Twentieth-Century America.* New York, 1992.

Smith, Paul, ed. *The Historian and Film.* Cambridge, 1976.

Sobchak, Vivian C. "Beyond Visual Aids: American Film as American Culture." *American Quarterly* 32, no. 3 (1980): 283–93.

Sobchak, Thomas, and Vivian Sobchak. *An Introduction to Film.* New York, 1987.

Sorlin, Pierre. *The Film in History: Restaging the Past.* Totowa, N.J., 1980.

Staiger, Janet. *Interpreting Films: Studies in the Historical Reception of American Cinema.* Princeton, N.J., 1992.

Stempel, Tom. *Framework.* New York, 1988.

Stern, Fritz, ed. *The Varieties of History: From Voltaire to the Present.* New York, 1957.

Suid, Lawrence H. *Guts and Glory.* Reading, Mass., 1978.

Susman, Warren. *Culture as History: The Transformation of American Society in the Twentieth Century.* New York, 1984.

Toplin, Robert Brent. "The Filmmaker as Historian." *American Historical Review* 93, no. 5 (Dec. 1988): 1210–27.

———, ed. *Hollywood as Mirror: Changing Views of "Outsiders" and "Enemies" in American Movies.* Westport, Conn., 1993.

Tudor, Andrew. *Image and Influence.* New York, 1974.

Vogel, Harold L. *Entertainment Industry Economics.* New York, 1986.

Walkowitz, Daniel J. "Visual History: The Craft of the Historian-Filmmaker." *The Public Historian* 7, no. 1 (Winter 1985): 53–63.

White, David Manning, and Richard Averson. *The Celluloid Weapon: Social Comment in the American Film.* Boston, 1972.

White, Hayden. "Historiography and Historiophoty." *American Historical Review* 93, no. 5 (Dec. 1988): 1193–99.

———. *Tropics of Discourse: Essays in Cultural Criticism.* Baltimore, Md., 1978.

Whitfield, Stephen J. *The Culture of the Cold War.* Baltimore, Md., 1991.

Williams, Christopher. *Realism and the Cinema: A Reader.* London, 1980.

Wills, John E. Jr. "Taking Historical Novels Seriously." *The Public Historian* 6, no. 1 (Winter 1984): 39–44.

Zinman, David. *Fifty Grand Movies of the 1960s and 1970s.* New York, 1986.

INDEX

ABC Television, 35
Abzug, Bella, 206
Academy of Motion Pictures Arts and
  Sciences, 26
AFL-CIO, 214
Africa, 160
African Americans, 4, 11, 17–18, 26–
  27, 34–35, 43–44, 130, 219, 222
After the Fact, 51
Agnew, Spiro, 187
Alabama, 33
Allende, Salvador, 108, 110, 112–18,
  120–21, 123
All Quiet on the Western Front, 89
All the King's Men, 21
All the President's Men, 20, 179–202, 277
American Clothing and Textile Work-
  ers Union, 214–15, 217, 219
American Foreign Service Association,
  112, 123
American Historical Review, 8, 76
American Telephone and Telegraph
  Co., 206
American University, 53
Angola, 76
Arcadia, La., 151
Argentina, 108
Arnold, Gary, 198
Asseyeu, Tamara, 205–8, 210–13
Astor Theatre, 99
Atlantic City, 138
Atlantic Monthly, 71
Attack on Terror, 31
Attenborough, Richard, 8, 55
Attonasio, Paul, 14
Austria, 82

Bancroft, Anne, 206
Bancroft, George, 7
Bandura, Albert, 153
Bank of Commerce and Credit Inter-
  national, 15
Barker, Bernard, 191
Barrow, Blanche, 151
Barrow, Buck, 151
Barrow, Clyde, 130, 134–35, 138–50,
  152
Battle Cry of Freedom, 11
Battle of the Bulge, 169
Bay of Pigs invasion, 61
Beatty, Warren, 131, 143, 148
Belgium, 82
Belin, David, 67, 69, 71
Benton, Robert, 141–44, 147, 150
Berkowitz, Leonard, 153
Bernstein, Carl, 20, 181–86, 189, 191–
  96, 198–200
Bible, 71
The Big Parade, 89
Birth of a Nation, 1, 18
Blackboard Jungle, 133
Black Fury, 209
Blakey, G. Robert, 71
Blockade, 89
Blue Collar, 210
Bolsheviks, 165
Bond, Julian, 35
Bonnie and Clyde, 19–20, 127–54, 226
Boone, James, 221
Boritt, Gabor, 225
Born on the Fourth of July, 48–49
Boston after Dark, 171
Boyum, Jay Gould, 198

Bradlee, Ben, 184–85, 189
Bradley, Omar, 160, 169, 171
Brando, Marlon, 133
British, 167–68
Bronx, 138
Brooke, Alan Francis, 167
Brown, Carolyn, 221
Buchanan, Pat, 41, 43
Bundy, McGeorge, 58
Burbank, Calif., 189
Burns, Ken, 4–5, 7
Bush, Clyde, 223
Butch Cassidy and the Sundance Kid, 185
Buxton, George Edward, 90

California, 189
Cambodia, 76, 173
Camelot Productions, 53
Campaign Financing Act, 197
Canby, Vincent, 112, 139, 198
The Candidate, 182–83
Cantor, Eddie, 152
Capra, Frank, 54
Captain Blood, 89
Carlyle, Thomas B., 7
Carter, James Earl (Jimmy), 197–98
Casablanca, 89
Casey, Phil, 148
Castro, Fidel, 59–61, 66, 76
Catholic World, 99
CBS Television, 70
Central Intelligence Agency. *See* CIA
Chandlee, Harry, 89, 93–96
Chaney, James, 27–28, 31, 33–36, 43
Chaplin, Charles, 100
Charleston, S.C., 3
Chicago, 212
Chicago Sun-Times, 35, 70
Chile, 18, 104–11, 113–18, 121, 123
China, 82, 193
Chomsky, Noam, 57
Christie, Julie, 209
Churchill, Winston, 160
CIA, 49, 60, 65–66, 71, 73, 75–76,
    104, 114–15, 117–18, 174, 182,
    195, 197
Cineaste, 76–77

Civil Rights Act, 40
Civil War, 4, 5, 11, 25, 225
Clawson, Ken, 199
Clayburgh, Jill, 209
Cohen, Jacob, 64
Colesberry, Bob, 32–33
Collins, Stephen, 190
Colson, Charles W., 199
Columbia Pictures, 143, 210
Commentary, 64
Committee on Ballistic Acoustics of
    the National Research Council, 63
Committee to Defend America by Aid-
    ing the Allies, 84
Committee to Reelect the President.
    See CREEP
Commonweal, 99
Confession of a Nazi Spy, 88–89
Congressional Record, 91–92
Congress of Racial Equality, 27, 35–36
Connally, John, 62, 72
Conrack, 298
Cooper, Gary, 94
Coppola, Francis Ford, 161
Costa-Gavras, Constantin, 52, 107,
    109–11, 113, 118, 121–24
Costner, Kevin, 55, 62, 64
Covert Action in Chile: 1963–1973, 112
Cowan, Samuel K., 92
Cox, Archibald, 192, 199
CREEP, 190, 192, 195–96
Crist, Judith, 140
Crossfire, 52
Crowther, Bosley, 134, 137–40, 148
Crystal Lee: A Woman of Inheritance, 205
Cuba, 49
Cuban Missile Crisis, 53, 61
Cubans, 60, 65
Cuskelly, Richard, 170
Cutting, Corporal, 91
Czechoslovakia, 82, 107

Dafoe, Willem, 31
Dallas, 50, 68, 141
Dallas Conspiracy, 51
Davis, Nathaniel, 104–5, 112, 120,
    123–24

Dead Certainties: Unwarranted Speculations, 7
Dean, James, 133
Deep Throat, 194–95
Delgado, Bill, 33–34
DeMille, Cecil B., 87
Democratic National Committee, 197
Dillinger, John, 145, 148
The Dillinger Days, 141, 145, 148
The Dirty Dozen, 133
Disney Channel, 2
Don Quixote, 114, 171
Dowell, Pat, 76
Dumas, Alexandre, 7
Dunaway, Faye, 131, 148, 201

Earl Scruggs and His Foggy Mountain
     Boys, 133
The Economist, 41
Eisenhower, Dwight D., 60, 160, 165,
     167, 169
El Salvador, 106
Ephron, Nora, 186
Epstein, Edward J., 71
Equal Rights Amendment, 206
Erlichman, John, 183
Ervin, Sam, 192, 199
Esquire, 141
Evika, George Michael, 76
The Execution of Charles Horman, 106,
     114, 118, 120
Exner, Judith, 59
Eyes on the Prize, 43

Farago, Ladislas, 159–60
FBI, 26, 28, 30–32, 34–41, 43, 57, 59–
     60, 65, 68, 73, 75–76, 149, 174,
     195, 197, 226
Federal Bureau of Investigation. *See*
     FBI
Federal Communications Commission,
     15, 193
Ferrie, David William, 71
Field, Sally, 207, 209
Finkel, Abem, 89, 91–92
F.I.S.T., 210
Flynn, Earl, 171, 186

Fonda, Henry, 70
Fonda, Jane, 206, 209
Ford, Gerald R., 67, 71, 194, 197–98
Ford, Glenn, 133
Foreign Relations of the United States, 57
France, 82, 160
Frank, Harriet, 209
Freedom of Information Act, 57, 106,
     197
Freedom Summer, 26
The Front, 208
The Front Page, 187

Gable, Clark, 171
Gallup poll, 83
Gandhi, Mohandas Karamchand (Ma-
     hatma), 55
Gandhi, 8, 55
Garrison, Jim, 49, 52, 54–56, 60, 64–
     65, 71–72
Gelb, Leslie, 74
Georgia, 33
Gerelmo, Chris, 29–33, 36–38, 41–44
Geritol, 14
Germans, 165
Germany, 160
Giancana, Sam, 59
Giglio, James, 57
Gilman, Richard, 140
Glory, 11
The Godfather, 153
Gold Diggers of 1933, 89, 152
Goldman, William, 185–86, 189–90,
     192, 200–201
Goldwyn, Samuel, 89
Goodman, Andrew, 27–28, 31, 44
Goodman, Carolyn, 44
The Good, the Bad, and the Ugly, 133
Goodwin, Richard, 15, 16
Graham, Katherine, 184
The Grapes of Wrath, 97, 146
Great Britain, 98, 168
Great Depression, 139, 144–45, 210
The Great White Hope, 208
Green Berets, 71
Griffith, D. W., 18
Grundmann, Roy, 76

Gulf of Tonkin Resolution, 58
Guzman, Enrique, 119

Hackman, Gene, 31, 37, 131, 151
Halberstam, David, 33, 41
Haldeman, H. R. (Bob), 173, 183
Hall, Donoho, 93
Hall, Jacquelyn Dowd, 207
Hamer, Frank, 130, 149
Harlan County, U.S.A., 212
Hart, Jeffrey, 113
Hatch, Robert, 199
Hauser, Thomas, 104–5, 114, 116,
    118, 122–23
Hawks, Howard, 89
Hedgepath, Maurine, 221
Hersh, Seymour, 199
Hillsboro, Tex., 150
Hitchcock, Alfred, 133, 141
Hitler, Adolph, 82, 160
Hoffa, James R. (Jimmy), 210
Hoffman, Dustin, 189–90
Hoftstadter, Richard, 66
Holland, 82
Holocaust, 51
Holtzman, Elizabeth, 206
Hoover, J. Edgar, 28, 37–38, 60, 174
Horman, Charles, 105–7, 109, 111,
    113, 117, 119, 121–23, 226
Horman, Ed, 104–7, 109–11, 113, 119,
    122–24
Horman, Elizabeth, 104, 107, 123
Horman, Joyce, 106, 109, 119
House Assassination Committee, 64
Houston, 149
Howard, Larry, 50
Huevel, William vanden, 197
Hugo, Victor, 6–7
Huie, William Bradford, 31
Humphrey, Hubert H., 195
Huston, John, 89
Huston, Tom, 174

The Illiad, 6, 76
The Imperial Presidency, 197
Indo-China, 82
Inside Hoover's F.B.I., 31, 38

Inter-American Development Bank,
    114
Iran-Contra scandal, 15

Jackson, Henry M., 195
Jawarski, Leon, 192
JFK, 1, 9, 16–17, 45–80, 226
JFK Information Center, 50
"JFK Study Guide," 69
Johnson, Lyndon Baines, 26, 28, 37,
    38, 40, 50, 55, 57–58, 61, 68, 72–
    73
Joint Chiefs of Staff, 50
Jones, Daniel, 150–51
Jordan, Barbara, 207
Joseph, Robert, 148–49
Josephson, Julian, 92–94
J. P. Stevens Co., 204–5, 212, 214–15,
    217–18, 222

Kael, Pauline, 132
Kauffmann, Stanley, 71, 198
Keaton, Diane, 206, 209
Kennedy, John F., 17, 46–47, 49–50,
    52–61, 63, 67–68, 70, 72, 75, 130,
    226
Kennedy, Robert F., 58–59, 68
Kennedy and Vietnam, 52
Kent State, 106
Khrushchev, Nikita, 53
The Killing Fields, 5
King, Coretta Scott, 35
King, Martin Luther, Jr., 35, 37, 68
Kissinger, Henry, 118
Klein, Herbert G., 199
Kleindienst, Richard, 187
Klute, 186
Kopple, Barbara, 212–13
Korean War, 137
Kovik, Ron, 49
Krause, Arthur, 106
Krause, Doris, 106
Krauthammer, Charles, 73
Kroll, Jack, 198
Kuhl, Charles H., 168
Ku Klux Klan, 27–32, 34–39, 42–43
Kurosawa, Akira, 19, 52, 67, 77

Ladies Home Journal, 206
Lafayette, Ala., 33
Lambrakis, Gregorios, 107
Lancaster, Burt, 162
Lane, Mark, 71
Lardner, George, Jr., 70–71, 74
Lasky, Jesse L., 87–90, 92–93, 95, 100–101
Leab, Daniel, 4
Lee, Crystal, 205, 207, 209, 211–14, 216, 218–19, 221–23
Leifermann, Henry P., 205, 209, 212–13
Leigh, Janet, 133
Lend-Lease Act, 98
Leslie, Joan, 94
Lewis, Anthony, 73–74
Lewis, Eddie, 107–8
Lewis, Flora, 111–12
Lewis, Mildred, 107–8
Liberty Lobby, 50
Lincoln: A Novel, 223
Little Caesar, 89
Liuzzo, Viola, 40
London, 98
The Longest Day, 159
Los Angeles Herald-Examiner, 113, 170
Los Angeles Times, 40, 148–49
Lousiana, 130, 134, 149
Lynch, Dorothy, 221

Macaulay, Thomas B., 7
MacNamara, Robert, 58
Mafia, 30, 54, 59, 61, 65–66
Mailer, Norman, 74
Malcolm X, 130
Malcolm X, 5
Mallory, Robert, 221
Maltin, Leonard, 72
Manchester, William, 66
The Man Who Shot Liberty Valance, 31
Marrs, Jim, 52, 65
Marston, David W., 29
Marvin, Lee, 31
MCA/Universal Studios, 107, 109
McCarthy, Frank, 158–59, 161–62, 171

McCarthyism, 71
McGovern, George, 196
McGregor, Clark, 199
McLaine, Shirley, 206–7
McPherson, James, 11
Mead, Margaret, 174
Meagher, Sylvia, 51
Meet John Doe, 97
Melanson, Philip, 51
Memories of Hadrian, 6
Meridian, Miss., 27
Methvin, Henry, 151
Mexico, 47
MIBURN, 32
Midler, Bette, 206
Midnight Express, 48
MIR, 116–17
Missing, 18, 103–25, 226
Mississippi, 17, 28, 30, 32–33, 35–36, 39–41, 43
Mississippi Burning, 25–44, 226
Mitchell, John, 174, 198
Mitrione, Daniel, 117
The Molly Maguires, 208
Montgomery, Sir Bernard Law, 160, 165, 167–68
Montreal, 139
Morganstern, Joseph, 135–36
Morris, Yancey, 138
Movement of the Revolutionary Left. *See* MIR
Mr. Deeds Goes to Town, 97
Mr. Smith Goes to Washington, 54, 56, 97
Muskie, Edmund, 195
My Lai, 121
My Son John, 71

The Nation, 49, 140, 199
National Commission on the Causes and Prevention of Violence, 153
National Labor Relations Board, 216–17
National Organization of Women, 206
National Security Memorandum 263, 50, 56–57
Nazis, 165–66
NBC Television, 14, 33–34, 225, 226

Neshoba County, Miss., 28
Newman, David, 141–44, 147, 150
Newman, John, 51–52
New Orleans, 49, 54, 62, 72
New Republic, 71, 140, 198
"New Sentimentality," 141, 143
Newsweek, 72, 99, 135, 198, 206
New York City, 27, 30, 82, 97–98, 144, 208
The New Yorker, 157
New York Post, 29
New York Times, 40, 70, 73–74, 77, 111–12, 134, 138–39, 148, 171, 198
New York Times Magazine, 7, 205
New York University, 48
Ngo Dinh Diem, 57
Nightline, 35
Nixon, Richard M., 114, 173–75, 181, 187–88, 193–94, 196, 199
Nixon administration, 20, 115, 193, 200
Norma Rae, 20–21, 203–23, 227
North, Edmund, 161
North Carolina, 20, 211, 213
Northwestern University, 143
Norway, 82
Nye, Gerald P., 83, 100
Nye, Russell B., 6
Nye Committee, 83

O'Donnell, Ken, 58
On the Trail of the Assassins, 49–50
Opelika, Ala., 212
Operation Mongoose, 61
Orion Pictures, 30
Oswald, Lee Harvey, 47, 60, 62, 64, 68, 71

Pakula, Alan J., 186, 188–91, 200–201
Palance, Jack, 111
Pall Mall, Tenn., 92
The Paranoid Style in American Politics, 66
Parallax View, 186
Parenti, Michael, 4
Paris, 182

Parker, Alan, 26, 30–33, 36, 38, 41–44
Parker, Bonnie, 130, 134–35, 138–50, 152
Parkland Hospital, 63–64
Parkman, Francis, 7
Parsons, Estelle, 131, 151
Pasteur, Louis, 85
Patterson, Basil, 197
Patton, Beatrice, 159
Patton, George S., 19–20, 155–77, 227
Patton, George S. III, 159
Patton, 19–20, 155–77, 227
Patton: Ordeal and Triumph, 159
PBS Television, 2, 4, 42–43
Penn, Arthur, 135–37, 139–40, 143–44, 146–47
Pershing, John Joseph (Gen. Black Jack), 99
Pesci, Joe, 71
Petras, James, 76
Philadelphia, Miss., 27, 32–33, 38, 43
Pile, Rosier, 90, 92, 96
Pinochet, Augusto, 108, 121
Platoon, 48
Platte City, Mo., 151
Poitier, Sidney, 133
Poland, 82
Pollard, Michael J., 131
Pratt Institute, 182
Prentice-Hall, 49
Prescott, William H., 7
Price, Cecil, 32
Prouty, L. Fletcher, 50–51
Psycho, 128, 133
Public Enemy, 133
Pulitzer Prize, 11, 56, 193

Queens College, 27
Quiz Show, 14–16

Radical Republicans, 18
Ramage, Tom, 171
Ranier, Peter, 113
Rashomon, 19, 52, 67, 78, 113
Raskin, Marcus, 10, 76–77
Rather, Dan, 74
Ravetch, Irving, 209

Ray, Michele, 107
Reagan, Ronald, 106, 210
Rebel without a Cause, 133
Redford, Robert, 14–15, 180–91, 200–201
Redgrave, Vanessa, 206
Reds, 5
Red Scare, 49, 208
Remembering America: A Voice from the Sixties, 15
Rhineland, 82
Richard III, 43
Riefenstahl, Leni, 72
Ritt, Martin, 208–14, 223
Roanoke Rapids, N.C., 20, 205, 215–16, 218, 221–23
Robards, Jason, 184
Rocky, 210
Roe v. Wade, 206
Rogers, William, 173
Rommel, Erwin, 164, 167
Roosevelt, Eleanor, 99
Roosevelt, Franklin D., 98–99, 152
Roosevelt, Theodore, 6
Rose, Alex, 205–8, 210–13
Roselli, Johnny, 61
Rosenstone, Robert A., 8–9, 77
Rostow, Walt Whitman, 58
Royko, Mike, 149
Ruby, Jack, 68
Rusconi, Jane, 51, 76
Rusk, Dean, 58
Russell, Jane, 92
Russians, 163, 165–66

San Clemente, 173
Sands of Iwo Jima, 163
Sarris, Andrew, 134
Scarface, 133
Schaffner, Franklin, 161–62, 168–69
Schama, Simon, 6–7
Schickel, Richard, 41
Schjeldehl, Peter, 171–72
Schlesinger, Arthur M., Jr., 56, 58, 73, 197
Schneider, Rene, 115, 120
Schwerner, Michael, 27–28, 31–34, 43

Scott, George C., 157, 161, 166–67, 170–71
Scott, Peter Dale, 51
Segovia, Spain, 169
Segretti, Donald, 192, 195–96
Senate Intelligence Committee, 112
Senate Select Committee on Campaign Practices, 192
Sergeant York, 18, 81–101
Sergeant York: His Own Life Story and War Diary, 92
Sergeant York and His People, 92
Shakespeare, William, 6, 41, 43, 140
Shaw, Clay, 49, 52, 54, 56, 60
Sheridan Square, 49
Shreveport, 151
Sidey, Hugh, 173–74
Sienkiewicz, Henryk, 6
Sigmund, Paul, 118
Simon, Neil, 182
Sirica, John, 192
Sitkoff, Harvard, 37, 40
Skeykill, Thomas, 92
Sklar, Zachary, 49, 50, 74, 76
Sloan, Hugh, 190
Slotkin, Richard, 12–13
A Soldier's Story, 160
Sorbonne, 107
Sorlin, Pierre, 4–5
Sounder, 208
South Carolina, 4
Soviet Union, 53, 61–62, 98, 159, 193
Spacek, Sissy, 110, 206
Spain, 160, 169
Spartacus, 107
Spy Saga, 51
Stagecoach, 128
Stans, Maurice, 199
State of Siege, 107
Steel, Ronald, 57
Stewart, Donald, 107, 114, 121–22
Stewart, Jimmy, 54
Stokes, Louis, 75
Stone, Oliver, 1, 9, 16–17, 46–47, 50–55, 57–59, 64–78
Streep, Meryl, 206, 209

Student Non-Violent Coordinating Committee (SNCC), 36
Supreme Court, 71
Susman, Warren, 12
Sylvester, Arthur, 159

Tanner, Alice, 221
Taylor, Bennett, 221
Taylor, Maxwell, 58
Tennessee, 90, 92–94, 207
Tet Offensive, 156
Texas Rangers, 149
The Texas Rangers, 149
Texas School Book Depository Building, 62
Thatcher, Margaret, 210
Three Days of the Condor, 182
Three Lives for Mississippi, 31, 36
Tillman, Captain, 90
Time, 41, 99, 128, 135, 140, 186, 206
Toland, John, 141, 145, 148
Tolstoy, Leo, 6–7
Towne, Robert, 145–46
Trafficante, Santos, 61
Triumph of the Will, 72
Truffaut, François, 143
The Turning Point, 206
Twentieth Century–Fox, 156–58, 160, 173, 210–11, 214
Twenty One, 14
Tyson, Cicely, 206

United Kingdom, 168
United Mine Workers, 222
Universal Pictures, 143
Universal Studios, 160
The Untouchables, 142
Uruguay, 107–8
U.S. Agency for International Development, 107
U.S. Air Force, 50
U.S. Army, 158
U.S. Congress, 93
U.S. Department of Defense, 158–60
U.S. Department of State, 106, 110, 123
U.S. House of Representatives, 75, 97

U.S. House Select Committee on Assassinations, 75
U.S. Senate Foreign Relations Committee, 114, 122–23
U.S. Senate Interstate Commerce Committee, 100
U.S. Senate Select Committee on Intelligence, 112, 114
U.S. Senate Select Committee to Study Government Operations with Respect to Intelligence Activities, 115–16

Valenti, Jack, 72
Vallee, Rudy, 152
Van Doren, Charles, 14–15
Van Wegenen, Lola, 182
Variety, 139, 170
Vesey, Denmark, 3–4
Vidal, Gore, 225–26
Vietnam, 20, 46, 52–58, 61, 71, 121, 129, 136–37, 156–58, 162–63, 170–72, 174–75, 226
Vogue, 140, 206
Voting Rights Act, 40

Waldorf Astoria, 97
Walkowitz, Daniel, 8–9
Wall Street Journal, 56, 170, 198
Wallis, Hal, 89–92
War and Peace, 6
Warner, Harry, 100
Warner, Jack L., 89, 143
Warner Brothers, 69, 82, 88, 99, 128, 180, 210
War Powers Act, 197
Warren, Earl, 71
Warren Commission, 46, 55, 59, 62–67, 69, 72–73, 75, 226
Warshovsky, Reuben, 216–17, 221
Washington, George, 70, 99, 165
Washington, D.C., 41, 104, 189, 191
Washington Post, 20, 68, 70–71, 73–74, 77, 180, 182, 184–85, 187, 190–93, 198
The Waterfront, 209
Watergate, 15, 110, 180–81, 184, 189–92, 194, 196–98, 200

Watson, Nate, 95
Wayne, John, 166
Webb, Jim, 161
Webb, Walter Prescott, 149
Weisberg, Harold, 70, 72
Welles, Orson, 89
Welsh, Neil J., 29
We're in the Money, 152
West Point Peperell, 215
Westport, Conn., 137
Wicker, Tom, 70, 74
The Wild Bunch, 133
The Wild One, 133
Will, George, 46
Williams, Gracie, 91, 94, 96
Williams, Joseph, 222
Willingham, Calder, 161–63
Willis, Frank, 190
Willis, Gordon, 186
Willkie, Wendell, 100
Wilson, Woodrow, 87
Wiseman, Frederick, 29
Woodward, Bob, 20, 180, 182–86,
    188–95, 198–201

Worker City, Company Town, 8
World War I, 13, 84, 86–87, 91, 96,
    99–100, 226
World War II, 18, 84, 88, 98–99, 158,
    160, 164–67, 174
Wycherly, Margaret, 94
Wyler, William, 161

Yale University, 47–48, 51
York, Alvin, 83–87, 89, 90, 92, 96
*Young Mr. Lincoln: A Guide to the Study of
    the Historical Philosophy*, 70
Yourcenar, Marguerite, 6

Z, 107, 108
Zanuck, Darryl, 158–59, 161, 171, 173
Zapruder, Abraham, 62, 64
Ziegler, Ron, 187
Zivkovich, Eli, 216–17, 219, 221–22
Zola, Emile, 85
Zollo, Fred, 29, 31, 36, 42–44
Zukor, Adolph, 87
Zwick, Edward, 11

ROBERT BRENT TOPLIN, professor of history at the University of North Carolina at Wilmington, is the film review editor of the *Journal of American History*. He is the author of numerous books and articles on film and history and on U.S. and Latin American history. In addition, he was the principal creator of dramatic films that appeared on PBS television and the Disney Channel, including *Denmark Vesey's Rebellion, Solomon Northrup's Odyssey* (which won the Erik Barnouw Award from the Organization of American Historians), *Charlotte Forten's Mission,* and *Lincoln and the War Within.*

UNIVERSITY OF ILLINOIS PRESS
1325 SOUTH OAK STREET
CHAMPAIGN, ILLINOIS 61820-6903
WWW.PRESS.UILLINOIS.EDU